From the great Gaels of Ireland
Are the men that God made mad.
For all their wars are merry,
And all their songs are sad.

- G. K. Chesterton,
The Ballad of the White Horse

Author

Dan Holden was born in Eugene, Oregon, the son of a former Brooklyn Dodger minor leaguer and the grandson of a former Canadian NHL defenseman. He majored in Journalism at Oregon State University where he wrote for several college publications and played a little rugby.

Holden researches and writes articles that focus on historical subjects; primarily Irish history. For three years his articles appeared monthly in the *Irish American* newspaper which served Philadelphia, PA and the upper Delaware valley under the byline, *Holden's Historical Review*.

His articles have been featured in *Military History* magazine, *RUGBY* Magazine, *Inside Hockey, Boxing News, The Oregonian, Eugene Register-Guard, Seattle Times, Winnipeg Tribune, Lethbridge Sun Times, DIVER* magazine, as well as numerous on-line publications.

Holden has been in the insurance risk management field for over three decades and has written for a number of insurance and risk management publications (which he finds slightly vapid).

In 2003 he wrote a book about his grandfather and the part he played in the birth of professional hockey in North America. The book became well-known in hockey circles and he was eventually asked to submit copies to the Hockey Hall of Fame in Toronto, Ontario as well as to the office of former Canadian Prime Minister, Stephen Harper.

Holden holds dual citizenship with the United States and Canada. He can't skate.

Recommendations

"Dan Holden packs a great deal of fascinating and inspiring stories into his book. Thoroughly researched and written in an engaging style, this eclectic collection of stories brings to life some remarkable characters of the Irish and Irish American past. Read this book and you begin to understand what has sustained the Irish people through so many centuries of trial and tribulation." – *Edward T. O'Donnell, author of 1001 Things Everyone Should Know About Irish American History.*

"Dan Holden's collection of stories provides an informative and exciting mix of the unique Irish experience around the world and across centuries, Readers will find an easy read packed with keen insight on historical characters and backed with solid research on the Irish character. A must read for those interested in Irish history." – *Dennis P. Heron, Editor & Publisher, The Irish Eye.*

"Daniel Holden's book is an extraordinary feat, a fusion of historical reportage, surprising anecdotes, and provocative argument. Anyone curious about Ireland's past won't come away disappointed." – *Darren Holden, native of Mooncoin, Kilkenny, Ireland, top 10 recording artist in Ireland and member of the Irish folk group, The High Kings*

"This is a great read for those interested in the rather complex and tumultuous history of Ireland. Offered in a chapter by chapter approach, it's not only educational but enjoyable as well." – *Mick Mulcrone, Professor of Journalism, University of Portland.*

Irish History

Beyond Shamrocks & Shillelaghs

Dan Holden

Irish History: Beyond Shamrocks & Shillelaghs

978-1-59330-905-3

Printed in the United States of America

This book is dedicated with love to my daughters, Rachel and Kathleen; my mother, Charlotte; my brother, Chris; my grandchildren, Santana, Elena, and Analia…to all of the Irish Holdens who came before me and will come after.

And to my father, Danny…in a world of saints and sinners he was a wee bit of both.

Go gcastar ar a chéile arís muid

Introduction

Many years ago I was approached by an independent newspaper and asked to write a monthly piece on Irish history. Apparently I was becoming somewhat well-known in certain circles for the articles I had published in various magazines and newspapers in the US and Canada. This particular publication served Pennsylvania and the upper Delaware Valley, and they were seeking more experienced writers to take them to the next level.

I chose the title, *Holden's Historical Review* as the name of my monthly "column." The paper would not dictate the terms, select the topics, nor influence my writing in any way. A writer's dreams come true. So for the next three years I produced articles for the approximately 10,000 subscribers.

For this book, I have selected the articles I consider to best exemplify the Irish traits of tenacity, perseverance, and the desire for freedom…at whatever the cost. Transversely, I also became keenly aware of the frailty of the Irish nature and the propensity to go to battle for the sake of a good fight.

I am reminded of the quote by Sidney Littlewood, *"The Irish don't know what they want and are prepared to fight to the death to get it."*

Sláinte!

Acknowledgements

A special thanks to the many friends and family who inspired me over the years to continue writing, as well as those who had a positive influence on the course of my life from either a creative perspective or the mere fact they were always present. *Go raibh maith agat.*

Darren Holden, Gerald & Lucille McAleese, Sarah Molloy, Becki Glaubitz, Jeff Prechtel, Bill & Cherie Wheatley, Larry Holden, Linda Macdonald-Lewis, Christel Thorson, Monee Dartt, Kevin Hollowell, Brian Gannon & Laura Pulido Gannon, Lanette Hanson, Cindy TenHarkel Langston, David O'Longaigh, Jim Ford, Mark Beairsto, Pete Ducich, Mike Cronan, Dan Wyant, Harold Dorn, Ken Higgins, Jerry Gjesvold, Bill Starnes, and Jerry Andrews.

And to the friends who said what I didn't know would fill a book. Well, here it is…

What's the use of being Irish
if the world doesn't break your heart?

- John F. Kennedy

Contents

1916: The Easter Rebellion

Culture, Mythology, Arts

Brian Boru
Emperor of Ireland

"They are inflamed with the desire
of violating the fairest daughters
of this land of beauty,
and enriching themselves
with the spoils of sacrilege and plunder."

**- Brian Boru to his troops at Clontarf, prior to battling
the Danes in 1014**

To truly comprehend the impact Brian Boru had on Ireland,
one must understand Irish society and politics as it existed over
2,000 years ago, as well as the fearful role played by the Vikings
in shaping that history.

At the time of Brian Boru, Ireland was a fragmented,
aristocratic warrior society with over 200 tribes. Each tribe
had its own chieftain (or king), who fought to control lands in
territories ruled by five provincial kings.

They constantly fought with each other over territorial
expansion, as well as possessions. Provincial kings owed taxes,
and warriors, to a high King, or "Ard Ri." The Ard Ri not the
king of Ireland, but was merely the *king of kings* and the man
with the strongest personal army.

In the midst of this territorial squabbling were the intermittent
Viking raids. These Scandinavian adventurers, known as
"Ostermen," (Old Norse for *"men of the east"*), first arrived in
Ireland in 795 A.D. Because the Irish had inferior weapons, no
fleet, and no political unity, the Irish were an easy mark for the
marauding and far more organized Vikings.

For the next 25 years the Vikings (or "Norsemen") arrived
by longboat. They came ashore as small raiding parties and

averaged one hit-and-run attack per year, usually targeting undefended monasteries for their treasure, stores of provisions, potential slaves, and women.

"The Annals of Clonmacnois" recorded the sentiment of the Irish at the time, *"As many women as they could lay hands upon, noble or ignoble, young or old, married or unmarried, whatever birth they were, were by them abused most beastly, and filthy, and such of them as they liked best, were by them sent over seas into their own countries there to be kept by them to use their unlawful lusts."*

The scattered attacks ended around 830 ADonly to be replaced by a full scale invasion when large Viking fleets arrived in the rivers of Liffey, Boyne, Shannon, and Erne.

Feeling bolder, the Vikings began to plunder inland locations. They would terrorize the Irish for weeks and months at a time before returning to Scandinavia for the winter. Eventually they saw no reason to return home, so they begin setting up permanent residence.

By the mid-800s the Irish began to unify and put up a stronger resistance. They even won a few battles over the Norsemen. But try as they might, they weren't able to drive out the Vikings. The best hope they had was to constantly harass the Norsemen hoping they would tire of the pesky Irish and go home. But in 914 AD, another Viking fleet landed at Waterford, starting a whole new phase of plundering and the Irish were simply overwhelmed.

Eventually the Vikings were traveling to and from Ireland so often they established settlements at Wexford, Waterford, Cork, Limerick, as well as Dublin. These would become the first towns in Ireland.

Those Vikings who stayed in Ireland began to develop trade and marry into Irish families. Viking leaders would become much like other rulers in Ireland and even joined in the wars between rival Irish kings. Soon it became difficult to tell friend from foe; Norseman from Irishman.

While some Vikings settled down to a peaceful farming existence, other Vikings kept invading from the north in hopes of gaining riches. The Vikings who became farmers would fall prey to Vikings who continued to plunder. And so this odd dance between the Irish and the Norsemen continued until the mid-900s.

In 941 A.D., Brian mac Ceinneidigh ("Son of Kennedy") was born to a relatively minor king of the Dalcassian (Dal Cais) tribe in the Kingdom of Thomond (Co.Clare). Brian was the 12th son of Kennedy of Thormond.

His eldest brother, Mahon, succeeded to the throne of Munster when the current king died. Mahon was engaged almost constantly in war with the Danes, and with the Leinstermen who were in alliance with them. Many Leinstermen, including Sitric Silkbeard of Limerick, joined forces - not so much for love of the Danes - but for hatred of the Dal Cais. *My enemy's enemy is my friend.*

Mahon once considered peace with the Vikings, but Brian urged armed resistance. Brian had fought the Vikings all of his life, and he vowed to rid the country of the invading Norsemen.

In 959 A.D., Mahon and the Munstermen attacked the Vikings at Clonmacnois. In 965 A.D. they destroyed the Viking town of Limerick, and in 968 A.D.they fought a decisive battle with the Norsemen, and their Irish supporters, at Sulchoid, about two and a half miles northwest of Tipperary. The Sulchoid battle lasted from sunrise until midday and ended in the complete rout of the Vikings. The Norse prisoners were then gathered on a hill of Spaingel, near Limerick, and *"every one that was fit for war was put to death and every one that was fit for a slave was enslaved."* Brian mac Ceinneidigh would give no quarter to the Norse invaders.

Then came the Battle of Bealach Leachta in 978 A.D. which marked the first major defeat of the Vikings in Ireland. It also established Brian as a serious contender for role of Ard Ri.

The battle was the climax of a power struggle between the Dal Cais of North Munster and the Irish Lords of Carbery who had allied themselves with the Vikings. During the battle, Mahon of the Dal Cais was captured by Imer, King of the Limerick Vikings.

Imer delivered Mahon into the hands of the O'Mahoney's - who had allied themselves with the Vikings - and they executed Mahon at Aghabullogue. With Mahon dead, Brian, now 35 years old, was the new King....and he came seeking revenge for his brother's murder.

Brian tracked Imer to a monastery on Scattary Island and cut him down. Imer's sons, and any other Vikings in the vicinity, were also slaughtered. He was without mercy. Before he left he made sure he desecrated the church for harboring Imer.

With Imer out of the way, Brian now held both Limerick and Munster. He tracked down and killed Clan Chieftain O'Donovan, also a Viking ally, further eliminating any opposition.

Then Boru set his sights on the man who killed his brother and he challenged the army of Maolmuidh of the O'Mahoneys to do battle at Bealach Leachta.

A fierce battle waged all day on the riverside plain. Brian's army had swelled to considerable size as many minor chieftains began to recognize (and fear) his potential strength.

The O'Mahoneys had the support of what remained of the O'Donovan clan and 1,500 Danes. Maolmuidh and his troops were forced back during the battle, and Maolmuidh took refuge at Leach Dubh (the current site of Macroom Golf course), where he was found and killed.

As a final punishment for killing his brother, Brian Boru had Maolmuidh buried on the north side of a hill where the sun never shines and the harsh winds would always blow.

Following the battle, Brian Boru was crowned King of Munster. Three standing stones were erected on the site of the battle (of which two remain to this day). He then made his way to Connaught and Leinster in 997 A.D. where he met with

Mael Sechnaill (successor to Domnall Ui Neill, King of Tara). Between the two they divided the whole of Ireland.

Not all of Brian's subjects were happy with their king. In 999 A.D., the people of Leinster and Dublin (primarily the Norse) rose up against Brian, but were defeated at Glenn Mama. The King of Leinster was taken prisoner by Brian.

The King of Viking Dublin, Sitric Silkbeard, was defeated by Brian's forces later that same year. In 1002 A.D., Brian demanded that Mael Sechnaill recognize him as King of Ireland. Mael was all too happy to capitulate rather than end up buried on the windy side of a hill.

Thus, Brian Boru, the 12th son of Kennedy of Thormond, became the High King of Ireland, ending the dynasty held by the Ui Neill family for 600 years.

As is customary for the Ard Ri, Brian asked for tribute, mostly cattle, to which he was given the title "Boru" ("of the cow tribute").

About this time Brian had set aside his troublesome wife, Gormlaith, a princess of Leinster, by an earlier marriage. She was the mother of Sitric Silkbeard, King of Viking Dublin, and one of Brian's most bitter enemies.

Gormlaith was a royal pain in the arse who proved time and again she could not be trusted. So Brian simply cut her loose. This affront incensed Silkbeard. Gormlaith and her brother, Maelmora, King of Leinster, encouraged Sitric to rally their Viking allies from Scandinavia and overthrow the High King.

So bent were they on overthrowing Brian, that Sitric offered his mother in marriage to the man who killed Brian Boru. Therefore, after a decade of relative peace, a new Viking invasion force set sail from Scandinavia, the Orkney Islands, and the Isle of Man, encouraged by Sitric and other disaffected Irishmen who resented Brian's power and policies.

It is said that once the Viking ships arrived they filled Dublin Bay. When he learned of the invasion, the aging Brian (now approximately 88 years old) sent word to his allies in Ireland.

This included both his Viking allies and the great Gaelic clans including Tadhg Mor O'Kelly and Brian's old rival and now friend, Malachi Mor. Once his troops arrived, Brian took up his sword and went to meet his enemies, marching across Ireland from Kincora to Clontarf.

Although the battle has gone down in history as Irishmen versus Viking (primarily the Dublin Vikings), it was actually a battle between the Vikings and the men from Munster. To add to the confusion, there were Irish who fought with the Vikings, most notably the men from Leinster who hated Brian. There were even Vikings who fought with Brian. It was all very political.

Surrounded by his Dal Cais knights, Brian marched into Leinster at the head of 30,000 men in three divisions. He was joined there by Malachy II, King of Meath. He encamped, as he had done the year before in the battle against Maelmordha, near Kilmainham.

After both armies viewed each other - each trying to develop a winning strategy - the leaders agreed the fate of Ireland would be determined by the outcome of the battle on the plain at Clontarf.

Brian offered the Danes battle on Palm Sunday, which they declined. But on Good Friday the Danes indicated they were ready for battle.

The right wing of the Irish army was comprised of Dal Cais knights, the household troops of Ireland. Next to the knights were the nobility of Munster, and Malachy with the forces of Meath. This wing was to be commanded by Brian's son, Prince Murrough. On the left wing were the troops of the King of Connaught made up of the O'Kelly Clann of Ui Maine (Cos Galway and Roscommon), the Damnonians, and detachments from other troops.

At sunrise, on Good Friday, April 23, 1014, at the small fishing village of Clontarf, the elderly King Brian Boru rode in front of his army holding a gold-hilted sword in one hand, and a crucifix in the other. He reminded his warriors of the day selected by the pagan invaders to offer battle, and exhorted them to conquer or die:

"On your valor rests the hopes of your country today; and what surer grounds can they rest upon? Oppression now attempts to bend you down to servility; will you burst its chains and rise to the independence of Irish freemen? Your cause is one approved by Heaven.

You seek not the oppression of others; you fight for your country and sacred altars. It is a cause that claims heavenly protection. In this day's battle the interposition of that God who can give victory will be signally manifested in your favor.

Let every heart, then, be the throne of confidence and courage. You know that the Danes are strangers to religion and humanity; they are inflamed with the desire of violating the fairest daughters of this land of beauty, and enriching themselves with the spoils of sacrilege and plunder.

The barbarians have impiously fixed, for their struggle, to enslave us, upon the very day on which the redeemer of the world was crucified. Victory they shall not have!

From such brave soldiers as you they can never wrest it; or you fight in defense of honor, liberty and religion, in defense of the sacred temples of the true God, and of your sisters, wives and daughters.

Such a holy cause must be the cause of God, who will deliver your enemies this day into your hands. Onward, then, for your country and your sacred altars!"

King Brian then waved his sword and the crucifix, signifying he was ready to die for the cause of Christianity and for his native Ireland.

He proceeded, amidst the wild shouts of his troops, toward the Dal Cais troops to take his station among them and lead the advance. However, all of the chiefs interceded and implored him to let his son, Murrough, lead the battle and that Brian should retire to his tent due to his great age.

After protesting, he reluctantly agreed. The Irish army then called on their chiefs to lead them in to battle. The Dal Cais, leading the way, raised the sunburst flag standard of Fingal – the "Gall-Greana" or (Blazing Sun) marked with the arms of the O'Brien, the hand and sword, bearing the inscription *"Victory or Death."*

As they approached the Danes, the Dal Cais were forced to dismount. Their horses could not traverse the large ditches in front of the Dane positions. The Danes allowed the Irish to remount and then the two armies charged each other. The collision of rushing men was loud and chaotic as wooden shields banged together and steel swords and battle-axes clashed.

The Irish were outnumbered, and Prince Murrough was heard to shout *"this is the time to win fame, for the greater the enemy the greater the glory!"* The battle was closely engaged with battle-axe and sword, spear and dagger. Other Irish divisions joined the fight and engaged the Danes in fierce hand to hand combat.

The battle lasted a full day and changed hands several times. At one time during the battle, Murrough lifted the standard of Fingal and waved it yelling, *"before the hour's end this standard will float over the Danish camp, or over my dead body!"*

The Irish chieftains, invigorated by Murrough's words, charged the Danes. Thrown into panic and confusion, the Danes finally broke rank and fled to their ships. Many of the Vikings drowned in the process, or were killed before they reached the sea.

The aftermath of the battle was grisly. Malachi's own chronicler described blood dripping from the trees, and the nearby River Tolka turned red.

As the battle waned, Prince Murrough stopped at a creek to bathe his bruised and battered sword arm in the cool water. At that moment, a straggling party of Danes retreating from the field stumbled across him, and seizing the opportunity, they attacked. Murrough, even with his incapacitated right arm, was able to fend them off. He dragged the coat of mail over one

Dane's head and placed the point of his sword against the Dane's body, and then leaned on it, pierced his body. At the same time the Dane was able to snatch Murrough's scimitar from his girdle and plunged it into the Prince's breast. The Dane died instantly. Prince Murrough was gravely wounded and died the next day.

Brian remained in his tent awaiting word of the battle. He was guarded by a "fence of shields" composed of chosen warriors who surrounded him with shields locked together. The king is said to have knelt on a cushion with his psalm-book open before him.

Corcoran, one of Brian's marshals, was the first to reach Brian with the news of Murrough's serious injury. Brian, upon hearing the sad news, thought the Danes had won the day. He directed Corcoran to flee to Armagh with the other chieftains, and that he would remain behind, *"I came here to conquer or die."*

At that instant, Brodar, a Viking Chieftain, and two other Danes, were running from the battlefield when they spied King Brian's tent. The Danes killed Brian's bodyguard and entered his tent. Brian seized his great two-handed sword and with one blow cut off the legs of the first Dane that entered his tent. Brodar, entering next, struck Brian on the back of the head with his battle-axe. Brian was able to decapitate Brodar, and then kill the third Dane, before collapsing and dying.

The great High King, Brian Boru, had died in the midst of what would become his greatest victory. It was a costly victory for the Irish. The king himself was dead, as was his son and heir apparent, Prince Murrough, along with Murrough's son, Turlough. Many sons of Ireland died that day.

At the conclusion of the battle, the soldiers disbanded, each returning to their own clans and territory. Donchadh, Brian's son who had been away on a foraging expedition and had taken no part in the battle, took command.

The death of Brian and Murrough brought about the displacement of the Dal Cais and the restoration of Malachy to the throne. For a hundred years after the death of Brian, rulers of powerful provincial families fought bitterly for supremacy. But none of them had any lasting success.

Brian Boru has gone down in history as the man who defeated the Vikings. This is fact. Occasionally historians will go too far and infer that he actually forced the Vikings out of Ireland. That is simply not true. The Vikings never left Ireland. They merely continued to work and trade as before in the cities they had already established.

What the Battle of Clontarf did accomplish was put an end to Viking dominance. The Norsemen would never again undertake the invasion of Ireland. Unfortunately, the petty bickering over territory resumed after Brian's death and kept the clans fragmented and at each other's throats.

This lack of unity enabled the Norse invaders to maintain their Danish coastal strongholds in Dublin. That is, until the Normans would arrive on the beaches of Co. Wexford four centuries later.

The Norman Invasion of Ireland

*"Contrary to the conditions of our treaty of peace,
you have invited a host of foreigners into this island...
either restrain in future the irruptions...
or I will certainly have your son's head cut off,
and send it to you."*

**- Rory O'Connor, King of Connaught, in a message to
his enemy, Dermot MacMorrough, King of Leinster**

The long struggle between the English and Irish can be traced directly back to the Norman invasion of 1169, when an Irish chieftain asked England's King Henry II for help in defeating his rivals. This would be an unfortunate miscalculation on the part of the chieftain, one in which Ireland would pay dearly for nearly 800 years.

The Normans were the descendents of the original Vikings, or "Norse men." They were also called "North men" (because they came from the North), and in later years the name evolved into a shorter version called "Norman."

Inheriting the Scandinavian propensity for invasion, the Normans actually were involved in four known conquests. The first was the conquest of an area in France, now known as "Normandy," named for the Normans who carried out the invasion. The second invasion occurred in 1016 and was the conquest of southern Italy and Sicily. The most well known invasion was the 1066 conquest of England by the Duke of William. This particular invasion transformed England from a German-speaking Saxon country to a French-speaking Norman property. And finally, there was the 1169 invasion and (partial) conquest of Ireland.

At the height of their power, the Norman kings and warlords had some degree of political control over Normandy, Southern Italy, Sicily, England, Wales, parts of what is now Yugoslavia, Turkey, Ireland, and, according to some historians, small parts in the north of Africa.

The political climate in Ireland at the time was one of inter-tribal rivalries, as it had been for centuries. Only Brian Boru had been able to all but stop such feuding, but upon his death at Clontarf in 1014 the bickering resumed.

In the mid-1100s a great rivalry for the high kingship of Ireland existed between Muirchertach MacLochlainn of Tirowen, a cruel and violent man, and Rory O'Connor (Ruadri Ua Conchobair) of Connaught. Dermot MacMorrough (Dairmait Mac Murchada), the King of Leinster, allied himself with MacLochlainn, and Dermot's greatest foe, Tiernan O'Rourke (Tighernan Ua Ruairc), King of Breifne, allied himself with O'Connor. Dermot and Tiernan were, themselves, bitter rivals contending for the middle kingdom of Meath.

Dermot MacMorrough was a savage brute, so it was not surprising for him to throw in his lot with MacLochlainn. Dermot had gained his Leinster kingship by killing two Leinster princes and blinding another. This did not endear him to his subjects. In a time of savagery and vicious ambition he had no equal.

In 1152, Dermot struck a mighty blow by abducting Dervorgilla, the wife of Tiernan O'Rourke, while O'Rourke was on a pilgrimage to St. Patrick's Purgatory in Loch Dearg. This sealed the hatred between the two kings.

There has long been a debate as to whether she went willingly, as she had ample opportunities to escape. Some say she even hatched the plot herself having long entertained a passion for MacMorrough. If that were true, it made things even worse. It has been further surmised that Dervorgilla grew tired of looking at her rather unappealing husband who was known as "Monoculus," or "One-Eye."

Gerald of Wales (1146-1223) left an account of the incident:
"*...and she, who had long entertained a passion for Dermot, took advantage of the absence of her husband, and allowed herself to be ravished, not against her will. As the nature of women is, fickle and given to change, she thus became the prey of the spoiler by her own contrivance. For as Mark Anthony and Troy are witnesses, almost all the greatest evils in the world have arisen from women.*"

Later, she must have come to her senses, or Dermot grew tired of her, as she returned home a year later. Regardless, not one to forget a slight, it took O'Rourke 14 years to build a power base sufficient enough to exact revenge on the man who stole his wife. And even though he did regain her in 1153, it wasn't enough to quench his thirst for vengeance.

When MacMorrough's strong ally in the north, O'Loughlin of Tir-Eoghan, died in 1165, Dermot, the King of Leinster, was weakened to the point where it was at last feasible to move against him.

Fearing his vulnerable position, and realizing how much his own countryman had grown to hate him, Dermot sailed to Bristol, to the Norman court of Henry II. Dermot found Henry fighting in Acquitaine, and told his sob story. Capitalizing on what appeared to be a win-win situation, the king agreed to aid the Irishman as *"vassal and liegeman,"* but could not afford to send his own troops due to his prior financial commitments.

Dermot was then given permission by Henry to recruit the support of the Marcher Lords of South Wales. At first, he could find no takers. After much searching, and a promise of land and his daughter's hand in marriage, he found a taker.

A powerful warlord named Richard FitzGilbert de Clare, Earl of Striguil and 2nd Earl of Pembroke, known as "Strongbow," was the first to answer the call. De Clare was a Norman-Welsh prince, and as such was expected to provide for a great many landless relatives. Essentially, he needed to secure some sort of wealth, and occupation, for them without draining his own purse.

Strongbow was deeply in debt since his father's death, and spent a great deal of time avoiding creditors. Ireland seemed the perfect escape. However, he was in disfavor with Henry II and dared not go without his expressed permission. Therefore, Strongbow sent his half-brother, the Norman-Welsh Robert FitzStephen who agreed to help Dermot in exchange for the town of Wexford as payment.

In early May 1169, three single-masted longships beached at Bannow Bay, Co. Wexford, having sailed from Milfordhaven in Wales. On board were 390 soldiers: Norman knights and half armored-clad horsemen, Welsh archers, and Fleming mercenaries. Another force of 300 men led by Maurice de Pendergast landed at Bannow Creek, south of Wexford, and camped on an island. When Dermot heard the news of their landing, he quickly assembled 500 of his former subjects and hurried to meet them.

FitzStephen and Dermot wasted no time and made straight for Wexford, which, at the time, was still ruled by Norse-Irish. The townsmen advanced to meet the Norman army in battle. But the men of Wexford were overwhelmed by the Norman horsemen, and retreated back into their town, burning all the outlying buildings.

FitzStephens then laid siege to the town. His armored warriors moved into dry trenches around the city, while his archers covered them by raking the wall-towers. The Normans then heaved their siege ladders against the walls and clambered to the top. The men of Wexford mustered a great defense by throwing down large stones and wooden beams, and managed to repulse the attack.

Frustrated, FitzStephens called off the attack, and withdrew to the harbor. Undaunted, FitzStephens regrouped and assaulted the town the next morning. By now the men of Wexford were tired of battle, and with the help of bishop mediators, negotiated a peaceful settlement. Dermot then gave the town to FitzStephens. In an unusual twist, the townspeople then joined the Normans and Leinstermen and ravaged the territory of Ossory. At the end of the raiding campaign, two hundred heads were laid at the feet of Dermot. He turned the heads one by one, raising his hands in joy and shouting each time he recognized an enemy. According to Gerald of Wales, *"among them was one he hated above all others, and taking it up by the ears and hair, he tore the nostrils and lips with his teeth in a most savage and inhuman way."*

Gerald, in a rather ethnocentric manner, also described the primitive nature and battle methods of the Irish they encountered: *"They go to battle without armour, considering it a burden and esteeming it brave to fight without it. They are armed with three kinds of weapons: short spears, light darts, and heavy battle-axes of iron, exceedingly well wrought and tempered. These they borrowed from the Norwegians.*

In striking with the battle-axe they use only one hand, instead of both. When all other weapons fail, they hurl stones against the enemy. Their clothes are made after a barbarous fashion. Their custom is to wear small close-fitting hoods, hanging below the shoulders. Under this they use woollen rugs instead of cloaks, with breeches and hose of one piece, usually dyed.

The Irish are a rude people, subsisting on the produce of their cattle only and living like beasts. This people, then, is truly barbarous, being not only barbarous in their dress, but suffering their hair and beards to grow enormously in an uncouth manner."

Later, Maurice FitzGerald, a comrade of Strongbow, would land at Wexford with 140 Norman-Welsh warriors. He and Dermot would then march on Dublin ravaging and burning the surrounding territory.

Rory O'Connor, a clan chieftain, gathered his army and marched to intercept Dermot and FitzStephen. However, the Norman army requested a parley, hoping to avoid battle.

O'Connor agreed, but only if Dermot made some act of submission and the foreigners should immediately depart for Britain. Dermot accepted the first condition, and offered his son as hostage. He then secretly agreed to (or pretended to agree) that he would convince the foreigners to leave Ireland.

Rory then acknowledged Dermot as the king of Leinster. Now drunk with power, Dermot MacMorrough believed he could seize the high kingship. On the advice of FitzStephen and FitzGerald, Dermot again asked for Strongbow's help. When permission finally arrived from Henry, Strongbow agreed to help MacMorrough by commanding a force of volunteers sufficient to defeat his enemy. For this, the Irish king promised the hand of his daughter, Aoife ("Eva") and the succession of his kingdom when he died. However, due to Irish law, the kingdom was not his to give, and he bloody well knew it.

In 1170, Strongbow arrived in Ireland, bringing with him 200 armored horsemen and 1,000 Welsh archers and other soldiers. He had already sent an advance group of warriors who had set up a beachhead near Waterford. However, the Viking-Irish townsmen savaged this scouting party.

When Strongbow finally arrived, he sought revenge for the annihilation of his advance party, and then made straight for Waterford. In a relatively short amount of time, Strongbow's men had torn down a stone wall and entered and taken Waterford, slaughtering the inhabitants and putting the two Danish rulers to death.

On hearing of the invasion, Dermot hurried south with his daughter, Aoife. The marriage between Strongbow and Aoife was then celebrated amid the still bloody scenes.

Now, joined by Dermot, FitzStephen and FitzGerald, Strongbow set his sights on Dublin. The hapless city was caught unawares, and immediately negotiated for peace. While talks ensued, a group of Normans stormed the walls and seized the city.

Dermot, crazed with multiple successes, then raided the territory of his greatest enemy, Tiernan O'Rourke. Furious, Rory O'Connor send a message to Dermot reminding him of his peace agreement: *"Contrary to the conditions of our treaty of peace, you have invited a host of foreigners into this island… either restrain in future the irruptions… or I will certainly have your son's head cut off, and send it to you."* Dermot refused to comply with the agreement, and his son was subsequently executed.

Dermot's luck eventually ran out, or perhaps it was karma, as he died a few months later of natural causes, leaving Strongbow in command. After Strongbow crushed a general revolt of the Leinster Irish and Osterman (Vikings), he proclaimed himself "Lord of Leinster."

Exceedingly jealous - and fearing Strongbow's new found power in southwestern Ireland - Henry II ordered the Normans to return on penalty of losing their lands in England. He also refused to allow any ship to sail to Ireland. This loss of reinforcements and supplies fell hard on Strongbow, but he was still able to hold his conquered territories.

After repeated commands by Henry to return to Britain, Strongbow finally complied. Upon his arrival at Henry's court, Strongbow humbly laid his conquests, cities and territories at his angry monarch's feet. He only asked that he be made Henry's tributary from Leinster.

Henry always wanted to invade Ireland; it was part of his master plan. But it seemed he always had other pressing issues that needed his attention. Now it was time to assert his authority.

On October 17, 1171, Henry II landed in Waterford with a large army. He had received approval from the newly elected English Pope, Nicholas Breakspear (Adrian the Fourth) on the grounds that morale in Ireland had become corrupt, and religion almost extinct. His sole purpose was to bring the *"barbarous nation within the fold of the faith and under church discipline."*

Henry was hardly the one to espouse religion. He led a brutal life, was a supporter of the "anti-Popes," and was accused of, and nearly excommunicated for, instigating the murder of Thomas Beckett.

In his Irish campaign, Henry received recognition and hostages from the Osterman (Vikings) of Wexford as well as from other kings in Ireland.

Henry made a formal grant to Strongbow of Leinster in return for homage, fealty, and the service of 100 knights, reserving for himself the city and kingdom of Dublin, plus all seaports and fortresses. Strongbow was in no position to bargain.

When King Henry finally left, the Irish kings quickly realized they had meekly welcomed a foreign king on to their land. Ashamed, and then angry, they began to rise up against their oppressors to drive them out of Ireland.

No longer awed by the Norman warrior mystic, the Irish began to defeat their enemies. But it was too-little too-late. The Normans were already engrained, physically and politically, having made many Irish allies. They had thrust deep into the country; settling and fortifying with their massive stone-built castles. Much like the Vikings before them...the Norman weren't going anywhere.

Despite a few wins, the Irish were no match for the Normans. Try as they might, the Irish were defeated by the superior training, skill, and discipline of the Norman invaders. Their strange appearance, combined with their foreign allies, shocked the Irish who had never seen armored men before.

The Normans, whom the Irish called "Franks" because they spoke French, had far more sophisticated weapons. The Irish fell like oak trees as the vicious Normans slaughtered entire communities sweeping from town to town. This type of mass slaughter was barbaric to the Irish, and simply made no sense. But the Normans got their point across

According to the author Michael Greaney, at that time in history the Irish fought either unarmored or utilized old-fashioned scale armor. They did not normally fight from horseback, and when they did, they rode bareback because stirrups had not yet been introduced into Ireland.

The weapon most commonly used was the ax, supplemented with the short Irish spear. These weapons were hardly a match for the superior Norman chain mail and swords. The Irish were also a citizen army. They fought when they had to, and then returned to work their farms. They were no competition for a professionally trained military force.

The Normans only conquered less than half of Ireland. This was due to part to the local resistance, as well as political decisions by the Norman kings themselves.

Many of their potentially powerful and most troublesome barons were based in the borderlands. Thus, they were too busy to meddle in the king's affairs as they were constantly defending themselves from the smaller Celtic tribes who often attacked with little prompting.

The way the Irish conducted warfare was much different than the Normans. This resulted in a kind of "stalemate" according to author David Nicolle in his book, *The Normans*. The North men fought to dominate people and land, while the native Irish fought only to dominate people. The country was very underpopulated, at least in the north. The inhabitants were semi-nomadic and pastoral, their main wealth being cattle. It was therefore counterproductive to slay too many of the Irish. Instead, molesting, plundering, and limited but highly visible destruction by the Normans were designed to extort tribute and obedience. Sort of a shock-and-awe strategy.

Most warfare consisted of cattle raiding with minimal casualties. When the Normans tried to hold a piece of territory, the Irish inhabitants often destroyed their homes, burned their crops, and quickly migrated to another area. The Normans would then retaliate by trying to force Gaelic chieftains to return the refugees and encouraging foreigners to settle the vacated land. In response, the Irish concentrated on guerrilla warfare in the marshes and forests where the Normans technological advantages were less effective.

Many historians have adopted Gerald of Wales' version of the Norman Invasion; one in which the brave but few Normans outmaneuvered and outwitted the entire native population. That is how the English wished to view the scenario.

Playing it down slightly, the Irish would consider the invasion to be only a minor nuisance. Historically, they were accustomed to foreign invaders. The Vikings came, conquered, and were assimilated into Irish society. So the Normans would be as well. They would also enter into Ireland's ongoing tribal warfare, as had the Vikings before them. The Normans would adopt the Irish language and customs, and become, *"Hibernicis ipsis Hibernior"* (More Irish than the Irish).

As the years went by, the native Irish would accept the Normans and life continued as before. Absolute control of the country was never established. However, enough of Ireland had been taken by the Normans that it would be considered an English possession. And the ramifications would prove to be sad and perilous for the Irish for the next 800 years.

Grace O'Malley
Pirate Queen of Connaught

*"Is it trying to hide behind by backside you are –
the place you came from?"*

**- Grace O'Malley to her cowardly son, Tibbot, during
battle**

Little has been written about Grace O'Malley. Perhaps, in
a male-dominated clan society, a female leader was an affront
to the male ego. However, modern historians are only now
discovering that not only was Grace an anomaly, but she ranks
as one of the most intriguing figures in early Irish history.

Born Grainne Ni Mhaille in County Mayo in 1530, she
was the daughter of Sea Captain Owen "Dubhdarra" (Black
Oak) O'Malley, who, by the Brehon legal system, was elected
chieftain of Umhall Uachtarach (Baroney of Murrisk).

The O'Malley clan claimed descendancy from Brian Boru's
brother, Orbsen, and thus were set down in the "Books of Rights"
as the tributary kings to the provincial kings of Connaught. The
O'Malley's were also known for their sailing prowess since 1123,
and traded regularly with Scotland and Spain. Not surprising is
the O'Malley family motto which is "Terra Marique Potems,"
("Powerful by land and sea.")

As a young girl, Grace longed for the open sea, and begged
her father to allow her to travel on one of their ships to Spain.
Her father refused. Her mother scolded her, telling her the
life of the sea was no place for a young lady. Undeterred,
Grace disappeared for a few minutes, and then returned with
her long hair cut short like a boy. Apparently her family was
greatly amused and gave her the nickname "Grainne Mhaol (or
Granuaile) meaning "bald" or "cropped hair."

It wasn't long before Grace began accompanying her father on trading missions. Once, upon returning from a trip to Spain, their ship was attacked by an English vessel. Grace had been instructed to hide below deck if they were ever attacked, but in this case she refused. Instead, she climbed up onto the sail rigging and watched the battle from above.

She spotted an English pirate sneaking up behind her father with a dagger. Grace leapt off the rigging, and on to the pirate's back, screaming the entire time. This outburst distracted the pirates, and caused enough of a diversion that the O'Malley's were able to regain control of the ship and defeat the English pirates.

In approximately 1546, when Grace was 16, she married Donal O Flaitbheartaigh (O'Flaherty) who was next in line to be head of the clan and chief of all Connaught. He was known as Donal-an-Chogaidh ("Donal of the Battles") for his fierce disposition and bad temper. In those days the marriages were often arranged, and it is safe to assume this marriage was of a political nature. O'Flaherty also possessed the castles of Bunowen and Ballinahinch, which made him a good catch. It was also a plus that the O'Flahertys were also a seafaring clan.

Over the course of their 19-year marriage, Grace learned more about seafaring from Donal and the O'Flaherty clan, which added to the knowledge she had already attained from her the O'Malley clan. Grace was soon commanding the O'Flaherty fleet of ships and ruled the waters surrounding their lands. It was said you could identify her ships by the flags bearing the sea horse of the O'Malley's and the lions of the O'Flahertys floating proudly fore and aft from the mastheads of her galleys.

Grace and Donal would have three children: Owen, Murrough, and Margaret. Over time she would surpass her husband in importance, actively engaging in politics, tribal disputes, fishing and trading.

Considering them far too dangerous, the city of Galway closed their gates to the O'Flahertys, and so Grace and Donal were forced to trade with Munster, Ulster, Scotland, Spain, and Portugal.

Not one to forget a slight, Grace would swoop down in her fast galleys and waylay any ships sailing from Galway. Then she would negotiate with the ship's captain for a suitable price for safe passage. If they refused, she would give her men leave to pillage and plunder. People soon learned that to cross Grace was a bad decision indeed.

During the 1560s, Murrough O'Flaherty ("Murrough of the Battle Axes"), a young chief, was making his presence known. After defeating the English Earl of Clanrickard in 1564, the Queen of England offered him the position of Chief of all of Iar Connaught in exchange for a promise of submission. Murrough accepted, and thus became "The" O'Flaherty (signifying Clan chief) ousting the current chief - and the fellow who would have been the next-in-line chief - Donal, Grace's husband.

Before he had a chance to finagle his way back to the top of the clan, Donal was later killed in a battle against the Joyces who were seeking revenge for his capture of the island castle of Caislean-an-Circa.

Donal fought like a demon and earned the posthumous nickname, Donal-an-Cullagh ("the Cock"), for his great courage. Grace also fought the Joyces with ferocity and earned the nickname "the Hen." The castle was henceforth called "Hen's Castle." Later she would defend Hen's Castle from an English siege in which she ordered the lead roof be melted down for ammunition, and proceeded to route the English.

After Donal's death, Grace found herself unable to collect her portion of her husband's estate per Irish law. Apparently the O'Flaherty clan did not recognize that particular Gaelic custom. Grace was then forced to rely on the O'Flahertys for support, which she detested.

Disgusted and embarrassed, she decided to set out on her own, and she sailed back to O'Malley territory with 200 followers where she set up her headquarters on Clare Island in

Clew Bay. This way she could monitor the ship traffic along the coast. With her combination of piracy, and charging for safe passage, she did very well.

On St. Brigid's Day, Grace and her forces were on pilgrimage at a holy well on Clare Island when she heard news of a ship floundering near Achill. She set sail, but when she discovered the ship it had already been broken in to pieces on the rocks. However, they did manage to rescue a young man named Hugh de Lacy, who was near death and sprawled on the rocks.

Grace nursed Hugh him back to health and the two fell deeply in love. Sadly, he was killed shortly thereafter by the MacMahons of Ballycroy while deer hunting.

Grace, full of rage, wasted no time in avenging her lover's murder. She tracked down the MacMahons, destroyed their boats, and personally slew those responsible for Hugh's death. Still not satisfied, she sailed back to their castle of Doona in Blacksod Bay, routed its inhabitants, and installed her followers there. After this episode she was known as "The Dark Lady of Doona."

In 1566, Grace married Richard-an-Iarainn ("Iron Dick Burke"). This was purely a political move so Grace might obtain the only portion of Clew Bay not in the hands of the O'Malleys.

Legend has it that Grace traveled to Castle Rockfleet, knocked on the door and proposed marriage to Richard for a period of one year. She explained the union would enable both clans to withstand the impending invasion by the English (who were slowly taking over the adjacent Irish lands).

Under Brehon law, marriage was a contract of mutual benefit for the participants, and divorce was simple and uncomplicated. Therefore, exactly one year later, after Grace had thoroughly installed herself in Rockfleet, and upon Richards' return from battle, she called down from the ramparts of the castle, "I dismiss you!" apparently offering him the option to end the marriage. He must not have accepted her dismissal as they remained married until he died 17 years later.

Grace and Richard's union produced one child, Tibbot-na-Long ("Theobald of the Ships"). Grace now had four children. Tibbot (or "Toby") was born on the high seas while Grace was returning from a trading mission. The day after the birth they were attacked by Turkish pirates. The captain informed her that the battle was not going well. Grace leapt out of bed wrapped only in a blanket, *"May you be seven times worse this day twelve months, who cannot do without me for one day,"* she said as she stormed the deck and fired her blunderbuss killing the Turkish captain. She then rallied her crew and defeated the Turks, captured their ship, and hung their crew.

Grace was a warrior, and as such had little patience for cowardice. Once when she was fighting the Stauntons of Kinturk Castle, her son, Tibbot, faltered and drew back to shelter behind his mother. *"An ag iarraidh dul I bhfolach ar mo thó ín"* ("Is it trying to hide behind by backside you are – the place you came from?") she asked. Mortified and embarrassed, Tibbot stood his ground and the Stauntons eventually surrendered.

Her maritime activities became so well-known (and feared) that on March 8, 1574, English Captain William Martin lead a force of ships and troops and laid siege to Grace in Rockfleet Castle. She rallied her defenses, and on the 26th turned the siege in to an attack. Captain Martin was forced to beat a hasty retreat after barely avoiding capture. This victory only enhanced her reputation as a ferocious fighter and not someone to be messed with.

It was about this time that many of the Irish chieftains - tired of the constant battles with the English - began to submit to the English throne.

In March 1576, *The* O'Malley (Grace's father had died by this time) was summoned and gave submission in Galway to Sir Henry Sidney in that he agreed not to participate in the current rebellion.

By 1577, the pressure from the English was steadily increasing. Survival in Ireland became the rule of the day. So, in hopes of advancing her husband's career and alleviating some pressure on herself, Grace finally presented herself to Sir Henry who wrote, *"There came to me also a most famous feminine captain called Grany Imallye, and offered her services unto me, wheresoever I would command her, with three galleys and 200 fighting men, either in Scotland or Ireland...This was a notorious woman in all the coasts of Ireland."*

On April 30, 1583, Richard died of natural causes (although some sources said he was executed by the English). Knowing that, once again, she would have no rights to her husband's property, she established her own claim. Therefore, with her followers, she absconded with 1,000 head of cows and mares and departed for Carrikahowley in Borosowle.

By this time Grace was getting on in years. Perhaps her senses weren't as keen, because at age 56 she was captured by Sir Richard Bingham, a ruthless Governor appointed by the Queen to rule over the regranted Connaught territory.

Bingham had dedicated himself to the eradication of the Gaelic way of life by force, if necessary. Soon after his appointment, Bingham sent guards to arrest Grace and have her hanged. Grace was apprehended, along with members of her clan, and scheduled for execution.

At the last minute, Grace's son-in-law, "Devil's Hook Burke," offered himself as hostage in exchange for the promise that Grace would never return to her rebellious ways. Bingham released Grace, but was determined to keep her from power and make her suffer for her insurrection.

Over the course of time, Bingham took away 1,000 of Grace's cattle and horses; forced her in to poverty; and orchestrated the murder of her eldest son, Owen. In her own words Grace described the account of the brutal treatment of her son, *"The next night following, a false alarm was raised in the camp in the dead of the night, the said Owen being fast bound in the cabin of Grene O'Molloy, and at that instant the said Owen was cruelly murdered, having 12 deadly wounds, and in that miserable sort he ended his years and unfortunate days."*

Grace then fled to Ulster for three months, under the protection of the O'Neills and O'Donells, while she regrouped and planned her next move.

In 1588, Grace received the Queen's pardon in Dublin. At that time many ships of the invading Spanish Armada ships were driven onto the West Coast by high winds. Some then unfortunately fell prey to the O'Malleys.

In the early 1590s Grace was virtually penniless due to the relentless efforts of Bingham who was determined to destroy her. There was a rather large rebellion brewing and Bingham feared Grace would join the fight against the English. She did exactly that.

He later wrote in a letter to an acquaintance that Grace was, *"a notable traitoress and nurse to all rebellions in the province for 40 years."* Once, during the rebellion, her son Murrough O'Flaherty sided with Bingham against her. Incensed, Grace rallied her ships and landed in Ballinehenchie where Murrough lived. She then proceeded to burn his town, steal his cattle, and murder several of his men. Murrough should have known better than to cross his mother.

In 1593, Grace began petitioning the Queen of England demanding protection from Bingham, but received no response. Later the same year, her son Tibbot, and her stepbrother Donal-na-Piopa ("Donald of the Pipes"), were arrested and thrown in to prison. This was the final straw. Since the Queen would not respond to her letters, she decided she should visit the Queen in person to request the release of her kin as well as help in regaining the lands and wealth that were rightfully hers.

Grace set sail and somehow managed to avoid the English patrol boats that littered the seas between Ireland and England. That in itself was an amazing feat. She then made her way up the Thames. Few Irish chieftains would set foot on English soil… especially Grace with her reputation of thwarting English ships.

It is unknown why the Queen agreed to meet with Grace rather than have her killed on the spot. But they did meet. Grace was fluent in Latin and thus was able to converse freely with the Queen. Grace explained that her actions in the past were not rebellion but rather acts of self-defense. She told how her rightful inheritances from her two husbands' deaths were wrongfully withheld.

During the meeting, Grace sneezed in the presence of the Queen. A member of the Queen's court, in an act of politeness, handed Grace an attractive and expensive lace handkerchief. She took the delicate cloth and proceeded to blow her nose loudly, then tossed the kerchief in the fire. The Queen scolded her saying the handkerchief was meant as a gift and should have been put in her pocket. Grace replied the Irish would never put a soiled garment into their pocket and apparently had a higher standard of cleanliness. After a period of uncomfortable silence, nervous laughter then erupted. The Queen was amused.

Upon hearing that Grace had taken her grievances to the Queen, Bingham sent a letter denouncing her again as a "notable traitor." But Grace had already won over the Queen who agreed to her requests. The Queen then commanded Bingham to free Grace's son and brother, and that Grace be given her property as well as a stipend with which to live. In exchange, Grace promised to fight any enemies of England. Bingham first tried to ignore the orders, but later relented. He did release the two captives, but never returned her rightful possessions.

On the way home from England, Grace stopped at Howth to restock, which was the main port of Dublin at that time. She went directly to the Lord of Howth seeking hospitality, as was the Gaelic custom. The gates of the castle were locked before her, and the servants would not let her in as the Lord was at dinner and was not to be disturbed. Furious at this breach of hospitality, she came upon the heir of Howath and seized him on the way back to the ship.

The Lord of Howath traveled to Connaught to negotiate for the return of his son for any ransom. Grace scorned the offer of ransom and demanded in return that his gates never be closed to anyone seeking hospitality. Furthermore she insisted that an extra place always be set at the table…a practice that exists to this day at Howth Castle.

Unfortunately, Sir Richard Bingham still found ways to harass Grace, despite orders to the contrary from the Queen. Grace, fed up, fled to Munster in late 1594 – 1595. Since all of the promises made to Grace by the Queen were not kept, she considered all bets off and put to sea again. For the next several years Grace involved herself in the war against England aligning herself with her old friends the O'Neills and the O'Donnells.

Grace died in poverty in 1603 about the time the O'Neills and O'Donnells were defeated at the Battle of Kinsale. Bingham's antics eventually caught up with him and he was forced to flee England to avoid imprisonment.

Grace O'Malley remains one of Ireland's most famous warriors, but is probably one of the least known. There are no references to her in the annuls of early Irish history; probably because the official chroniclers of the day refused to recognize a female chieftain.

Much of the history of the Pirate Queen of Connaught comes from the letters written to the Privy Council in Ireland or England, by the various statesmen of Queen Elizabeth who visited Connaught.

The one invaluable and undisputed document written in July 1593 contains Grace's answers to eighteen questions put to her by the Queen concerning herself and her activities.

Grace's impact on Irish history was obvious during the Wexford Rebellion of 1798. A song sung by survivors of the Ballinamuck Battle summed up their feelings:

"T'was a proud and stately castle in the years of long ago,
When the dauntless Grace O'Malley ruled a queen in fair Mayo.
And from Bernham's lofty summit to the waves of Galway Bay,
And from Castlebar to Ballintra her unconquered flag held sway."

Shane *"The Proud"* O'Neill

"I am not ambitious for the abject title of Earl.
I have gained that kingdom by my sword,
And by my sword I will preserve it!"

- Shane O'Neill to Queen Elizabeth when offered an English title

By the end of the 15th century, central English authority in Ireland had virtually disappeared. England's focus was on its Civil War ("Wars of the Roses") and they had little time to concentrate on Irish matters. That left Fitzgerald, Earl of Kildare, to control the island by utilizing military force and alliances with lords and clans around Ireland.

Around the country, local Gaelic and *Gaelicized* lords expanded their powers at the expense of the English government in Dublin. Ireland was growing more powerful.

It was during The Reformation in 1532 in which Henry VIII broke with Papal authority that fundamentally changed Ireland. While Henry VIII broke English Catholicism from Rome, his son, Edward VI, would break with Papal doctrine entirely.

While the English, Welsh, and later the Scots, accepted Protestantism, the Irish remained hard core Catholics. This decision would affect their relationship with England for the next four hundred years, and it coincided with the Reformation when the English, recognizing the rising power in Ireland, decided to re-conquer and colonize the island. This sectarian difference meant the native Irish and the (Roman Catholic) Old English would be excluded from political power.

In 1536, Silken Thomas Fitzgerald went into open rebellion against the crown in response to King Henry's crack-down on the Irish. The English were able to put down the uprising, but Henry VIII resolved to bring Ireland under English government control

so the island would not become a base for future rebellions or
foreign invasions of England.

Another political implication of the re-conquest was their core
belief that the Irish were lewd, uncivilized, and total incapable
of ruling themselves. At least that is how it was rationalized by
the English, and subsequently gave them the right to meddle in
Irish affairs and ultimately control the island.

This belief was a result of the vastly different social attitudes
of the English and the Irish. For example, Irish Gaelic marriages
were far more flexible than English marriages, and Irish
women were more gregarious than their introverted English
counterparts. Irish women drank alcohol, presided over meetings
and festivals, and kept their own names after marriage. They
could even divorce their husbands at will. All of these customs
were deplorable to the English, and served to further solidify
their opinion of rampant Irish immorality.

Henry began his re-taking of Ireland in 1541 by upgrading
the island from a lordship to a full Kingdom - and then had
himself proclaimed King of Ireland. With the institutions of
government in place, the next step was to extend the control of
the English Kingdom of Ireland over all of its claimed territory.
This took nearly a century, with various English administrations
in the process either negotiating or fighting with the independent
Irish and Old English lords unwilling to hand over their land.

One of the most effective ways to conquer the Island was to
repopulate it with Protestants. From the mid-16th and into the
early 17th century, England carried out a policy of colonization
known as Plantations. Scottish and English Protestants were
sent as colonists to the provinces of Munster and Ulster, and the
counties of Laois and Offlay.

These settlers, who were British and Protestant, would
eventually become the ruling class of Ireland. To make matters
worse, a series of Penal Laws discriminated against all faiths
other than the established Anglican (Church of England). The
principal victims of these laws were the Catholics.

While the English were able to control the island, they could not successfully convert the Catholic Irish to their Protestant religion. The brutal methods used by crown to subjugate Ireland heightened resentment of English rule.

It was during the "Tudor re-conquest" that Sean an Diomais (Shane O'Neill) was born; the son of Conn "The Lame" Bacach O'Neill and Sorch, the daughter of Huge O'Neill, Chief of the Clanaboy O'Neill's.

Little is known about Shane's youth. Historians do know that Shane's mother, Alice Fitzgerald, was Conn's first wife, and the daughter of the 7th Earl of Kildare. She died shortly after Shane was born, and Shane was fostered by the Donnelly family, who raised him until his early teenage years.

The records show that Shane went largely unnoticed until around 1550, when he joined forces against the English and their allies, and began to assert his claim to the family holdings.

As he grew, he often came to blows with anyone who dared question what he perceived to be his rightful inheritance. Shane believed he was predestined to rule.

At the same time, his father, Conn, who was trying to hold on to his territory, was under increasing pressure from four distinct groups vying for power in Ulster. They included the English; the rightful family of O'Neill (hereditary rulers) to which he belonged; a splinter group of O'Neill's called the "Clanaboy O'Neill's" (his wife's clan); and a group of rebellious Scots largely led by the Clan MacDonnell of the Isles.

With the Scots to the Northeast; Clanaboy O'Neill's to the East; and the English to the South; the problems faced by Conn trying to rule his territory weighed heavy. He was often forced to make, and then break, alliances in order to maintain power. The English had promised their support if he would allow himself, and his people, to be subjugated.

Frustrated, Conn chose to accept the English title of the "1st Earl of Tyrone" and swear allegiance to England. This was a common bribe used by the English, and Conn wasn't the only

Irish chieftain to acquiesce. So Conn Bacach O'Neill, former O'Neill clan chieftain, became an Irish/English Lord.

Instead of alleviating his problems, his new title only ignited an enormous family feud. Some family members began to bicker over who would rightfully inherit the chiefdom once Conn is gone. Gaelic custom dictates the successor to a chiefdom be elected from within his own kinsmen.

The English insisted on succession by the first born son or *primogeniture*. So if Conn was, in effect, an English Lord, shouldn't the English custom be followed?

This conundrum created a conflict between Shane, who wanted to be Chief, and the Earl's eldest surviving (yet illegitimate) son, Matthew.

Other members of the family were less concerned about succession. They considered Conn a traitor for kowtowing to the English. Whatever the political ideology, Conn's nephew (the elected heir), and many of Conn's sons, including Shane, chose to wage war against Conn.

Initially, Conn's army prevailed and he routed a number of his family members. Then he launched a surprise attack against his son, Feardorcha, whom the English had named, "Baron of Dungannon." This was a costly battle for Conn, who saw his army defeated and himself arrested. Feardorcha subsequently attacked all the remaining O'Neill's, and quickly became the scourge of the Irish for siding with the English.

During this inter-family warfare, Conn's illegitimate son, Matthew, was raised at the English court and declared heir to Conn over Shane, his legitimate son. This did not set well with Shane, who swore revenge.

On Conn's death, Matthew became Baron of Dungannon. He had little time to enjoy his new title as he was promptly murdered in the night by Shane's supporters.

The title then passed to Matthew's son, Brian, who was dispatched by Shane's followers just as quickly.

In 1562, the title passed to Matthew's youngest son, Hugh O'Neill. Convinced he would be murdered – and rightly so - he fled to safety in England.

With Hugh out of the country, Shane busied himself by establishing his authority in Ulster. He immediately had himself elected *The* O'Neill, which in Irish Gaelic custom meant he was the Clan High Chief of all the O'Neills. According to English law this was an illegal self-anointing. However, in the Irish custom, Shane had just as legitimate a claim to be The O'Neill as any of his rivals.

Shane strategically allied himself with the MacDonnell clan, Scottish rebels who had previously settled in Antrim in the North of Ireland. Together they rose up against the English Queen.

Shane hated the English, and especially their Queen. Not so much because he wanted the power they had, but also for personal reasons.

According to legend, Shane entered into an agreement with Richard Creagh, appointed Papal Archbishop of Armagh under Shane's rule. Shane expected the support of Creagh in stirring up disaffection in his province. Instead, the Archbishop steadily preached loyalty to the Crown even from the pulpit of Armagh Cathedral.

On one occasion Shane attended a service along with six hundred of his fighting men. They were there to hear a sermon that Shane had beforehand instructed his archbishop to preach to encourage his followers to attack their English enemies. Instead, the sermon was addressed to encouraging loyalty in the troops. Shane was furious, and he swore, "with most loud angry talk" to destroy the Cathedral; which he in fact did a few days later.

Shane swore that there was no one he hated more than the Queen of England and his own archbishop, and never again would he hear him preach to the native Irish of English loyalty.

When Queen Elizabeth ascended to the throne in 1558, she was inclined to come to terms with Shane, who after his father's death functioned as de facto chief of the formidable O'Neill clan. In order to deal with the Scots in Ireland, she would have to deal with Shane.

In 1561, Queen Elizabeth tried to have Shane assassinated by ordering Thomas Radclyffe, 3rd Earl of Sussex, to poison his wine. Twice Sussex tried and failed as the plots were discovered beforehand. Infuriated, Shane now had a legitimate reason to continue his criminal conduct. Having failed a number of times to eliminate the crafty Irish chieftain, the English Queen was forced to give in to his demands.

She agreed to recognize his claims to the chiefdom, thus 'dethroning' Hugh O'Neill, son of the murdered Matthew, baron of Dungannon. However, the Queen would only do this if Shane agreed to submit to her authority and that of her skivvy deputy, the Earl of Sussex. O'Neill refused. He would not put himself in the power of a man who had tried to poison him twice.

Shane then made other outrageous claims that were so irrational Elizabeth regretted she ever broached the subject with Shane. The Queen began to give serious consideration to subduing Shane and restoring Hugh O'Neill to Clan Chief.

At this time in Irish history there were three powerful contemporary members of the O'Neill family in Ireland – Shane O'Neill; Sir Turlough O'Neill; and Hugh O'Neill, 1st Baron of Dungannon. Turlough had been elected *Tainiste* (second and successor) when his cousin, Shane, was inaugurated as *The* O'Neill.

However, Turlough wasn't satisfied being second fiddle. He had planned to unseat his cousin while Shane was in England at the request of the Queen. The scheme failed. As soon as Shane returned to Ireland he quickly re-established his authority. In spite of Sussex, Shane renewed his warfare against the O'Donnells and the MacDonnells, to force them to recognize O'Neill dominion in Ulster.

Beyond frustration, Queen Elizabeth finally authorized Sussex to attack Shane on the battlefield. But two separate expeditions by Sussex failed to accomplish anything except cause destruction in O'Neill's country. Shane eluded Sussex, and made him look foolish.

The Queen decided to take a gentler, kinder approach, much against the wishes of Sussex who wanted him treated with contempt. She was afraid Shane might end up working for the Spanish, and that concerned her greatly. So she permitted him to return to Ireland, recognizing him as "The O'Neill" and chief of Tyrone.

The Queen even extended a royal invitation to Shane. Actually, it was more like an arrest. Convinced that the Queen would not harm him because of her formal invitation, Shane accepted, and the Queen received him graciously in London in December 1561.

Upon their arrival, the redoubtable chief and his retainers, all in their native attire, were viewed with curiosity and wonder. To the English, the Irish looked like a band of barbarians. Shane strode through the court between two lines of gawking courtiers; and behind him marched 200 galloglasses, their heads bare, their long hair curling down on their shoulders and clipped short in front just above the eyes. They wore a loose wide-sleeved saffron-dyed tunic, and over this a short shaggy mantle of wolf-skin flung across the shoulders. They also carried battle-axes.

When Shane was presented to her royal majesty, he threw himself face down on the floor at her feet and let out a long, wolfish howl. The Queen and her court were dumbfounded. Then he stood up and identified himself by speaking only in Gaelic, so neither the Queen nor her nobles could understand a word. This was equally puzzling to the Queen.

On the 6th of January 1562, Shane made formal submission to the Queen in presence of the court and the foreign ambassadors. As he "negotiated" with the queen, he made it abundantly clear that he saw himself as her equal.

The queen was not pleased, and so she *invited* Shane to stay and enjoy her hospitality for the next five months before allowing him to leave for home. Basically, he and his men were under house arrest…but in a polite way.

Historians believe the crown took advantage of his presence and made him sign documents against his will. Although he signed them, it would seem he had no intention to carry them out.

He returned to Ulster in May 1562 with the Queen's pardon, all his expenses having been paid by the English government. Shane remained indignant at being forced to sign conditions, and he felt his good nature had been disrespected. So he disregarded the contracts he previously signed, and renewed the war against England.

When the news reached the Queen, she was furious. Sick of the quarrel, she instructed Sussex to end the nonsense by offering Shane "reasonable concessions." Her instructions were carried out, and peace was signed in November 1563 in O'Neill's house at Benburb. This time the terms were to Shane's advantage.

After this peace accord was reached, things remained quiet for some time. Historians have said that Shane "the Proud" was blind to the Irish enemies he was making. Instead of working to unite the Irish against a common enemy, he forced his authority on them which only created more enemies – and he had plenty of those on the English side already.

Nonetheless, using his new found recognition by the Queen, and agreeing to subjugate the Scots, O'Neill now turned his hand against the MacDonnells, claiming he was serving her Majesty the Queen of England in harrying the Scots.

He fought an indecisive battle with Sorley Boy MacDonnell near Coleraine in 1564, and the following year marched from Antrim through the mountains by Clogh to the neighborhood of Ballycastle, where he slaughtered 700 MacDonnells at the Battle of Glentasie and subsequently took Sorley Boy prisoner.

This victory greatly strengthened Shane O'Neill's position. At first the victory gave great joy to the English; but when they realized how much it increased his power, their joy soon turned to jealousy and fear.

The Queen sent two commissioners to meet with Shane, who spoke the following: *"For the queen, I confess she is my sovereign: but I never made peace with her but at her own seeking. My ancestors were kings of Ulster, and Ulster is mine, and shall be mine. O'Donnell shall never come into his country, nor Bagenall into Newry, nor Kildare into Dundrum or Lecale. They are now mine. With the sword I won them: with this sword I will keep them."*

Sir Henry Sidney, one of those of met with Shane, declared that *"Lucifer himself was not more puffed up with pride and ambition than O'Neill."*

Arrogant, and full of himself, Shane attacked the O'Donnell's who were approaching on his western flank. Hugh O'Donnell chief of Tirconnel, had made a prior plundering excursion into Tyrone, Shane's territory, in 1567. Shane had decided to retaliate by crossing Lough Swilly into Tirconnell, but when he encountered O'Donnell's troops at the other side he was utterly routed. 1,300 of Shane's men died – most drown while trying to escape. Shane barely escaped with his life.

Shane the Proud didn't handle this defeat well. Some historians believe he lost his mind, or his heart, or both, because he chose to place himself at the mercy of the Scots, whose undying enmity he had earned by the defeat at Glenshesk two years before.

In a move that has bewildered historians for ages, Shane wandered into their camp at Cushendun on the Antrim coast in 1567, with only fifty followers, trusting in the Scots generosity.

They initially received him with a show of welcome and cordiality. Nevertheless, at the celebratory party on June 2, 1567, the wine began to flow and soon the MacDonnells became angry and resentful. As far as they were concerned, no amount of merriment could make them forget the slaughter at Glenshesk

In the midst of the festivities, the MacDonnells raised a dispute, most likely prearranged, and after seizing their arms, they massacred Shane and all his followers.

Some historians contend that a spy, hired by Thomas Radclyffe, 3rd Earl of Sussex and the Lord Deputy, was sent to the banquet to murder Shane. That does seem plausible given the number of time Radclyffe attempted to kill Shane. Other historians believe the instigator of the assassination was a "Captain Piers," a renowned soldier and one of Queen Elizabeth's favorites whom she often called upon for such nasty deeds.

Hot-headed Scots, or a paid assassin, either way the result was the same - Shane the Proud ended up on the wrong end of a Scottish dirk. No longer would he be a thorn in the side of the English.

Shane was buried at Glenarm, but not before the MacDonnells lopped off his head, covered it in preservative tar, and transported the gruesome article to Dublin. They hoped their macabre gift would help ingratiate them with the English, as well as the Queen, who had considered expelling the entire clan from Ireland.

When Shane's head arrived in Dublin, government officials were delighted. They placed the head on the pole thrust horizontally from the northwest Dublin city gateway, where it remained for several years.

The Lord Deputy then sent a hastily written note to Queen Elizabeth to relay the delightful news. Shane O'Neill, Captain and Clan Chief of Northwest Ulster, had been slain.

Once again, an Irishman had tried to block England's total conquest of the island and failed.

The Spanish Armada Smashes into Ireland

"Once they hit the storm,
the most severely damaged Spanish ships
floundered briefly, then sunk like stones."

– Irish governmental records, 1588

In 1588, the most powerful and best-equipped army in all of Europe belonged to Philip II, the King of Spain. Dubbed "The Army of Flanders," this force had all but crushed the Dutch protestant revolt in the northern provinces of the Spanish Netherlands.

Having temporarily routed the Dutch, Philip now wanted to stab at the heart of the Protestant revolt – England. To do so, he needed the help of his majestic Spanish Armada, the mightiest naval fleet in the world.

Philip knew he could not ultimately defeat the Dutch until he had conquered England and put an end to a long time religious rivalry between Catholic Spain and Protestant England. That would entail dethroning Queen Elizabeth and reconverting England back to her Catholic roots. This plan consisted of the coordination of a fleet of warships to sail from Spain, and an army from the Netherlands, to create a simultaneous invasion of England.

The main reason King Philip wanted to crush England was to overthrow the Protestants ruled by Queen Elizabeth I. In 1588, Spain controlled what was called the Spanish Netherlands, but is today known as Holland and Belgium. During that period, the English had aided the Dutch Protestants in Holland, which greatly angered the King of Spain. Holland wanted its independence, and bitterly resented being forced to join the Catholic Church - especially at a time when Protestant ideas were percolating.

Many of the Dutch were forced to practice Protestantism in secret for fear of the Spanish religious police called "The Inquisition," whose main duties were to chase down, persecute, and torture Protestants until they either converted to Catholicism or admitted they were heretics. The latter admission usually resulted in death.

There was other rationale for the attack on England, besides the religious element. The Spanish wanted retribution for the English "sea-dogs" who had been causing a great deal of damage to Spain's silver trade. Privateers, such as Sir Francis Drake, attacked Spanish shipping off of the West Indies costing Spain vast sums of money. The English may have viewed Drake as a hero; to the Spanish he was a pirate scoundrel employed by a heathen Queen.

With England under his control, Philip could dominate the English Channel and his ships would have easy passage from Spain to the Spanish Netherlands. Spanish troops stationed there could be easily supplied, and therefore a significant army could be in place as long as necessary.

King Philip also had a personal stake in the attack. He had been married to Elizabeth's half-sister, Mary, during the time when England was ruled by the Catholics. But one year prior, in 1587, Mary Queen of Scots, a Catholic, was executed in England on the orders of Queen Elizabeth. She had made it clear that if she became Queen of England, Philip should inherit the throne after her death. Even though that wish went unfulfilled, Philip still believed he had a moral obligation to ensure no more Catholics would be arrested, or executed, in England.

Chosen to lead the mighty Spanish Armanda was the Lord High Admiral, Marquess of Santa Cruz, Don Alvaro de Bazan the elder, a veteran sailor, and the only experienced naval commander that Spain possessed. He was King Philip's obvious choice. Other experienced commanders included Juan Martinez deRecalde, who had traveled this route before, including sailing past the Irish coast which was normally given a wide berth by the Catholic Spaniards.

The planning needed to prepare the Armada was tremendous. Cannons, guns, gunpowder, swords and many other weapons were needed, and Spain bought them from whomever they could. A number of merchant ships were converted to naval vessels, and other ships carried only supplies for the Armada such as 600,000 pounds of salted pork, 14,000 barrels of wine, 40,000 gallons of olive oil, 11,000 pairs of sandals, 5,000 pairs of shoes, 11 million pounds of ships biscuits, not to mention 728 servants and 180 priests.

Word of the preparation eventually reached England, and in 1587, Drake "singed the King of Spain's beard" by sailing an English fleet into Cádiz Bay, one of Spain's main ports, occupying the town for three days, destroying 31 enemy ships as well as a large quantity of stores and capturing 6 ships, and disrupted coastal shipping. Santa Cruz sailed in pursuit of the fleeing English ships, but eventually pounding storms forced him to return to Lisbon without exacting revenge.

This was a valiant preemptive strike by the English, but Spain had plenty of ships, so they just shrugged it off. What's one year, more or less? However, the attack did more than delay the launch of the Armada for one year. During the time it took Spain to repair their damaged ships, Admiral Cruz, who had been ailing for some time, died suddenly on February 9, 1588.

The Armada, now fitted and ready to sail, was without its most experienced naval veteran. This was a bad omen.

Dismayed but undeterred, King Philip selected a replacement - a very rich and successful infantry general named Alonso Peréz Guzmán, Duke of Medina Sidonia.

Though a competent field general, Medina Sidonia had never been to sea, and when he did, he got sick. He was a foot soldier, not a sailor. The Duke himself, realizing the absurdity of the King's decision, protested the appointment due to his own admitted inexperience in naval matters. However, the King insisted. So the man who would lead the world's most powerful naval fleet, with no prior nautical experience, and prone to puke at sea, was ordered take his troops across the narrow end of the North Sea and attack England, the most powerful nation in the world at that time.

It should be noted that although this great fleet has been called the "Spanish Armada," it actually included ships manned by Portuguese, Italians, Germans, Dutch, Flemings, Irish, and even some English opportunists.

With the new general in command, the Armada set sail on July 19th 1588. The fleet of 130 ships - including 22 fighting galleons - sailed in the traditional crescent shape which offered their ships the most protection. The larger but slower galleons were in the middle of the crescent and were protected by the faster, smaller boats that surrounded them. Smaller ships known as zabras and pataches supplied the galleons. Medina Sidonia's force also included 30,000 men - mostly infantry.

The voyage went smoothly, and the Armada faced little opposition as it approached the English coast of Cornwall ten days later. Cornish fishermen, angling off the English coast, watched in amazement as the massive Armada sailed by. The Spanish knew they could not keep their arrival a secret, so they didn't even try. They were hoping the English would spot the powerful Armada and tremble in fear at its approach.

As the Armada sailed up the English Channel, it was attacked by an English force lead by Sir Francis Drake, whom the Spanish loathed because of his privateer attacks on their ships. But the attack did little damage to the Armada. The English, firing from their coastal forts, watched as their ammunition bounced off the hulls of the well-built Spanish ships. Even the smaller English ships, swarming around the large Spanish vessels like gnats, were no match for the Armada.

Throughout the whole of its journey from Spain, until they reached the east side of the English Channel, the Armada went virtually unmolested save for the brief skirmish with Drake. The formidable crescent shape formation served its purpose as opaque armor; much like the Roman infantry who locked shields to form an impenetrable phalanx.

Lord Charles Howard of Effingham, High Admiral of England, was the first to intercept the Armada near Plymouth with a much larger English fleet. For the next week the English and Dutch ships, led by Lord Howard, Sir John Hawkins, Sir Martin Frobisher, Lord Henry Seymour and Sir William Winter, made small hit and run attacks on the Spanish off of Plymouth, Portland Bill, and the Isle of Wight. Although they were able to inflict some damage, they could not break the Armada's crescent-shaped defense.

So the English bided their time, hoping for their luck to change. It did change, but for the worse, when on August 4th, a strong wind caused the Channel to become rough, and the smaller English ships were tossed about as if they were toys. The Spanish, with their heavier vessels, used the wind to move quickly to the European coastline where they intended to pick up Spanish troops to assist in the invasion of England.

However, stopping to load those troops proved to be the chinch in the Spanish armor. When the fleet slowed, as it approached the Spanish Netherlands, it lost its crescent shape, and effectively dismantled their mighty shield. Medina Sidonia also discovered, to his dismay, there was no port deep enough for the fleet to stop and load the troops. The best he could do was to harbor at Gravelines near modern day Calais, France, and wait for the troops to come to them. On July 27th 1588, the mighty Spanish fleet moored - and waited.

Without their crescent formation the Spanish were virtually helpless, and outnumbered ten to one by the combined English and Dutch navies. Now their heavier, bulkier design was a disadvantage – quite different than when they were out in open sea.

This time the lighter English ships, sleek and more maneuverable, had the upper hand. They also had better equipment, and sailors who were expert cannoneers, trained for blasting ships out of the water. Conversely, the Spanish relied more of infantry weapons, and their ships carried infantry soldiers, not professional sailors. The Spanish sailors were prone to boarding and engaging in hand-to-hand combat. But if the English kept the Spanish at arms-length, there would never be a *mano a mano* battle.

Now the English had their enemy hemmed into a port and began systematically picking them apart. It was the worst possible scenario for the Spaniards. With all their weaknesses exposed, they were simply fish in a barrel to the English ships who absolutely pummeled them.

Ceasing an opportunity, Sir Francis Drake loaded eight rickety ships with flammable material, lit them on fire, and sailed them into the heart of the armada. Although the Spanish had heard about these crewless English "Hell Burners" - and even posted sentries to keep watch - the floating bombs still drifted toward the fully armed fleet. Each Hell Burner carried enormous amounts of gunpowder meant to blow enemy vessels out of the water upon impact.

As the Spanish spotted the burning ships bearing down on them, each vessel in the Armada panicked and endeavored to break out of Gravelines to save itself. Awkwardly jockeying for position, the ships set sail to avoid the Hell Burners. One Spanish ship was struck and erupted into flames on impact. Panicked sailors leapt over the side of the burning ship and into the sea. Four Spanish galleons chose to stand their ground and fight Drake, even though they were hopelessly outnumbered.

Three of these galleons were sunk within minutes, and 600 men were killed and 800 wounded. But they succeeded in keeping the English from attacking the rest of the Armada who fled to open seas. The weather once again favored the Spaniards as a storm arrived and aided in the Armada's escape. Medina Sidonia later wrote that the Armada was, "saved by the weather, by God's mercy..."

Meanwhile, the rest of the fleet was frantically trying to escape to the deep waters of the North Sea. Anticipating that particular escape route, the English/Dutch fleet had blocked off any chance the Armada had of sailing west in the English Channel. Therefore, when the Armada reassembled into a fleet, it could only head east, up the coast of England, and around the north of Scotland. From there the Armada could sail past the western Irish coast and back to Spain. And so they began the long journey home. Or so they thought.

After the Battle of Gravelines, the English examined their ships and discovered they had suffered little hull damage. The Spanish vessels, however, were severely damaged by canon fire, much of it below the waterline, and were rapidly taking on water as they escaped. It was now a race to get home before they sunk.

Hundreds of years later, divers would recover Spanish cannon balls used during the Battle of Gravelines. It showed the Armada's ammunition to be badly cast. The iron lacked the correct composition and was too brittle, causing the balls to disintegrate on impact, rather than penetrating the hull. Several guns were found to also have been badly cast, and also of inadequate composition, increasing the danger of bursting and killing the Spanish gun crews.

The Spaniards also carried guns of significantly greater weight than the English fleet. Study of the wrecks found off the Scottish and Irish coasts showed the largest guns not to be part of the ships' armament, but a siege train to be used on land after the invasion. More evidence the Spaniards were prepared for a land invasion, but ill equipped for naval battle.

Once out to sea, and free of the Dutch and English fleets, a meeting of the remaining Armada commanders was held on the Spanish flagship. Some commanders proposed a course for Norway, others opted for Ireland. Medina Sidonia made his choice, and his instructions were issued to the fleet:

"The course that is first to be held is to the north/north-east until you be found under 61 degrees and a half; and then to take

great heed lest you fall upon the Island of Ireland for fear of the harm that may happen unto you upon that coast. Then, parting from those islands and doubling the Cape in 61 degrees and a half, you shall run west/south-west until you be found under 58 degrees; and from thence to the south-west to the height of 53 degrees; and then to the south/south-west, making to the Cape Finisterre, and so to procure your entrance into the Groin or to Ferrol, or to any other port of coast of Galicia."

According to these instructions, the ships were to approach the coast of Norway, before steering to the meridian of the Shetland Islands and on to Rockall Island. This allowed safe passage inside the southern tip of the Shetlands, with the fleet clearing the coast of Scotland at a distance of 100 miles.

Once out in the broad Atlantic, the commanders were to steer to a point 400 miles beyond the mouth of the River Shannon on the west coast of Ireland, leaving a clear run to northern Spain. They were told by Medina Sidonia to avoid Ireland at all costs because of the overwhelming English presence. Before the Armada left Spain, he had been informed that landing on the Irish coast was risky at best, and quite possibly fatal.

The Armada followed the appointed course, clearing the North Sea and sailing into the Atlantic from North Uist in the Hebrides Islands, until it found itself off Rockall (the most isolated sea-rock in the world). Existing log-books show that the fleet accurately estimated its distance from the Irish coast at this point as "95 leagues."

However, their supplies on board were not enough for such a journey and many of the crews were reduced to eating rope for survival. Fresh water quickly disappeared. But that was nothing compared to what lay ahead.

As the Armada sailed around the north of Scotland in mid-September, it ran head-long into one of the worst storms in history. Irish governmental records at the time stated the storm was, "...the like whereof hath not been seen or heard for a long time." Once they hit the storm, the most severely damaged Spanish ships floundered briefly, then sunk like stones.

At Rockall, a portion of the fleet led by Juan Martinez de Recalde deviated from Medina Sidonia's instructions - whether by choice or out of necessity is not known. It is possible that the formation of the fleet was broken in heavy weather or fog, or possibly during the storm itself.

After seven long weeks at sea, the proximity of the Irish coast made landfall a good option so they could take on supplies and effect repairs. So choosing to ignore Sidonia's warning to avoid Ireland, 28 ships headed for the Irish shoreline. Perhaps Recalde made this decision because of his prior knowledge of the area, including sailing around the coast of Ireland.

Only 84 ships followed Medina Sidonia's flagship on the appointed course around Scotland and the Shetland Islands. Most of those vessels made it home to Spain where the sailors reunited with families and slept in warm beds. The fate of those who chose to disregard the warning and land on the Irish coast wasn't nearly as pleasant.

The portion of the fleet that descended upon the Irish coast in 1588 included several galleons, but most were merchant ships which had been converted for battle and were now leaking heavily. Most of their anchors were missing and they were sailing with severely damaged masts and rigging. Within days, this lost fleet had made landfall in Ireland.

The head of the Irish crown government at Dublin was Lord Deputy William Fitzwilliam. In August of 1588, Fitzwilliam was presented with misinformation that the battle in the English Channel had actually been won by the Spanish, and not the English, and the invasion of England was imminent. The information given to Fitzwilliam also implied that the entire Spanish fleet was about to fall on the coast of Ireland and subsequently join forces with the Irish rebels and slaughter the inhabitants, especially in territories that were beyond the control of the crown government. As one might imagine, the degree of alarm at Dublin was extreme.

But reliable intelligence was soon received at Waterford and Dublin that the Spanish had actually lost the battle, and now their crippled ships were smashing onto the Irish coastline from Ulster to Munster. Not wanting to take any chances, and with fewer than 2,000 troops to maintain their hold on Ireland, the English troops in Ireland resorted to the practice of exterminating the invaders. There would be no prisoners.

Fitzwilliam immediately issued an order to apprehend and execute all Spaniards on the spot. Even the use of torture was sanctioned in pursuit of the Spanish survivors; and those aiding them were to be charged as traitors and summarily executed as well.

The first landfall of the Armada ships was in the southern province of Ireland, which had recently been colonized by the English in the Plantation of Munster. There could have been no worse place for the Spaniards to land. Fitzwilliam received orders from London to lead an expedition there, and intelligence from the governor of Connacht soon confirmed that further landfalls were being made throughout the west and north of the country.

The first sighting of Armada ships was in the River Shannon estuary. There were seven Spanish ships anchored safely at Scattery Roads. An attempt to land was repulsed, although certain supplies were secured while repairs were undertaken.

One of the ships, the Annunciada, was scuppered, with the crew transferring to the Barco de Danzig, which managed to make it safely back to Spain.

Recalde's squadron consisted of three ships: the San Juan de Portugal (1,150 tons/500 men/20 guns), the San Juan de Bautista (750 tons/243 men), and another small vessel - almost certainly a Scottish fishing smack that had been seized to assist with navigation and inshore work.

As the ships made their way through a storm to the coast of Kerry, the ship's lookouts sighted Mount Brandon on the Dingle peninsula, and to the west the lofty Blasket Islands, a complex archipelago studded with reefs.

Recalde steered toward the Blaskets in search of shelter, and chose to ride on a swell through a tight gap at the eastern tip of the Great Blasket Island. His galleon made it through to calm water and dropped anchor over a sandy bottom beneath sheer cliffs. The Bautista and the smack soon followed. Recalde sailed through the gap between the tip of the Great Blasket and Carraig Fhada (right-of-center) to enter the sound (foreground). Lookouts for the English crown watched his arrival from a cliff-top in the Dingle peninsula.

The ships remained within their shelter for several days. An army of English soldiers arrived in Dingle to guard against a Spanish landing.

Recalde sent a reconnaissance party ashore, but all eight members were captured and summarily executed. At one stage a westerly gale caused the Portugal to collide with the Bautista, and when the wind died down another ship, the Santa Maria de la Rosa (900 tons/297 men/Guipuzcoa squadron), entered the sound from the north and fired a gun as a distress signal.

As the tide ebbed, Recalde's ships held their anchorage in the more sheltered part of the sound, while the Rosa drifted and then simply sank - leaving one survivor for the English to interrogate. The survivor's information was that the captain of the Rosa had called the pilot a traitor and run him through with a sword just as the ship began to sink

Two more ships then entered the sound - the San Juan de Ragusa (650 tons/285 men), the other unidentified. The Ragusa was in distress and sank - perhaps on striking Dunbinna Reef. The Bautista attempted to take advantage of an ebb tide and sail south out of the sound, but ended up tacking about on the flood tide to avoid the numerous reefs before sailing through the north-west passage.

After a difficult night, the crew was dismayed to find themselves at the mouth of the sound once more. But the wind blew from the south-east, and the Bautista finally escaped on the 25th of September and made it home to Spain through a terrible storm.

Three days later, Recalde led the remaining ships out of the sound and brought them to Spain. The stress must have proved too much for Recalde, for he died not long after his arrival home.

The sloop Nuestra Senora del Socorro (75 tons) anchored at Fenit, in Tralee Bay on the coast of Kerry, surrendered to crown officers. The 24 men on board were taken into custody and marched to Tralee Castle were they were subsequently hanged from a gibbet.

Off the coast of County Clare, numerous ships of the fleet were sighted. Four were reported at Loop Head, two of which were wrecked, including the San Esteban (700 tons/264 men) at Doonbeg, and probably the heavily damaged San Marcos (790 tons/squadron of Portugal/409 men/33 guns) at Spanish Point inside Mutton Island. All survivors were put to death by the Sheriff of Clare, Boetius MacClancy, most likely at Gallows Hill (Cnoc na Crochaire).

At Liscannor, the oar-powered galleass Zuñiga (290/Naples) anchored off-shore with a broken rudder, having found a gap in the Cliffs of Moher, which rose straight up from the sea over 220 meters. The ship came under surveillance by the Sheriff of Clare and, when a cock-boat was sent ashore in search of supplies, the Spanish were attacked by English forces and had to withdraw to their ship. One captive was taken and sent for interrogation. The Zuñiga escaped the coast with favorable winds, put in at le Havre, and finally made it home to Naples, Italy in the following year.

La Trinidad Valencera (1,000 tons/Levant squadron/360 men/42 guns) was taking on more water than could be pumped out as it approached the Irish coast. Nevertheless the 264 men in the Barca de Amburgo - another ship that was practically swamped in the heavy seas - were taken on board. Now overloaded with Spanish soldiers, the Trinidad anchored in Glenagivney Bay in

Co. Donegal, where she listed to such a degree the order was given to abandon ship. Some locals were paid for the use of a small boat, and over the course of two days all 560 men were ferried to shore.

The survivors of the Valencera and Amburgo then began a seven day march inland, hoping to find food and shelter. Instead, they encountered a force of English/Irish cavalry under the command of the foster-brothers of Hugh O'Neill, 3rd Earl of Tyrone. Upon pledges of safe conduct for their delivery into the custody of Fitzwilliam - given in the presence of the Earl of Tyrconnell - the Spanish laid down their arms.

Despite assurances, the Earl of Tyrconnell had the noblemen and officers separated from the rest of the crew, and 300 of the ordinary men were systematically massacred. One hundred fifty were able to flee the slaughter and disappeared through the Irish bog. Some were found by "Sorley Boy" MacDonnell at Dunluce, or at the house of Redmond O'Gallagher, the bishop of Derry. Eager to help the Spaniards, they were sent on to Scotland and freed.

The 45 Spanish noblemen and officers were marched to Dublin, but only 30 survived to reach the capital, where they were dispatched to London for ransom. O'Neill was furious that Tyrconnell had betrayed the Spanish, and he made efforts to aid all survivors within his territory.

As the Armada ships were wrecking up and down the Irish coast, survivors were delivered to Galway from all over the province. In the first wave of seizures, 40 noblemen were reserved for ransom, and 300 men were put to death. Later, on the orders of Fitzwilliam, all the noblemen except two were executed, along with six Dutch boys who had fallen into custody afterward. In all, 12 ships were wrecked on the coast of Connacht, and 1,100 survivors were put to death.

The Falco Blanco (300 tons/103 men/16 guns) and the Concepcion of Biscay (225 men/18 guns) and another unknown ship entered Galway Bay. The Falco Blanco was grounded at

Barna, 5 km west of Galway city, and most of those on board made it to shore safely. The Concepcion was grounded at Carna 30 km further west, having been lured to shore by the bonfires of the sea-faring O'Flaherty clan.

Three ships were wrecked on the coast of Sligo, with 1,800 men drowned and perhaps 100 making it to shore. Among the survivors was Captain Francisco de Cuellar, who gave a remarkable account of his experiences in the Spanish fleet as well as time spend avoiding capture in Ireland.

In September, at Tyrawley in County Mayo, a galleon was wrecked, and of the men who came to shore, 80 were killed by gallowglass (foreign mercenary) warriors. Seventy-two (along with a bishop) were taken into custody for the crown and put to death at Galway on Fitzwilliam's orders. Tradition has it that another ship was wrecked in the vicinity, near Kid Island, but no record remains of this event. Also, the Gran Grin was wrecked at the mouth of Clew Bay, the ancestral home of Clan Chieftain Grace O'Malley.

Another disabled ship, the merchant ship, La Rata Santa Maria Encoronada (419 men/35 guns), made a run for the Irish coast in desperate need of repair, along with 4 other ships of the Levant squadron, plus four galleons. The Rata carried an unusually high number of noblemen from the most ancient families of Spain - chief among them Don Alonso Martinez de Leyva - as well as the son of the Irish rebel, James Fitzmaurice Fitzgerald.

The Rata was skillfully handled along the northern coast of Mayo, but could not clear the Mullet Peninsula, and so anchored in Blacksod Bay on the 7th of September. The wind picked up and the anchors dragged, until the ship was driven on to Ballycroy strand. All the crew made it to shore under the leadership of de Leyva.

The resourceful Spaniards then seized two castles and fortified them with munitions and stores from their beached ship. Then they torched the ship. Unfortunately, the rebel's son died on board before they landed. He was subsequently placed in a cypress chest and cast into the sea.

The Spanish soon moved on to another castle, where they were met by a host of fellow survivors who had been on board another ship that glided into the bay without masts. De Leyva's makeshift army now numbered 600.

Not overly alarmed as yet, the Governor of Connacht decided to let them be rather than risk a bloody confrontation.

After a few days, two more ships of the Armada entered Blacksod Bay - the merchant ship, Nuestra Senora de Begona (750 tons/297 men) and the transport, Duquesa Santa Ana (900 tons/23 guns/357 men).

De Leyva and his 600 men boarded the Duquesa. The Nuestra Senora sailed straight for Santander, Spain arriving some time later. The Duquesa, however, was somewhat damaged, and decided to sail north for Scotland. Stormy weather soon grounded the Duquesa in Loughros Bay in Donegal. All aboard reached the shore safely, and to their delight, they had actually arrived in friendly Irish territory.

De Leyva, who had been seriously injured when a capstan malfunctioned, pitched camp on the shore of the bay for nine days. Finally news came of another ship of the fleet, the galleass, Girona, which had anchored in Killybegs Harbor while two other ships had been lost on attempting to enter the harbor.

With the assistance of friendly Irish chieftain, MacSweeney Bannagh, the Girona was repaired and set sail in mid-October with 1,300 men on board, including de Leyva.

This story had no happy ending however, as a gale struck and the Girona was driven ashore at Dunluce in County Antrim. There were only nine survivors, who were transported to Scotland by Sorley Boy MacDonnell. The bodies of 260 men washed ashore over the next several days.

All in all, as many as 24 Spanish ships were wrecked on a rocky Irish coastline spanning 500 km from Antrim in the north to Kerry in the south, and the threat to Crown authority was no

more. Most of the survivors of the numerous wrecks were put
to death, and the remainder fled across the sea to Scotland. It is
estimated that 5,000 members of the Spanish fleet perished in
Ireland.

By the end of September 1588, the queen's deputy,
Fitzwilliam, reported to her secretary that the Armada alarm
was over. Soon after, he surmised that only about 100 survivors
remained in the country.

In 1596, an envoy of King Phillip II of Spain arrived in
Ireland to make inquiries of survivors and was successful in
locating only eight Spanish sailors.

Of the 120 ships in the Armada, half were lost, many just
slipping silently beneath the waves. The remaining fleet limped
back to Spain in poor condition. The engagements between the
Armada and the English fleet at Eddystone, Portland, Isle of
Wight, Calais and Gravelines caused many casualties.

Of the Spanish Armada's complement of 30,000 soldiers and
sailors, 20,000 were killed during the various battles, or when
their vessels smashed onto the Irish coast. Those that survived
the shipwrecking were executed by the Irish inhabitants.

Before the end of the Anglo-Spanish War, Ireland would play
another part in Spanish strategy. 3,500 Spanish troops landed in
the south of Ireland in the autumn of 1601 to assist the Ulster
rebel, Hugh O'Neill, at the height of the Nine Years War (1595-
1603). However, this expedition failed, and Spain and England
finally agreed to peace in 1604.

The Spanish gradually reasserted their dominance at sea,
and booty from the New World flowed in to the royal treasury at
an increased rate.

Following the peace, Elizabeth's successor, James I,
neglected his fleet and chose to secure crown influence in Ireland.
In 1607, the chief rebels (who were sympathetic to Spain) fled
the northern province of Ireland, and the English re-conquest of
the country was perfected upon the seizure and colonization of
their territories in the Plantation of Ulster in 1610.

The Spanish Armada proved to be an expensive disaster for Spain, but for the English it was a much celebrated victory which made Sir Francis Drake even more of a hero. It even affected the way the English Tudors celebrated Christmas. From that day forward, Queen Elizabeth ordered that everybody should have goose on Xmas Day as that was the meal she had eaten on the evening she learned that her glorious navy had defeated the Armada.

As to whether any of the Spanish castaways settled in Ireland and procreated - there was actually little to induce the shipwrecked soldiers to stay. The Spanish considered the Irish to be savages, and they saw the island as a cold and forbidding place - totally lacking sophistication.

But a few Spaniards did stick around; and several participated in a combined force of Scots and Irish to defeat an English army at Ballyshannon in northwest Ireland in 1597.

It is safe to assume the Armada's survivors did not make much of a dent on the ethnic makeup of the country. This shatters the long held myth that the "Black Irish" are the descendants of the Spanish castaways.

That's not to say that Spaniards never settled in Ireland. Spanish merchants did a brisk commerce in Irish ports for hundreds of years before and after the Armada's arrival. Some, no doubt, had children and/or took up residence in Ireland; but those numbers were nominal at best, and probably no different than any other seafaring ethnic group who decided to plant roots.

Robert Emmet
The Revolutionary

"When my country takes her place
among the nations of the earth,
then and not till then,
let my epitaph be written."

- Robert Emmet on his impending execution 1803

Why would a wealthy Irish Protestant take up arms against the British Army occupying Ireland, only five years after a similar rebellion met with disastrous results?

Long before the conflict in Northern Ireland took on overwhelmingly religious tones, Catholic and Protestant Irish men and women fought together for independence from Britain.

The most well-known joining of religious forces was the famous Wexford Rebellion of 1798, where Catholics and Protestants alike joined together in an ill-fated attempt to throw off the yoke of British tyranny. It is in the aftermath of the '98 Rebellion that the story of Robert Emmet truly begins. An Irish Protestant idealist with enough power and connections to effect change.

Emmet was born in Dublin in 1778 to Robert Emmet, State Physician of Ireland, and Elizabeth Mason. He was the youngest of 17 children, 13 of whom died at birth. He was the fifth child to be named Robert, after his father. He enrolled in Trinity College in Dublin in 1798, which was the path that members of the Irish-Anglican upper class trod on their way to high government and social positions. At the time of his enrollment, his older brother, Thomas Addis Emmet, had declared himself a member of the United Irishmen, and was one of the main architects of the '98 Wexford Rebellion...something that did not go unnoticed by Robert.

While attending Trinity College, Robert Emmet joined the Historical Society whose alumni included Theobald Wolfe Tone, the leader of the ill fated 1798 Irish rebellion. It wasn't long before Emmet, and his fellow Society members, incurred the wrath of the Board of Fellows of Trinity College for, "*entertaining republican principles and for making the Historical Society a theatre for the discussion of modern politics.*"

In 1798, in the wake of the Wexford Rebellion, the Lord Chancellor of Trinity began interrogating students regarding their views on Irish independence, and demanding they disclose the names of fellow students who were members of the United Irishmen. The inquest resulted in the expulsion of 19 students, including Robert Emmet.

Emmet then traveled to France in 1800 where, with exiled United Irishmen, he laid the plans for a French-aided uprising in the summer of 1803. He felt the time was right for another revolution, especially because of the possibility of yet another war between France and England. If this were to happen, Emmet theorized that Napoleon Bonaparte would most likely invade either England or Ireland.

The United Irishmen, both on the continent and in Ireland, were therefore prepared to sacrifice their just resentment against France, for her failure to keep her engagements with them in '98, and enter into a new alliance.

This time Emmet believed he had an absolute promise from the French of a large expeditionary force to aid in the rising in Ireland. There was also an understanding with - and guarantees of co-operation from - revolutionary societies in England and Scotland. He also had pledges from men of the highest social, military, and political standing in Ireland who promised financial backing and moral support. Emmet was certain he had 19 counties that could be relied upon to join the rebellion.

It certainly appeared that another effort at an uprising would stand a good chance of success. Therefore, having met with Napoleon, and convinced that a French invasion of Ireland was imminent, he returned to Ireland in the autumn of 1802. Against his brother's wishes, Robert Emmet committed himself to a revolution. After considerable planning and preparation, Emmet's revolution was ready.

Unfortunately, the rebellion got off to a bad start due to a series of blunders. Emmet was forced to act one week early, and without French assistance, when an accidental explosion destroyed one of his arms depots. Regardless of the lack of French help, he was still counting on the assurances that if Dublin rose, the rest of the country would follow.

Due to miscommunication, a band of outlaws, hiding in the Wicklow Mountains since 1798, never came to Emmet's aid. There were also a variety of foolish errors, which caused the insurgents to enter their war ill-equipped. Fuses and rammers were forgotten; fuses for grenades were mislaid; scaling ladders, pikes, and blunderbusses were not ready; and money to purchase additional weapons arrived late and was altogether insufficient.

One of the worse blows to the rebellion came when Bernard Duggan, a trusted Emmet insider, continuously fed information to the British Under-Secretary. From that ignominious start, the uprising then disintegrated into pure chaos.Hoping to recruit 2,000 men for the uprising in Dublin, only about 90 arrived at the rendezvous point, armed with pikes and blunderbusses.

On the night of Saturday, July 23, 1803, wearing a green and white uniform and brandishing a drawn sword, Emmet and his small, rag-tag troop marched on Dublin Castle.

Emmet moved toward the old Market House, but some of his men detached themselves and attacked the coach of Lord Chief Justice Kilwarden of Ireland, who happened to be traveling by. Kilwarden was dragged from his coach into the street. A man by the name of "Shannon" rushed forward and plunged his pike into the Chief Justice. Others followed. His Lordship became a pincushion.

Emmet had lost control of his men. He was attempting to restore order when word reached him of the Kilwarden murder.

Realizing his rising had transformed into a brutal and wild street riot, he dismissed his men. Suddenly a detachment of British military appeared and fired on the insurgents, who immediately fled in all directions.

Emmet was distraught and demoralized. He had hoped by seizing Dublin Castle, others would rise up and join him. Needless to say, this small band of revolutionaries never got anywhere near the Castle. By dispersing his followers, Emmet thought his men could fare for themselves until the promised French aid had arrived. What Emmet did not know is the French were not coming.

Once again the French had failed their Irish allies. Years later, Thomas Addis Emmet would refer to Bonaparte as, *"the worse enemy Ireland ever had."* Emmet, by now thoroughly disillusioned by his followers' lack of discipline and murderous rioting, abandoned the project and went in to hiding in the Wicklow Mountains.

Emmet's friends tried to convince him to flee the county, but he refused. He was determined to speak with his fiancée, Sarah Curran, before he decided whether to flee the country. Eventually, he returned to Dublin in an effort to see Sarah.

Unfortunately, a fellow named Malachy Delany, one who had donned a uniform and marched along side Emmett during the insurrection, had turned informer and notified the military of his whereabouts.

On August 25, at about 7:00 PM, Emmet was arrested. He tried to escape, but was pistol-whipped into submission by a British guard and taken to the infamous Kilmainham Jail.

On Monday, September 19, 1803, at the special commission before Lord Norbury, Robert Emmet was put on trial for high treason.

One of the three counsel assigned to Emmet was Leonard McNally, a paid informer for the crown. The Attorney-General, Standish O'Grady, read the indictment against Emmet, accusing him of organizing and inciting the rebellion. Then, one by one, witnesses testified in court to Emmet's personal involvement in planning the rebellion. They testified to Emmet supervising the making of weapons, overseeing the tailoring of green military jackets, his attempted alliance with France, and leading his men, with sword drawn, calling out, *"come on, my boys,"* as they marched down from Dirty-Lane and began firing their blunderbusses.

After a litany of witnesses and informers concluded their statements, effectively sealing Emmet's fate, he was asked the following question, *"What have you therefore, now to say, why judgment of death and execution should not be awarded against you, according to law."* Emmet, standing forward in the dock, in front of the bench, launched in to a most eloquent speech denying that he was an emissary of France, and that he had no plans what-so-ever to offer up his country to the French.

Emmet further stated that he only wished to procure for his country, *"the guarantee that Washington procured for America."* Although constantly interrupted, Emmet continued his lengthy oration. Finally, he spoke one last time. *"I have but a few words more to say. I am going to my cold and silent grave, my lamp of life is nearly extinguished. I have parted with everything that was dear to me in this life, and for my country's cause with the idol of my soul, the object of my affections. My race is run. The grave opens to receive me, and I sink in to its bosom. I have but one request to ask at my departure from this world, it is the charity of its silence. Let no man write my epitaph; for as no man who knows my motives dare now vindicate them, let not prejudice or ignorance asperse them. Let them rest in obscurity and peace; my memory be left in oblivion, and my tomb remain uninscribed, until other times and other men can do justice to my character. When my country takes her place among the nations of the earth, then and not till then, let my epitaph be written. I have done."*

Emmet was then sentenced to be hanged and beheaded, in deference to his aristocratic background, rather than death by firing squad or guillotine.

At about 1:30 P.M., Emmet was brought from his prison and placed in a carriage accompanied by two clergymen of the Church of England, to be conveyed to the place of execution in Thomas Street opposite St. Catherine's Church. He was dressed in gentlemen's clothes, having had his request to die in his uniform denied.

The carriage proceeded slowly through the streets, followed by a strong guard of cavalry and infantry. When they arrived at the makeshift scaffold, Emmet alighted from the carriage. He shook hands with a few gentlemen of the platform, then removed his watch and presented it to the executioner.

Showing no fear, Emmet assisted in adjusting the rope around his neck. Then a hood was placed over his head. Inside the hood was sewn a lock of Sarah Curran's hair. Twice Emmet responded to the executioner that he was not yet ready. Finally, before Emmet could respond a third time, the executioner tilted the plank on which Emmet stood, sending Emmet to his death.

After a significant period of time, the body of Robert Emmet was taken down and extended on the scaffold. Then his head was struck from his body, grasped by the hair, and paraded along the front of the gallows by the hangman, who proclaimed to the multitude, *"this is the head of a traitor, Robert Emmet!"*

Emmet's body was then removed, and with great privacy was buried in Dublin. The exact site of Emmet's grave has remained a mystery, although some speculate he was moved from his original gravesite at St. Michan's Church in Dublin to an unmarked grave, as he had requested in his final words.

A short time after the execution, a young woman passing by the site noticed dogs lapping up the blood of Robert Emmet. She called the attention of the soldiers of the Highland regiment who were guarding the scaffold. The soldiers were horrified, and chased the dogs away. Another spectator, loitering around the spot, dipped his handkerchief in the blood and held it to his bosom.

Like many Irish Republican martyrs, Robert Emmet was far more powerful in death than in life. He may have been a failed revolutionary, but his passion speech at his trial earned him a permanent niche in the history of Ireland.

Some historians refer to the insurrection of 1803, as an *aftershock* to the 1798 Wexford rebellion. Others call it the *final encore*. The truth is it was both. It was the end of armed rebellion in Ireland for quite some time, yet it was the spark for future revolutions to come.

Emmet's words were a source of inspiration for generations. There was a time in Ireland where every home proudly displayed a framed copy of his speech from the dock, or a painting of "Bold" Robert Emmet, wearing his green uniform, and leading his men in to battle.

Even Abraham Lincoln was said to have read his speech as a boy in his Kentucky cabin.

The Curse of Oliver Cromwell

"It is the righteous judgment of God
upon these barbarous wretches."

- Oliver Cromwell, defending his slaughter of the Irish at Drogheda, 1649

Historians could have never predicted that a commoner would one day become the most powerful man in England. From a fledgling interest in local politics, Oliver Cromwell would rise to become Lord Protector of England, depose the monarchy, and lay waste to Ireland in an inhumane manner of epic proportions.

Cromwell was born into a modestly wealthy family on April 25, 1599, in Huntingdon, England. Even though they were not a royal family, they were considered somewhat respectable. His father, Robert, was the younger son of a knight, and so Oliver inherited *"only scraps of poverty, barely enough to sustain gentle status,"* according to the Cambridge University Library. His grandfather lived in a large house just a mile from Huntington where he entertained kings and courtiers. No doubt Oliver was present during some of these gatherings.

Cromwell was educated at Huntington and later entered Sidney Sussex College in Cambridge, where he remained for only one year. His father died when he was eighteen, and three years later he met Elizabeth Bourchier while studying at Lincoln Inn's Court in London. They were married in 1620 and had eight children.

Elizabeth was the daughter of Sir James Bourchier who was well connected in the higher social circles. Through his in-laws, Cromwell made contact with wealthy London merchants and various puritan peers interested in colonial development, including the Earl of Warwick. Cromwell himself had some business failures and was forced to sell many of his possessions.

But later he would inherit a small estate from his childless uncle that would restore him to modest prosperity.

In 1626, at the age of 27, he had a *"religious experience"* and converted to Puritan Christian. Other historians claim what he actually had was a mental breakdown, and throughout the 1630s he became a man waiting for God to give him a job.

It was at this time that he became interested in local politics. He once remarked, *"if here I may serve my God by suffering or by doing, I shall be most glad."* He was a relatively quiet man, but nevertheless commanded tremendous authority when he spoke.

Impressed with Cromwell, the people of Huntingdon sent him to Parliament as their representative in 1628, where he became a member of the Puritan-led Independent Party. Cromwell quickly became an outspoken critic of the Bishops and one of the first to call for the established church to be pulled up *"roots and branches."*

The English Civil war erupted in 1642 and quickly involved every level of society through out the British Isles, including Ireland. On one side was Charles I and his supporters, who fought for traditional government in Church and State. Charles, a devout Anglican, was an uncompromising autocrat whose policies increasingly antagonized the powerful class.

On the other side were the supporters of Parliament who sought radical changes in religion and economic policy and a *"greater share of power at the national level."* Cromwell sided with Parliament, and took an active part in the war. When Charles I eventually fled to Scotland, the Scots captured him and turned him over to Cromwell in 1646. Cromwell was instrumental in having Charles I declared a traitor, which led to his execution on January 30, 1649. While this was being played out in England, the Irish were already engaged in their own rebellion against English Protestants. However, the English Civil War was about to bring the full might of the English armies down on Ireland.

The worsening conflict between the English King and Parliament encouraged the Irish to seek to recapture their previously forfeited lands. They also feared the suppression of the Catholic faith if the Puritans (led by Cromwell) were to triumph.

The pot boiled over on October 21, 1641, when the Irish rose up against the Protestant English landholders and settlers who possessed land that had previously belonged to the Irish.

In one night, all of Ulster was retaken. Leinster and Munster soon followed, and for the first time in hundreds of years the English were all but driven from the Island. Unfortunately, during the uprising a number of Protestant inhabitants were collateral damage, as if often the case in war. The uprisings continued, and in 1642 a Catholic government was formed in Kilkenny.

Whether they realized it or not, their uprising would place the Irish right smack in the middle of the English civil war. When the reports of the Irish atrocities reached England, it fanned the flame of disdain for the "uncivilized" Irish to a fever pitch. Pamphlets containing grossly exaggerated versions of the attacks circulated around London, as well as fantastic stories of Irish barbarism.

Soon English citizens began to fear the possibility of an Irish invasion of England, or perhaps even an uprising of English Catholics, or both. Even the English Speaker of the House was convinced there had been *"common counsel at Rome and in Spain to reduce us to Popery."*

Perhaps their fear was not entirely groundless, as Charles II had made it known his intentions of traveling to Ireland and using it as the staging area for an eventual invasion of England. There was a Royalist army already there and several other rebel armies were negotiating with Charles to assist in restoring him to the throne. The time had come for England to act, or in their view, risk being conquered by the barbaric, Catholic hoard. And they called upon their champion…Oliver Cromwell.

On August 15, 1649, Cromwell landed in Dublin with eight regiments of foot soldiers, six regiments of horse, and several troops of dragoons. He also brought a large supply of three other items: bibles, scythes, and sickles. The bibles were to be distributed amongst his soldiers as well to the *"poor unfortunate natives."* The scythes and sickles were to cut down the corn, so the Irish might be starved into submission.

From there he marched towards Drogheda. He also issued two proclamations: one against intemperance, as he could not afford to have drunken soldiers in camp. The other proclamation prohibited plundering "the country people." He knew that to allow plundering would negatively affect his strict military discipline.

What Cromwell also brought with him was the notion the Catholic Irish was uncivilized and barbarous. He came to despise the hierarchy and ritualism associated with Catholicism. Interestingly enough, he saw it as God's will that he destroy the Catholics.

Ormonda had garrisoned Drogheda with 3,000 of his best troops. They were partly English, and all Catholic, and were commanded by the brave loyalist, Sir Arthur Aston. This was the most important town in Ireland, and Cromwell was determined to lay siege to it, which included not only taking town, but slaying all inhabitants. There would be no quarter.

He encamped before the city on September 2nd, and in a few days had his siege guns posted on a nearby hill. When he gave the order to begin firing, he basically unleashed hell upon Drogheda. He pounded the city for several days, and on September 10 his cannonade blasted two breaches. Then Cromwell sent in his storming parties.

Earthworks constructed inside the town and garrison resisted bravely, but ultimately they were defeated. Apparently quarter was promised upon the defenders of the city, but it was later withdrawn. Cromwell later claimed he made no such promise. Sir Arthur Aston and his staff were disarmed and slain on the spot.

Cromwell's officers and soldiers then focused their attention on the rest of the inhabitants.

At the order of Cromwell, men, women, and children were put to the sword. The soldiers took particular pleasure in torturing and killing pregnant women, priests, and those caught with a rosary. This carnage took five days to complete.

A number of the townspeople fled to the safety to St. Peter's church on the north side of the city. But every one was hunted down and murdered. All defenseless. All unarmed. Others took refuge in the wooden church steeple, but Cromwell order it set on fire. Those who attempted to escape the flames were piked to death.

The "principle ladies" of the city had sheltered themselves in the crypts. But there was no safe haven. The ladies were discovered and executed.

"Neither youth nor beauty was spared," according to the author C. F. Cusak. As the soldiers continued to search for more victims, they often used the Irish children as shields when ascending into the lofts and galleries of the church. Cromwell later wrote an account of the massacre to the "Council of State." He stated *"it hath pleased God to bless our endeavors at Drogheda. After battery we stormed it. The enemy were about 3,000 strong in the town. They made a stout resistance. I believe we put to the sword the whole number of defendants. I do not think thirty of the whole escaped with their lives. Those that did are in safe custody for the Barbadoes."*

The ghastly massacre was beyond anything that had previously occurred in any battle of the English Civil War. But Cromwell felt justified: *"I am persuaded that this is a righteous judgment of God upon these barbarous wretches, who have imbrued their hands in so much innocent blood."*

In his victory announcement to Parliament, he spoke proudly of the massacre and bragged that all but two of the Friars in the town were killed by blows to the skull, or as he wrote, *"knocked on the head promiscuously."*

When word of the slaughter spread, the nearby garrisons of Dundalk, Trim, Carlingford, and Newry, quickly took flight. The town of Wexford decided to make a stand. Cromwell had already secured the route to Ulster, so he now set his sights on the southeastern port of Wexford where 3,000 men, under the command of Colonel Sinnot waited. They didn't have to wait long.

Cromwell arrived and immediately began a dialogue with four of the royalists. On one hand he was promising the inhabitants if they surrendered he would let them march out with full military honors. On the other hand, he was attempting to bribe Captain Stafford, the Governor of the Castle.

Once he realized Stafford could be bribed, he denounced the proposals as *"abominable and impudent."* The traitor Stafford then opened the gates and Cromwell's men rushed in. The besieged were *"amazed and panic-struck,"* not comprehending that anyone would allow the enemy to march right into their midst. Despite the surprise, the men of Wexford put up a *"stiff resistance"* according to Cromwell.

In truth, the Irish of Wexford probably did defend themselves as best they could, but Cromwell's comment is self-serving. In order to appear more heroic, the victor will always praise the might of the vanquished. But, in this case, it was just plain murder.

Cromwell's men began slaughtering the townsfolk, even as Cromwell still held in his hand the former offer of surrender that been drawn up by the townspeople and which he agreed. He later informed Parliament that he did not intend to destroy the town. But letters he wrote later congratulated his correspondents on the *"unexpected providence"* which had befallen him, and he said the Wexford massacre was in retaliation for wrongs inflicted on the *"poor Protestants."*

Cromwell's usually well-disciplined soldiers were allowed to run wild through the conquered town raping and murdering the inhabitants. Between 1,500 and 2,000 Irish soldiers, civilians, and priests were slaughtered.

The reign of terror seemed to have its intended effect, for a number of Irish fortresses surrendered soon thereafter without resistance. By the time Cromwell moved his army into winter quarters, most of the Irish coast belonged to the English.

By storming Drogheda and Wexford, and denying quarter to the garrisons of both (soldier and citizen alike) Cromwell escalated a cycle of inter-communal violence dating back for decades. In all, he captured 28 Irish towns and castles on or near the East Coast. He left the rest of Ireland, and the redistribution of 40% of the landmass of Ireland, to his successors.

Eventually Cromwell's campaign in Ireland began to run out of steam. Illness, and the need to man garrisons, reduced his army in size, and on December 2, 1649 he was forced to abandon the siege of Waterford.

He resumed his attack the next year, as a string of towns surrendered with good terms offered to inhabitants and defenders. His luck ran out on May 17, 1650 when he attacked Clonmel. As his men poured through the breached walls, they found themselves trapped by the army of Hugh Dubh O'Neill. Cromwell was soundly defeated, losing between 1,000 - 2,500 men. Cromwell didn't relay this particular news to Parliament, of course.

Despite the loss at Clonmel, Cromwell had defeated enough of Ireland to implement large-scale confiscation of land. He first targeted the "rebel" landowners for clearance.

The most guilty - including 105 rebel "chiefs" - were subject to execution, banishment, or transportation. Those landowners who showed *"constant good affection"* towards parliament were subject to various levels of forfeiture and transplantation to Connaught.

The Irish owners were driven off eleven million acres of land that was subsequently given to the Protestant colonists.

Cromwell then issued a proclamation: *"Irish landowners found east of the river Shannon after 1 May, 1654 faced the death penalty or slavery in the West Indies and Barbados. Those who did not leave their fertile fields and travel to the poor land west of the Shannon would be put to the sword."* The famous expression, "To Hell or Connaught" originated at this time, for obvious reasons.

In April 1650, Cromwell returned to England. Only a few Irish garrisons remained to be conquered. Six months later, the only resisting town, Galway, surrendered. Ireland was now completely under English domination.

Cromwellian rule in Ireland continued the traditional English policy of suppressing Catholics and establishing Protestantism.

Now that Cromwell had utterly defeated the Irish, the next phase in England's plan to keep the Irish subservient was to institute the Penal Laws of 1653. This made it illegal for the Irish to do the following:

- Exercise their Catholic religion
- Receive education
- Enter a profession
- Hold public office
- Engage in trade or commerce
- Live in a corporate town (or within 5 miles thereof)
- Own a horse of greater value than 5 pounds
- Purchase land
- Lease land
- Vote
- Keep any arms for their protection
- Be guardian to a child

Despite temporary success for the English, these drastic policies eventually backfired, as Ireland continued to cling to its Roman Catholicism. They educated their children behind hedges, modified their dancing to exclude arm movements, and redefined their ornate rosaries to a single decade that could be concealed in a pocket.

By 1656, many of the powerful classes wanted to return to the "old ways," so they created a new Parliament, a new House of Lords, and offered Cromwell the title of King, which he contemplated but later refused. He once said if he were 10 years younger, *"there was not a king in Europe I would not make to tremble."*

Cromwell's demise would come on September 3, 1658 when he succumbed to malaria, leaving his son Richard as his successor. His death would come just one month after his beloved daughter, Elizabeth, would die of cancer at the age of 29. Elizabeth's death undoubtedly weakened his constitution and his will to live.

Cromwell's body was embalmed and buried with royal ceremony in Westminster Abby. However, the son was no match for the father, and much of what Cromwell accomplished began to unravel. England returned to the monarchy in 1660, crowning Charles I's son (Charles II) as king.

Once Charles II was in power, he ordered the exhumation of Cromwell's body on January 30, 1661, the anniversary of Charles I's execution. The corpse was taken to Tyburn and the body was hung, in its shroud, from the gallows.

Before he was re-buried, in what is now believed to be in the Marble Arch area of London, his head was lopped off and stuck on a pole at Westminster Hall, where it remained for approximately twenty years. It was eventually rescued by a Cromwell supporter and is believed to be buried near Cambridge College.

Cromwell had gone from Commoner to Lord Protector, the most powerful man in England. On the way he had massacred thousands of Irish people (among many others), annihilated the monarchy, and championed the radical puritan cause.

To this day, historians have conflicting opinions about the man. Some see him as a defender of principles, liberty, and the advocate for religious tolerance. Others denigrate him as a murderer, bigot, psychopath, and omnipresent tyrant.

The Irish, however, have never wavered in their opinion of this man. Author W.C. Abbot writes the, *"conditions of the Cromwellian conquest and settlement left a heritage of hate among the defeated people scarcely equaled and seldom, if ever, surpassed in history."*

In Ireland he is still revered as a monster; a devil; the epitome of evil. The "Curse of Cromwell" is still uttered to this day by those who wish ill fortune on others.

Daniel O'Connell
The Liberator

"England is not my country.
Censure her as much as you please,
you cannot offend me. I am an Irishman…"

- O'Connell to a Frenchman who mistakenly chastised
him for being English, 1793

The O'Connell Clan had been a minor force in their part of Co. Kerry for at least two centuries. As wardens for the MacCarthy Mors, they had enjoyed the hereditary custodianship of a castle. Even after the brutal Protestant era of Oliver Cromwell and King William, they had retained possession of some of their land…an extremely rare fete for Catholics.

But the O'Connell's were crafty. Quirks in the law had favored them from time to time. And, according to Oliver MacDonagh in his book, *The Hereditary Bondsman*, the O'Connells *"also maintained a profitable French connexion (sic), a trade in priests and soldiers as well as brandy, silks and other luxurious contraband, throughout the eighteenth century."*

What also added to the continuation of the Catholic O'Connells was geography. No part of Ireland was less accessible or freer from state surveillance than flat, roadless, Iveragh, Co. Kerry. The coastline from Kenmare to Carragh was a series of contortions and indentations of small coves and beaches, which allowed for a copious sea trade in contraband. Because they were adept at recognizing and exploiting their natural resources, the O'Connell's had never been reduced to peasantry.

The eighteenth century O'Connells, lead by Daniel's Uncle, Maurice "Hunting Cap" O'Connell, melded with the Protestant Ascendency. As thoroughly organized smugglers, they supplied the local Anglican gentry with contraband. This rendered them extremely useful. It even purchased them practical immunity from the law.

Since Kerry was a wild and harsh terrain, it was not hospitable to Anglicization. Therefore a form of the old clan system survived, and families like the O'Connells retained considerable power over their immediate followers and dependents.

They and the other Catholic well-to-dos of the peninsula lived in a relatively comfortable system of limited mutual support, civil relations and cross-favors with their Protestant counterparts.

Sectarian suspicion and dislike were generally subordinate to business pursuits. However, it was well known that the Catholics remained subservient to the Protestants. Hunting Cap was painfully aware of this fact.

Cognizant of the systematic abasement of Irish Catholics, and the contempt and injustice of the ascendancy, he undoubtedly looked back in time when the O'Connells were Chieftains of the land and subservient to no one.

It was to this rather complex and unique society in which Daniel O'Connell was born on August 6, 1775 in a cottage close to Carhen, near Cahirciveen. Carhen and the surrounding land was one of several pieces of O'Connell property which the family was able to retain by virtue of leases pre-dating 1691, which passed to Morgan, Daniel's father, one of the older of the twenty-two children of Donal Mor and Maire Duibh O'Connell.

Daniel was the oldest of ten children born to Morgan and his wife, Catherine O'Mullane. Because it was customary in Gaelic society - but also because Daniel was born to a middle class household with brothers and sisters joining the family with regularity - that he was fostered-out in infancy and did not return to Carhen until he was four years old.

His surrogate mother was the wife of a herdsman on Morgan's own land. His foster home was a cramped and poorly ventilated mud cabin.

His first language was Gaelic, and he was immersed in the traditional culture of song and story of Co. Kerry. Despite his foster situation, he remained close to his biological parents.

Historians are quick to link this early exposure to the poor Irish peasantry; their individual thoughts and aspirations; which would serve him well in the years to come. Daniel was also influenced by the stories of his grandmother, Maire Duibh, known throughout Kerry as a Gaelic poet and rhetorician. She refused to adopt non-Gaelic ways as many of her peers had done.

An example of that refusal to change was epitomized by a scene at the deathbed of one of her many sons. She was outraged when her daughter-in-law knelt down to pray in silence by the bedside. Instantly, she broke into a torrent of poetic lamentation in Irish.

One of her daughters, Eileen O'Leary, would compose one of the most famous Gaelic laments to honor her husband, the outlaw Art O'Leary, who was shot and killed.

In some way, Daniel was caught between the old Gaelic world and post-Gaelic modern era. Perhaps this was his destiny; to be a man of two worlds. One who was comfortable with his Gaelic past, but able to understand and comprehend the nuances of the protestant ascendency.

Since Hunting Cap had no children of his own, Daniel became his heir apparent, and he went to live with Hunting Cap at Derrynane Abby. He was determined that Daniel's education should begin early, so he had him tutored locally.

He proved to be a good student, and in later years he would sit by the window and read for hours. He was eventually sent to St. Omer in France, along with his brother, Maurice, where he would complete his secondary education.

Not long after he arrived, he was accosted by a Frenchman who mistook him for an English student. Incensed, the Frenchman began to berate England for being a country far inferior to the France. Daniel calmly replied, *"Sir, England is not my country. Censure her as much as you please, you cannot offend me. I am*

an Irishman, and my countrymen have as little reason to love
England as yours have – perhaps less."

Daniel later went to Douai, but his time there was short due
to the French Revolution. He witnessed first-hand the brutality
and violence of such an uprising. This left such an impression
that from that day forward he deplored violence of any kind.

In 1793 the two O'Connell brothers returned home. By 1794
Daniel became a law student at Lincoln's Inn, London, and two
years later he transferred to the King's Inn in Dublin.

While in London, Daniel became interested in politics. He
read a great deal and was influenced by the ideas of radicals
such as Thomas Paine, Jeremy Bentham and William Godwin.
By the time he qualified as a lawyer in 1798, O'Connell had
committed himself to religious tolerance, freedom of conscience,
democracy, and the separation of Church and State.

For the next ten years Daniel built up his law practice while
remaining active in the movement to repeal British laws that
penalized Roman Catholics because of their religion.

It was through representing many Irish tenants against
English landlords that he saw first hand the effects of English
rule on the Irish.

The era of penal legislation in Ireland had ceased by this
time, mostly due to the Catholic Relief Act of 1795, and
Catholics were placed in many respects on a level with other
denominations. But they were still excluded from Parliament,
from the inner bar, and from the higher civil and military offices.
Even though Ireland was 80% Catholic, they were not allowed
to hold public office.

The Protestants had given every indication that no further
concessions would be given. O'Connell could not comprehend
why Irish Catholics, who paid taxes and were obedient to the
law, should not have a share in the spending of the taxes and the
making of the laws.

One step at a time within the legal system, O'Connell decided
to work toward liberating the Irish socially, economically, and

politically. His ultimate aim was "Home Rule" in which Ireland would be allowed to govern itself without interference from England. Daniel eventually joined the "United Irishmen," a group that had been inspired by the French Revolution. During the 1798 Wexford insurrection, O'Connell feared he would be arrested by the English authorities and went into hiding in Co. Kerry. Despite his radical views, Daniel opposed the rebellion. He argued the Irish people *"were not sufficiently enlightened to hear the sun of freedom,"* and that the insurrection would decrease rather than increase the desire for Irish liberation. Instead of rebellion, Daniel advocated using the machinery of Parliament to obtain political and religious equality.

The rebellion, and the terrible butchery that followed, confirmed his opinion that violence was not the way to gain equality. While he approved of the principles of the United Irishmen, their call for reform and for Catholic Emancipation, he abhorred their methods.

Disillusioned by the Wexford Rebellion, O'Connell ceased to be active in politics and concentrated on his law practice. Before long he had become the most famous barrister in Ireland.

Gradually, he did return to politics. From 1812 to 1817 the Irish government was little else than a long-sustained quarrel between O'Connell and the new chief secretary, Sir Robert Peel. Both were very determined individuals with strong beliefs, and they would be at odds with each other until the very end. Peel espoused privilege and ascendency and attacked and berated the Catholic leaders. O'Connell responded by calling him *"Orange Peel,"* because of his pro-Protestant stance.

In 1815, O'Connell harshly criticized the Dublin City Council (aka the "Dublin Corporation"). He called them bigoted and reactionary, and accused them of constantly defending the Protestant ascendancy.

In a public speech he referred to them as a *"beggarly corporation."* The alderman and councilors were outraged. When O'Connell would not apologize, he was challenged to a duel by corporation member, John D'Esterre, a noted duelist.

D'Esterre had expected O'Connell to back down in humiliation. Or, if O'Connell did fight, it would mark the end of O'Connell's career, either by death or dishonor. D'Esterre also knew that the Irish Bishops forbade dueling, and he counted on O'Connell not wanting to provoke an ecclesiastical response.

O'Connell surprised everyone...he chose to fight. To the Catholics, this duel epitomized their struggle. It was the Orange vs. the Green; Protestants vs. Catholics; Irish vs. English. And they came by the hundreds to support their man, O'Connell.

His friend and second, Major John "Fireball" MacNamara, a noted hothead and himself a participant in at least 57 duels, accompanied O'Connell to the dueling location outside.

At Bishops Court, Co. Kildare, the two combatants stood on the snow-covered ground facing each other. As the handkerchief was dropped, they raised their pistols and fired. D'Esterre missed, but O'Connell's shot struck D'Esterre in the hip and stomach.

The seconds then shook hands relieved that no one was killed and the matter of honor was now settled. Unfortunately, D'Esterre died two days later of his wound.

Although O'Connell maintained a stoic front, he bitterly regretted the deed. For the remainder of his life he never missed an opportunity to assist the D'Esterre family, and often tipped his hat as he walked past the D'Esterre's house. He also wore a black glove on his dueling hand whenever he received communion.

As far as the duel ending his career, it had just the opposite effect. The Irish Catholics loved a fighter, and O'Connell further endeared himself to the people. The Irish Bishops even turned a blind eye to the duel, as they had always looked upon O'Connell as a *"Catholic national champion."*

Although Daniel would eventually be acknowledged as the leader of the Catholic Emancipation movement, he became frustrated when the Catholic cause was not advancing. Until then, the campaign for Catholic Emancipation was mainly reserved for the intellectual minority and there was no informed public opinion on the subject.

In 1823, O'Connell, along with Richard Lalor Sheil and Sir Thomas Wyse, organized the Catholic Association, whose main purpose was to win emancipation *"by legal and constitutional means."* All Irish citizens, especially the poor, were encouraged to join.

O'Connell realized that a successful campaign needed money to pay for speakers, pamphlets etc… so he asked all Catholics to pay a "Catholic Rent" of 1 shilling per month. This stipend was collected after Mass on Sunday, and financed the Association's activities. It was also used as an insurance fund for members who were evicted for belonging to the Association.

The Priests were eventually won over, and churches became a recruiting and propaganda vehicle for the Association.

Many poor Catholics joined as part of a religious crusade. They had little to lose and everything to gain. In its first year of existence, the Association had an income of L1,000 per week (960,000 pennies a month) and at the end of the year it had L10,000 invested.

The campaign was non-violent, but agitation was constant. Agitation was the O'Connell way. Incitement through relatively peaceful means, rather than violence, was what O'Connell strived for.

The Catholic Association campaigned for the repeal of the Act of Union, the end of the Irish tithe system, universal suffrage and a secret ballot for parliamentary elections.

Although O'Connell rejected the use of violence, he constantly warned the British government that if reform did not take place, the Irish masses would start listening to the *"counsels of violent men."*

Any banding together of Catholics alarmed the Protestants, and by 1825 the Association gained enough power that the British government declared it illegal.

O'Connell had boasted that if the authorities tried to ban his organization he would "drive a coach and four" through the legal restrictions placed on it. Unfazed, and using his verbal and legal skills, he simply restructured the organization. He called the association a *"public and private charity"* that stood for *"public peace and tranquility as well as private harmony between all classes."* He was successful, as the authorities had no basis to ban the new association.

By 1826, the Catholic Association began supporting candidates in parliamentary elections. This was quite a change for the Catholic Irish who, since the Catholic Relief Act of 1793, had always voted as their landlords instructed.

Now they were able to vote however they pleased; and they cast their votes for candidates who supported emancipation.

Days before the election, members of the Catholic Association paraded up and down the streets of their towns wearing the color green, the symbol of Irish nationalism.

They had some great victories, including O'Connell who defeated C. E. Vesty Fitzgerald, President of the Board of Trade, in a Co. Clare by-election. However, as a Catholic, O'Connell was not allowed to take his seat. This presented quite a problem for Wellington. He could pass a Catholic Emancipation Act and let O'Connell take his seat or he could declare the election null and void and run the risk of violence in Ireland, and possible civil war.

Wellington wanted to avoid bloodshed at all costs. The Irish got their way, and in April 1829 the Catholic Emancipation Act was put through Parliament with a great deal of support from Lord John Russell and the Whigs.

This resulted in many Protestants losing important political offices they had held for decades. But the greatest victory was the passing of the Catholic Emancipation Act in 1829 which stated the following:

1) Catholics could sit as MPs at Westminster;

2) Catholics were eligible for all public offices except those of Lord Chancellor, Monarch, Regent, Lord Lieutenant of Ireland and any judicial appointment in any ecclesiastical court;

3) In Irish county elections the 40/-freehold qualification was

to be raised to $10 householder, which minimized the number of peasant voters.

O'Connell saw his victory as the first step toward Home Rule. But it was emancipation at a price. Not only was the Irish electorate cut drastically, but the peasants saw O'Connell as a traitor because of the $10 household fee needed in order to vote.

In the 1830s O'Connell became a major figure in the House of Commons. He was active in the campaigns for prison and law reform, free trade, the abolition of slavery, and Jewish emancipation. He was also a prominent figure in the campaign for universal suffrage. In 1841 O'Connell became the first Catholic Lord Mayor of Dublin since the time of James II.

After completing his year in office, he announced that he intended to concentrate on repealing the Act of Union. However, very few MPs in the House of Commons supported the repeal of the Union, and therefore O'Connell was left in a weak negotiating position.

Sir Robert Peel, now the English Prime Minister, decided to go on the offensive. He outlawed a proposed large meeting to discuss repeal at Clontarf.

Despite the fact that O'Connell suggested his followers accept this decision, he was arrested and charged with sedition. O'Connell was found guilty and sentenced to one year in jail, but on appeal it was reversed, and O'Connell left prison as a hero in the fight for freedom of speech and resumed his career.

In 1845 O'Connell was unable to persuade Parliament to take quick action to deal with the Irish Famine.

During this time the "Young Ireland" members of O'Connell's party began to advocate revolutionary doctrines that he had always opposed. They saw O'Connell's tactics as ineffective, and were confused by his endorsement of violence in defense of existing rights, but non-violence for securing new privileges.

Other followers began to resent his Catholic sectarianism, and felt he was replacing repeal with piece-meal reform in return for Irish parliamentary support.

In 1846, the Young Ireland group split from O'Connell's party, marking the decline of his authority. O'Connell was deeply distressed by this disaffection among the Irish.

By March 1847, O'Connell was old and sickly. His doctors ordered him to move to a warmer climate. Fearing that he was dying, and wanting to die in Rome, he set off on a pilgrimage.

When he reached Paris he was greeted by a crowd of radicals who wished to pay tribute to the man they described as the "most successful champion of liberty and democracy in Europe."

O'Connell never completed his journey to Rome. He died in Genoa on May 15, 1847. As requested, his heart was buried in Rome and his body in Dublin.

The Black and Tans:
The British Special Police in Ireland

"Come out ye Black & Tans!
Come out and fight me like a man.
Show your wife how you won medals
Down in Flanders.
Tell her how the IRA
Made you run like hell away
From the green and lovely lanes
Of Killeshandra!"

- Lyrics to the IRA Song,
"Come Out Ye Black & Tans"

In the years that followed the Easter Rising of 1916, the British became increasingly frustrated with the successful paramilitary tactics of the Irish Volunteers, a brazen secret army organized by Michael Collins.

The Volunteers would strike British occupying forces seemingly from nowhere and then vanish into the landscape. The British couldn't catch Collins who traveled around Dublin on bicycle in plain site marshalling his troops and arming them on a previously unprecedented scale.

Collins was becoming a dream come true for the Irish, and a nightmare to the British forces occupying Ireland. The "Big Fellow" masterminded impossible prison escapes, created vast underground intelligence networks, and outfitted his *"invisible army"* with an arsenal of weapons including Thompson submachine guns from America. For the first time the Irish were taking control of the centuries-old situation in their country.

Frustrated, the British retaliated in January 1920 by forming the Black and Tans to supplement the Royal Irish Constabulary

(RIC). The British were able to recruit demobilized British soldiers to maintain operational strength, following widespread resignations and dismissals from the RIC. They were former soldiers unable to find work elsewhere due to England's post-war economic depression.

Few employers were willing to give jobs to untrained men whose wartime experience had given them a taste for adventure and hardened them to violence and brutality. For 10 shillings a day, these men were able to return to the life of a "soldier."

When they arrived in Ireland, it was discovered there were not enough of the dark police uniforms to issue to the new recruits. Therefore the missing articles of clothing were replaced with khaki army uniforms. So they appeared in a strange mixture of khaki and dark green, some with khaki tunic and green trousers, others in all khaki, some with civilian hats, but most with green caps and black leather belts of the RIC. These multi-colored uniforms inspired the nickname, *Black and Tans*.

The name also served to symbolize their contrasting position: they were technically policemen, but they acted as an occupation army.

The Black and Tans were given a free hand in their fight against the Irish Republican Army and acted with extreme lawlessness and virtually no accountability. On June 17, 1920, Lt. Col. Smyth was appointed division commander of the RIC for Munster, and he spoke the following to his troops: *"...if a police barracks is burned or if the barracks already occupied is not suitable, then the best house in the locality is to be commandeered, the occupants thrown into the gutter. Let them die there - the more the merrier. Police and military will patrol the country at least five nights a week. They are not to confine themselves to the main roads, but make across the country, lie in ambush and, when civilians are seen approaching, shout 'hands up!' Should the order not be immediately obeyed, shoot and shoot with effect. You may make mistakes occasionally and innocent persons may be shot, but that cannot be helped, and you are bound to get the right parties some time. The more you shoot, the better I will like you, and I assure you no policeman will get into trouble for shooting any man…"* This carte blanche, supported by new Chief Secretary Sir Hamar Greenwood, included burning down homes and factories, torturing of prisoners, and the execution of hundreds of suspects without trial. Even Michael Collins' own mother's home was torched by the "Tans."

There was a second armed force known as the Auxiliaries, which was created in August 1920 to supplement the Black and Tans. The Auxiliaries were ex-officers, and tended to be slightly older, tougher, and supposedly more responsible than the Tans (although that can be disputed). They formed an elite commando-style force. They were paid 1 pound a day and, like the Tans, were allowed considerable freedom of action.

Towards the end of 1920 there were approximately 30,000 regular British soldiers in Ireland, as well as 11,000 police (including the Tans and Auxiliaries). The British soldiers remained, to some extent, outside of the struggle. This was partly because the IRA was reluctant to take on the experienced professional soldiers. From the British standpoint, they did not want to engage their forces and risk recognizing the IRA as a true army, and by the same token, be forced to recognize the Irish republic as well. Armed and active IRA members numbered little more than 3,000.

Despite their overwhelming numbers, the Black and Tans quickly discovered fighting the IRA was quite different than fighting the Germans.

The First World War had been conducted according to the international rules of war. The opposing armies were very clearly recognizable. They hunkered down in trenches that faced each other across a clearly defined "no man's land." They advanced or retreated, but clearly measured their progress by the amount of land they could defend behind their lines.

But in Michael Collins' guerrilla warfare there were no rules, no boundaries, no uniforms, and no front line. The enemy was invisible...and there were everywhere. An innocent looking group of bystanders could suddenly be transformed in to a detachment of armed men who could strafe an RIC patrol with gunfire and then slip away quickly to mingle with the local population.

On the morning of November 21, 1920, a group of Michael Collins' counter-intelligence men shot dead 14 British special agents. This led to reprisals by the Tans who surrounded Croke Park during a Gaelic football match. Ostensibly, they were looking to capture members of Sinn Fein, but they soon opened fire indiscriminately on players and spectators. They would kill 12 and wound hundreds before members of the Auxiliaries finally managed to get them to cease-fire.

This atrocious event would go down in history as the first *"Bloody Sunday,"* but, unfortunately, not the last in the history of Irish independence.

The Tans would later claim they were fired upon first, but offered no evidence what so ever. Among the dead was Michael Hogan, a player from Tipperary, who was unlikely to have had a gun during the game.

Later that night at Dublin Castle, drunken Black and Tans tortured three prisoners and finally bayoneted and shot them to death. Of the three, Peadar Clancy and Dick McKee were actually members of Collin's squad. But the third man, Conor Clune, was a completely innocent clerk from Co. Clare who had merely been in Dublin on business. The official report of the British Colonial government was *"shot while attempting to escape."*

On December 11, 1920, the Auxiliaries and the Tans went on a rampage of burning and looting in Cork. During the day, a party of Auxiliaries were ambushed by the IRA near Dillon's Cross outside of Cork city. Twelve Auxiliaries were wounded; one of who would later die.

Just a few weeks prior, Tom Barry had led an IRA ambush of Auxiliaries traveling in two lorries near Macroom Castle. All were killed except one.

As news spread of both ambushes the Auxiliaries and Tan became incensed. They began stopping trams and cars all over the city. At one point they beat a priest when he refused to say *"to hell with the Pope."* A number of houses in Dillon's Cross were set ablaze about 10:00 p.m. by the Auxiliaries who were then joined by many intoxicated Black and Tans.

The Tans soon spilled out in to the street and prevented the fire brigade from fighting the first fires. The fire quickly spread as the drunken Tans sliced open the fire hoses, further impairing the desperate fire brigade, and then began shooting their guns indiscriminately in the air.

It wasn't long before the Tans were running wild looting local stores. Many were seen carrying suitcases full of stolen goods.

Moving across the River Lee, they next set fire to the City Hall, and the Carnegie Library. When the fire brigade arrived on the scene to fight the new blaze, the Tans physically barred them from the hydrants.

The next morning, large sections of the city of Cork were smoldering ruins. Few ventured out for Mass that day. Sir Hamar Greenwood, Chief Secretary to Ireland, addressed the British Parliament several days later claiming the IRA had set all of the fires, and that the forces of the Crown has saved Cork from destruction.

This statement was made against such overwhelming evidence to the contrary that from then on in Ireland *"telling a Hamar"* became a synonym for lying.

The Auxiliary company - which ran amuck in Cork that night - was transferred to Dublin where they would later wear burnt cork pins on their glengarries to commemorate their *"glorious"* night. Their commanding officer returned to England, where he shot himself a few weeks later.

The Black and Tan brutality continued for the next year, including the sacking of Balbriggan, which offended both the Irish and those in England, leaving the town with the appearance of a Belgian village after it was ravaged by the Germans in WW1.

An Irish ballad of the time suggested as much: *"The Town of Balbriggan they burnt to the ground, while the bullets like hailstones were whizzing around."* The Tans were often seen speeding down the village streets of Ireland in their lorries, firing their rifles at random to the peril of anyone who happened to be in the way, often singing incongruously: *"We are the men of the RIC, as happy as happy can be."*

The Tans pushed their luck and soon learned they needed eyes in the back of their heads. It wasn't long before Collins men began picking them off; oftentimes one by one, sometimes in groups. No place was safe.

This constant fear began to wear on the Tans, and their nerves were strained. Their building anxiety occasionally exploded in even worse deeds of inhuman savagery. Violence begat violence, and in an attempt to quell the attacks upon their ranks, the Tan issued the following proclamation regarding their new post in Drogheda, the site of Oliver Cromwell's vicious massacre of the Irish: *"DROGHEDA BEWARE, If in the vicinity a policeman is shot, five of the leading Sinn Feiners will be shot. It is not coercion - it is an eye for an eye. We are not drink-maddened savages as we have been described in the Dublin rags. We are not out for loot. We are inoffensive to women. We are as human as other Christians, but we have restrained ourselves too long. Are we to lie down while our comrades are being shot in cold blood by the corner boys and ragamuffins of Ireland? We say 'never,' and all the inquiries in the world will not stop our desire for revenge. Stop the shooting of police, or we will lay low every house that smells of Sinn Fein. Remember Balbriggan. (By Order) Black and Tans."*

In this panicked state of mind, it was quite possible for an innocent man to be shot simply for having his hands in his pockets.

A perfect example was Timothy O'Connell of Ahakeera, Dunmanway who was arrested on the morning of January 2, 1921 about a mile from the scene of a recent Black and Tan ambush.

"I happened to be in bed when someone downstairs shouted 'Tans!' I slipped on my trousers and coat, the latter being the coat Pat Deasy had worn when he was mortally wounded in the ambush at Kilmichael about five weeks earlier. The bullet hole was plain to be seen, and God help me if the Auxies could only guess the truth. I ran from the house a short distance...when suddenly fire was opened on me from all directions...so I lay down by a low stone fence to escape their fire which was still kept up. They were shouting at me to come out...They hauled me to my feet...and seemed disappointed to have missed me at such short range. The next move was out to the road and on to the lorry. But before I was hoisted on to same I was given a few hefty wallops for good measure.

Before reaching Coppeen village, the lorries came to a halt. I was ordered down, and told to stand up by the fence. Five or six of them stood on the road with the rifles at the ready, and naturally I expected the volley any second...but it didn't come. We continued on to the village where they again stood me against the wall of Mr. Murphy's shop. I could see them in conversation with him (Mr. Murphy). Eventually one of them came over to me and said that I could thank this man (Mr. Murphy) for saving my life as they would have left my brains on the wall if he hadn't given them my name. They moved from Coppeen southwards towards Castletown...where they arrested an old man whom they terrified by placing grenades in his pockets with lengths of string attached to pull the pin and blow him up: they specialized in and enjoyed this kind of stuff.

The next and final move was to the headquarters in Dunmanway workhouse. I was led to the guardhouse where I had to take off all my clothes and thoroughly searched. I was ordered to dress. I was ordered to get to work turning this hand-pump to supply the house with water. This job lasted non-stop for over an hour, and by then my palms were raw and bleeding. I was almost too weak to stand. It was now almost twenty-four hours since I had any food, or even a cup of tea.

I was brought back to the guardroom where I lay on the floor until about midnight when three Auxies ordered me to get on my feet. I was led into the room...and when about halfway through the room, the leader, a great big savage, suddenly turned around...and lifted me off the floor with a punch. He didn't drop me. I kept on my feet and took at least a few more before I went down. I made no attempt to get up until (they) came at me with a bayonet, and after that I stood up with my hands high to guard my face. Once again the savage moved in with a few more haymakers, and put me down for the second time. The blood was almost choking me by then. Once more I was forced to stand up to face the puncher and take more punishment. Finally, I went down to stay. I asked them to shoot me. The big fellow said 'we wouldn't have your blood on our hands,' even though by then they had most of what I had on their hands and clothes as well as in pools on the floor. In the end one of the Auxies dragged me to my feet to the top of the stairs...the big one caught me with a kick, and set me tumbling down almost halfway.

The remainder of Timothy O'Connell's testimony included more physical and mental abuse over the next several months. Several times he had a gun held to his head and was told he would die.

At one point O'Connell and other Irish prisoners were shown an empty coffin and told it was for them. They were then forced to place the body of a young Irish Volunteer named Daniel O'Reilly in the coffin. He had been killed the night before. The arm of the Volunteer didn't fit in the coffin so the Auxie *"pushed the arm down with his boot, and not to gently either."*

On May 11, O'Connell was released conditionally, and was ordered to report back every Saturday morning at 11:00. *"Once I was outside that building, I prayed that the next time I would come face to face with that gang of murderers I would have a gun in my hands."*

It was these sorts of tactics that actually aided the cause of Irish independence by uniting the general population of southern Ireland against British rule.

The Irish people were fed up with being terrorized by the Tans. Originally considered a nuisance by many people, the Irish Volunteers soon were seen as the only defenders of public safety against the British forces.

Public opinion throughout England was also moving in favor of Ireland. Thus influencing the British government to grant dominion status to the Irish Free State in 1921 and resulted in the eventual disbanding of the Black and Tans.

The Tans had played a part in the long, sad history of Anglo-Irish relations. An old Volunteer commander once said the IRA never beat the Tans, *"It was the British people who did it."*

The Tans eventually returned home to England and joined the growing ranks of the unemployed. They might have been somewhat effective for a short time, but their brutal, sardonic tactics, supported by the English government, ultimately backfired on them.

The Tans are gone, but not forgotten. Even today, the Irish still sing about their cruelty:

"From Dublin to Cork and from Thurles to Mayo,
Lays a trail of destruction wherever they go;
With England to help and fierce passions to fan,
She must feel bloody proud of her bold Black and Tans."

Croppies Lie Down!
The Origins of the Protestant Orange Order

"We'll fight to the last in the honest old cause,
And guard our religion our freedom and laws.
We'll fight for our country, our King and his crown,
And make all the traitors and Croppies lie down."

- Lyrics to an old "Orange" Song

According to many historians, Orangeism is the ideology, which promotes and protects Protestant domination over Catholics in Ireland. What is rarely acknowledged, according to author Jacqueline Dana, is that Orangeism is not at its heart a Protestant cultural response to Catholicism, but a deliberate sectarian tactic engineered and promoted by the British throughout the centuries to keep the people of Ireland divided and easier to control.

The problem is much larger that the Protestants vs. the Catholics, or the Orange vs. the Green, but is in actuality merely a symptom of the most crucial issue facing Ireland - the persistent British imperial presence.

The seeds of *Orangeism* actually began at the time of the first Protestant settlements in Ireland in 1553. Protestants first came to Ireland as part of Catholic Queen Mary Tudor's wish to subdue the Irish people and bring the island under her rule. The Queen devised a plan in which English colonists would form settlements, or "plantations," in Ireland, clearing the land of the native Irish people.

Under her "Leinster Experiment," colonists would promise to bring sufficient English workers with them to Ireland so that they would not need to hire any native Irish laborers. The Irish were not so easily subdued, and they fought against the settlers.

The queen was never able to persuade enough colonists to travel to what was considered at the time a "dangerous and barbaric wilderness."

A second plantation was attempted in Munster in 1583, and hundreds of thousands of acres were confiscated from the native Irish for use by Sir Walter Raleigh and others. Again, this plantation was mostly unsuccessful, for there still were not sufficient inducements for English settlement.

In 1603, King James I launched a new campaign to colonize Ireland. Englishmen confiscated land in the northeast counties of Ulster, and soon settlers were enticed to Ireland from James' native land of Scotland.

Unlike the other attempts at Plantation, this one worked due to the similarities of language, culture, and the close proximity to Scotland. The only difference in this plantation was the majority of settlers were not Anglican but Presbyterian. There were considered "the dissenters" who refused to join the Church of England.

The Irish tried to take advantage of the English Civil War in 1641 by making a concerted effort to fight back against their English colonists. The Catholic clergy helped to organize a rebellion, which occurred in several areas on October 23, and for some time the native Irish attacked settlers, burned towns, and killed many.

The English fought back, but with so many of their resources being utilized to fight the civil war in England, they were unable to subdue the Irish. The Irish victories fanned the flame of anti-Catholic sentiment among the Protestants in Ireland and back in England.

Many tended to believe wildly exaggerated reports of vicious Catholic atrocities inflicted on the defenseless settlers. In 1649, King Charles I was overthrown, and Oliver Cromwell took power and wasted no time in crushing the Irish rebellion and securing a "Protestant Ascendancy" for Ireland.

Several thousand people were murdered outright, and thousands more would die of starvation and disease. Under the Act of Settlement of 1652, the Catholic population was forced to the less fertile land west of the Shannon River or face execution. This forced migration became known as *To Hell or Connaught!*

The English monarchy was restored in 1660, when King James II, a Catholic, succeeded his brother, Charles II, to the throne, and showed signs of raising his son and heir to be Catholic as well. Members of Parliament feared England would return to Catholicism, and in 1688 the members took it upon themselves to invite James' protestant daughter, Mary, and her husband William of Orange, to take the English throne.

Although this scenario was largely peaceful in England, battles were fought in Ireland between the Catholics who were loyal to James, and the Protestants who remained loyal to William and Mary. A decisive battle was fought at the Boyne River near Dublin in 1690, and as a result, James fled to France.

To the Protestants in Ireland at the time, and to their descendants, the most significant event was the siege of Derry in which, for 105 days, James II's forces laid siege to the walled city where 30,000 Protestants, refusing to surrender to a Catholic force, faced starvation and disease inside. The siege ended on July 28 when William's fleet arrived and forced James' forces to retreat.

After James' defeat, the English enacted a series of Penal laws to punish the Catholics who had remained loyal to James. These laws made it illegal for Catholics to vote, practice law, hold elected offices, or own anything more than small plots of land. Catholic education and public worship were also outlawed.

Through the 17th and 18th centuries Irish land continued to be confiscated by English and Scottish colonists. Landlords were becoming stronger of securing more and more land.

While the radicals of Belfast dreamed of liberty, equality and fraternity, and discussed the ideas emanating from France and

America, the small catholic and protestant farmers and weavers of Armagh were locked in a furious sectarian conflict.

In the 1780's this ongoing warfare became formalized with the creation of the Catholic Defenders movement and the Protestant *Peep-o-Day* boys (so called from their visiting the house of the loyal Irish at day break in search of arms).

Some historians believe this intensifying conflict may have been related to increased competition between weavers in a crowded linen market. Regardless, the outnumbered Catholics tended to get the brunt, and catholic refugees who fled into North Leinster and Connaught brought their Defender affiliations with them.

As the Defenders grew in size, and the movement spread into other regions, they became increasingly daring and overtly political in their objectives, which included their desire for an Irish republic.

The formation of Orange Order, or the Loyal Orange Institution of Ireland, occurred following the violent clash between armed Protestant bands and Catholic Defenders at a crossroads hamlet, named "The Diamond," near the village of Loughgall. Approximately 30 defenders were killed on September 21, 1795, while no fatalities were recorded on the Protestant side.

The "Battle of the Diamond" ranks as one of the more bloody encounters between the Protestant "Peep O'Day Boys" and the Catholic Defenders stretching back to the mid-1780s. The protestant version of the battle is that it was instigated by a *"Roman Catholic revolutionary brotherhood"* that were part of the *"ethnic cleaning"* program of the seventeenth and eighteenth centuries whose goal was to *"remove the Protestant witness from the Island of Ireland."*

According to official Orange Order history, after the battle *"the Protestants formed a circle, joined hands and declared their brotherhood in Loyalty to the Crown, the Country and the Reformed Religion."*

Each summer in Northern Ireland loyal fraternal orders – the Orange Order, the Apprentice Boys of Derry, and the Royal Black Institution – plan marches and parades to commemorate historical events of significance to the Protestant community. Marches sometimes precede or follow church services, although in recent years more and more marches not affiliated with a church service have been planned and executed.

The official "marching season" begins at Easter and continues until the end of August. There are between 2,500 and 3,000 processions and parades altogether in nearly every city, town, and village in the north of Ireland.

The parades are a display of pageantry. The color of the sash, the uniforms of the bands and the detailed paintings on the banners combine to make for a colorful spectacle. The banners and flags are full of religious, cultural, and political symbolism depicting biblical scenes, as well as famous people or events in history.

The Orangemen held their first Boyne Commemoration Parade on July 12, 1796, although they claim that parades had been celebrated in their community long before 1796. Since then, the parade has been a part of their tradition and heritage.

The Orangemen believe that through the medium of a parade the, *"...witness for their faith and celebrate their cultural heritage."* They also claim their celebration is no different than the Carnival in Rio, the Mardi Gras in New Orleans, an American 4th of July parade, or even St. Patrick's Day parades in the U.S. and Dublin.

While many of the parades are relatively harmless, and confined to primarily Protestant neighborhoods, a few parade routes lead through Catholic-nationalist neighborhoods. Parade organizers claim this is acceptable due to the fact that these routes are "traditional" having been mapped out during a time when those neighborhoods were predominately Protestant.

Catholics, on the other hand, do not welcome these intrusions and compare the parade to the Ku Klux Klan marching through an African-American neighborhood Mississippi. To them it is nothing more than a way for the Orange Order in Ulster to demonstrate their power and dominance and to provoke the Catholic people.

The banners and paintings unfurled during the parades further inflame the situation as they contain illustrations of Protestant victories over Catholics which are then waved under the noses of the Nationalists. The symbols of power are further expressed by the beating of the big "Lambeg" drums and the shouting of sectarian slogans such as *"Croppies lie down!"* and *"Taigs out!"* Both are derogatory names for Catholics.

The Catholic community has fought hard to have these parades re-routed away from Nationalist neighborhoods. What you have is a classic case of the Loyalist's right to free expression, assembly, and exercise of religion, versus the nationalist's rights to freedom from oppression and intimidation, and their freedom to protest.

The Orange Order claims their institution is based on a *"brotherly bond"* which unites all members in a spirit of tolerance towards those outside the brotherhood who differ from them in religious persuasion. In fact, they go even further to claim on their website they will not tolerate any brother who persecutes, injures, or upbraids any man on account of his *"religious opinions."* As devout Christians, they claim they would never condone such attitudes towards anyone of any faith, race, or creed.

However, the Orange Order handbook lists the following qualification for admission: *"An Orangeman should... strenuously oppose the fatal errors and doctrines of the Church of Rome, and scrupulously countenance any act or ceremony of Popish Worship; he should by all lawful means, resist the ascendancy of that Church..."* Further more, the handbook goes on to explain the violation that would lead to expulsion: *"Any member dishonoring the Institution by marrying a Roman Catholic shall be expelled; and every Member shall use his best endeavors to prevent and discountenance the marriage of Protestants with Roman Catholics."*

King William III Loyal Orange Lodge No. 11 (Portsmouth, England) is typical of many of the lodges. They see their continued existence as vital to the future of the English nation. They claim the Order stands for Christian faith and morality due to the *"serious decline in spirituality in the United Kingdom, and England in particular."* They claim the *"flower power"* generation of the 1960s did not create the liberal society they had promised, but rather an *"amoral, fragmented and confused society."* They also claim the maintenance of their national sovereignty that is threatened by break-up due to *"European federalism, militant Irish nationalism and Scottish nationalism."*

Regarding the situation in Ireland, the Orangemen state *"there is no convincing case that the rights of Ulster Protestants would be protected in a United Ireland."* Therefore they believe their freedoms are best preserved in a strong union between the four countries of the United Kingdom. Not only do they want to preserve the union, they claim they are best suited to do so because of their *"aspects of faith and culture."*

Authors note: In 1915, when my Uncle Larry Holden was 9 years old, his loyalist Grandfather, James Wilkinson (past president of the Winnipeg, Manitoba, Canada Loyal Orange Lodge), took him to march in an Orange parade in Winnipeg. After the parade, my uncle returned home proudly wearing his new Orange sash. Patrick Holden, his other Grandfather (a Catholic nationalist and member of the Ancient Order of Hibernians), met him at the door. Shocked and dumbfounded at the sight of the sash, Grandfather Holden thrashed the poor boy soundly for daring to march in a Protestant parade. *"What did I know?"* my Uncle would recall nearly 70 years later, *"I was only 9!"*

Bram Stoker
The Irishman Who Created *'Dracula'*

"I could feel the soft, shivering touch of the lips
on the super sensitive skin of my throat,
and the hard dents of two sharp teeth,
just touching and pausing there.
I closed my eyes in languorous ecstasy and waited,
waited with beating heart."

- Chapter 3, 'Dracula'

Author Bram Stoker has become the forgotten man of literature, and one of the few writers in history to have created a novel so immensely popular that it would come to over-shadow him, and diminish any of his other literary works.

One of many Irish writers who made their name abroad, but unlike his peers, he has never been properly honored in the country of his birth. Most people don't realize the man who created Dracula, the most evil creature in modern literature, was an Irishman.

Stoker was born in Dublin, near Clontarf, on November 8, 1847. Until the age of seven, Bram was so sick he hardly left his room. Sometimes his brother, Thornley, would come and show him the rocks and insects he had collected while playing outside.

Day after day young Bram would lie in his bed, gazing out onto the ships in Dublin Bay. His favorite time of the day was when his mother came to sit by his beside. She would tell him tales of Irish fairies who kidnapped young children, and of hideous creatures called vampires that walked the earth in search of human victims to quench their thirst for blood. These and other stories of the supernatural came alive in the ailing boy's imagination, and he soon began to make up stories of his own to amuse himself and pass the time.

There was never an explanation for his illness, but it may have been psychological according his family, which would account for his sudden and unexplainable recovery. Regardless, at the age of seven, young Bram began to walk. Afraid of a relapse, Bram would force himself to take long walks each day. Soon he joined the rest of the boys playing outside.

Bram was named after his father, Abraham, an Anglo-Irish civil servant in Dublin Castle. His mother, Charlotte, a charity worker and writer, had grown up in Co. Sligo, in the west of Ireland. She may have been as much as 20 years younger than Abraham. She was very formidable, and had great aspirations for her four sons, but little time for her two daughters. At one time, Charlotte became very angry when one of her sons placed second in an examination out of 1,000 students. She told him he had failed.

Bram grew up hearing stories about the great cholera epidemic that swept Western Europe and across Ireland in 1832. Charlotte and her family stayed inside their house, with the safety of fumigation, as their neighbor's were dying by the score. There was no rhyme or reason to the deadly epidemic. Some homes would be struck with the plague, while others would be spared.

Charlotte recalled the corpses that littered the houses on both sides of her home, and the tenacious coffin-makers who would knock on doors, touting for business. Eventually the coffin-makers became very persistent towards Charlotte's family, knowing they were still alive, but hoping they wouldn't be for long. Charlotte told one coffin-make that if he returned the next day she would through water on him. Sure enough, the very next day he knocked on the door, and Charlotte opened the door and threw a bucket of water in his face. Stunned, the coffin-maker shook his fist, and with a diabolical grin said, *"if you die in an hour you shall not have a coffin."*

Not only would coffin-makers besiege the homes, but looters would invade the houses of those that had died or were too sick to defend themselves. One dark night, Charlotte saw a hand reaching through the skylight. Seizing an axe, she reared back and cut it off with one mighty blow.

Once Bram recovered from his mysterious illness, his father began taking him to the theatre. After every performance the two would critique the plays, the actors, even the scenery. It was at this time that Bram began writing down all of the ghost stories told to him by his mother, as well as creating several of his own. Without realizing it, Bram had set the stage for his life's passion: writing and theatre.

His mother's stories of the epidemic, as well of tales of the Irish famine, certainly influenced Bram's early writings. One of his first stories was called *The Invisible Giant*, about a girl who tries to warn others about an impending plague. In his story, the "giant" is actually the plague itself, who moves silently, liked a cloaked demon, from person to person until all are dead.

Bram studied hard and became an exceptional student, despite his childhood illness. He had plenty of time to study thanks to his older sister, Matilda, younger brother, Tom, and his mother, Charlotte, who helped educate him while he was convalescing. The Reverend William Woods, who ran a private day-school in Dublin, also tutored him.

By the time he entered Trinity College he was a physically fit, tall, red-haired young gentleman. Know then as Abraham, he joined the Philosophical Society and became its president. He played on the football team and was unbeaten in "walking marathons," and after two years became the athletics champion of Trinity. He had come a long way from his years as a sickly, bed-bound youth.

The usual mild-manner Bram had a fiery and impetuous side. He once *"knocked down two ruffians and dragged them to the nearest police station"* when they tried to rob him as he returned to his hotel after a lecture at Edinburgh University. Another time he jumped into the Thames from a passing boat when he saw a man drowning.

Bram could apply this determined facet of his personality to the arts, where he once defended those who found the writings of Walt Whitman morally offensive.

A fan of romantic poets, he even began corresponding with Whitman and kept him updated on the controversy that raged in the Fortnightly Club, a group of Dublin men who met for free discussions. Whitman was grateful for the letters, especially in his declining years.

The two would arrange to meet in Philadelphia in 1884 and twice again in 1886. After Bram left their last meeting, Whitman was heard to say, "*what a broth of a boy he is! My gracious, he knows enough for four or five ordinary men...He's like a breath of good, healthy, breezy sea air.*" Bram very much cherished his 20-year friendship with Whitman, and was quite sad when the old poet passed away.

Bram graduated from Trinity in 1870, with honors in science, and returned to work on his MA. Like many college graduates, he quickly moved from the intellectual and social life of academia to the stogy work of a lowly clerk in Dublin Castle. Although the he found the life of a civil servant rather dreary, it would later inspire him to write his first book entitled, *Duties of Clerks of Petty Sessions in Ireland.* To this day, it is still considered a standard text.

It was also about this time he read the vampire book, *Carmilla,* written by Sheridan Le Fanu of Dublin, also a Trinity graduate. He became fascinated by the legend of vampirism, and did additional research on the vampire legends. He learned that vampire and vampire-like creatures existed in all cultures: from China to India to the Incan Empire, and that in Eastern European lore, there is not one kind of vampire but many. So the term "vampire" is as nebulous a category as "demon" or "witch." At this point the vampire research he conducted was nothing more than to satisfy his own curiosity.

Looking for more in life and remembering the good times he spent with his father, Bram began attending the Dublin theatre. He was particularly impressed with the actor, Henry Irving, playing the role of Captain Absolute in *The Rivals*. Bram became so enthralled with theatre, and with the work of the Irving, that he approached the proprietor of the *Dublin Mail* and offered to be their dramatic critic at no salary. All he asked is that he be given free tickets to the plays. The newspaper happily agreed.

Bram maintained his civil service job, but continued to write more and more. His first venture into pure horror would be the publishing of a four-part serial in the *Shamrock* entitled, *The Chain of Destiny*. It would include a character named *"The Phantom of the Fiend."*

In the summer, with the fee earned from *Shamrock*, he visited his parents who had relocated to Zermatt, Switzerland for financial reasons. He explained to his Civil Servant father that he was seeing an actress named "Miss Henry," and that he wanted to give up his job at Dublin Castle, move to London, and become an author. His father was aghast! He tried to convince his son not to leave a stable job. He also stated that actors and actresses are not *"altogether desirable acquaintances."* Bram apparently did as his father advised, as he remained with the Civil Service, and the mysterious "Miss Henry" seemed to have disappeared.

The actor Henry Irving returned to Dublin in 1867 in the role of "Hamlet." By now Bram had been writing as a dramatic critic for five years, and he gave Irving rave reviews for his portrayal of the melancholy Dane. Irving was so impressed, that he asked his manager to arrange a meeting with Bram. When the two met, they realized how much they had in common. Thus began a friendship and business relationship that would last a lifetime, and have a profound impact on Bram's career.

Eventually Bram became the Irving's manager, as well as Irving's London theatre, The Lyceum. This occurred shortly after his marriage to Florence, Oscar Wilde's first girl friend. Stoker and Oscar Wilde had been friends, and Stoker was particularly fond of Wilde's parents, Sir William and Lady Wilde, both keen Irish folktale collectors. Bram and Florence were married in St. Anne's Church on Dawson Street on December 4, 1878.

Five days after the marriage, he and Florence moved to England to manage the Lyceum. In between his strenuous theatrical duties, Stoker wrote short stories and novels. The success of the Lyceum was due to his careful management, which was in sharp contrast to Henry Irving's theatrical excesses.

By 1890, he began work on a novel that would draw together all of his interests: his love of the sea, his interest in the weather, and his fascination with the supernatural, and with vampires in particular. Seven years later, Bram sent the novel, The *Un-Dead* to the publisher, but quickly changed the name to *Dracula*.

The public didn't know what to make of the novel. Some found Stoker's tale of the blood-thirsty Transylvanian Count to be *"grotesque,"* while others described it as *"excellent...weird, powerful, and horrible."* The book was not a bestseller, but it did sell steadily. People were fascinated with the combination of sexual repression and Gothic horror. The story describes a world in which the rationality and science of the modern realm clashed sharply with Old World culture.

Most historians have settled on the fact that Stoker must have based his "Dracula" on a 15th century Romanian prince. Prince Vlad 5th of Wallachia lived from 1431 to 1476. Vlad was a bloodthirsty villain who delighted in torturing helpless enemies.

Examples of his maniacal behavior abound. He once invited the beggars of one town to a sumptuous feast, then locked the doors and set fire to the place with the justification that this prevented plaque and eliminated inferior stock.

When visiting ambassadors neglected to doff their turbans in his presence, he ordered that they should be nailed to their heads. He was known as Vlad Tepes (*tzepa* meaning spike) or Vlad the Impaler, owing to his penchant for impaling his enemies on tall spikes – an excruciating torture as the man was thrust downwards on to the sharp, oiled point. Gradually, his own weight would force this upwards, until the stake pierced so deeply that he died.

When one of his men commented on the screams and smells, Vlad had him impaled also, on a taller stake, stating, *"you live up there, yonder, where the stench cannot reach you."* In 1456, after one particular battle, Vlad impaled 20,000 Turks. To Romanians, Vlad was a great warrior and national hero. To the rest of the world, he was a savage beast.

In 1458, Vlad Dracula built the citadel of Bucharest. In his time there was no such country as Romania. The land consisted of the three states of Transylvania, Moldavia and Wallachia. The latter were united in 1859 and joined by Transylvania after the First World War to form Romania. It should be pointed out that Vlad Dracula was no vampire.

He was a brut in the most extreme way, but he was no vampire. However, there is just enough resemblance to the factual truth in Stoker's novel that many have assumed he based Dracula on Vlad the Impaler.

The name "Dracula" actually was given to Vlad's father, also named Vlad. On Februrary 8, 1431, Emperor Sigismund of Luxemborg conceded the ruler-ship of Wallachia to Vlad. Emperor Sigismund gave a necklace to Vlad and a golden medallion with a dragon engraved on it, the badge of the knights of the Order, bearing the name of the mystical animal.

Waiting for his coronation, Vlad and his family went to Sighisoara in Transylvania, where he set up a mint using the engraving of the medallion, a dragon, to emboss his coins. The Romanians, whose language was Latin, nicknamed Vlad, "Dracula," (from the Latin *Draco-Onis*, meaning Devil/Dragon). This nickname was eventually used as Vlad's descendents surname. Vlad had two sons, Vlad Calugarul (meaning "Vlad the Monk") and Vlad Tepes ("Vlad the Spike.")

It was Vlad Tepes whose barbarias acts would forever shape the name of "Dracula." Since Vlad Tepes always signed with his father's name, he became *Vlad Dracula*.

No evidence exists as to why Bram chose this 15th Romanian prince as the model for his fictional character. Some speculate that it was his friendship with a Hungarian professor from Budapest, and that this professor might have suggested the name of "Dracula." No one really knows.

Scholars have argued for decades over the true identity, or rather inspiration, for Dracula. Many believe that the actor, Henry Irving, was an important model for the Count Dracula, and that the novel was a kind of unconscious revenge against he man to whom Stoker gave so much. Others believe the dark-cloaked count, much like Stoker's earlier story, *The Invisible Giant*, is a symbol of disease. And, to dig even further, a possible symbol of tuberculosis, based on the symptoms of Dracula's victims.

However, the inspiration for Dracula may have come from an Irish legend, rather than the Transylvanian, Vlad the Impaler, according to Celtic history and folklore expert, Bob Curran, a lecturer at Northern Ireland's University of Ulster in Coleraine.

Dublin-born civil servant Bram Stoker had never visited Eastern Europe. So Curran surmises that Stoker may have based his creation on a fifth-century Irish chieftain from Londonderry in Northern Ireland, called "Abhartach." In the academic journal, *History of Ireland*, Curran claims that the lore surrounding Abhartach was that he was a tyrant and drinker of human blood. He drank tainted blood – *droch fhoula* in Gaelic (droc'ola) – and became a member of the "undead." He also rose from the grave to demand bowls of blood drawn from his subjects.

Curran adds that he could not be slain; only restrained in a grave when buried upside down under a stone after being stabbed with a sword made from yew wood. *"Can we really consign the vampire to some remote part of Eastern Europe?"* asks Curran. *"Stoker's experiences may have come more directly from Irish folklore."*

Dublin scholars also claim that Stoker was strongly influenced by the mummified bodies in St. Michan's Church in Dublin, where a branch of the Stoker family once owned an underground burial vault.

Stoker was also fascinated by the graveyard at Ballybough that was reserved for burying only the victims of suicide. Other aspects of Ireland are used as symbols in the novel, such as rats, fog, storms, gypsies, castles, abbeys and so on. Others have gone as far as to make the assumption that Dracula was synonymous with the oppressive British landlord system itself.

According to Classic Notes, *"Stoker was deeply concerned with sexual morality. Although his novel is full of racy subtext, possibly far more than the author intended, his own views regarding sex and morality were in many ways quite conservative. He favored censoring novels for their sexual content and considered racy literature dangerous for the ways that it nurtured man's darker sexual tendencies. Although Dracula has many scenes that seem to revel in sexual language and sensual description, these pleasures are sublimated to a Victorian and Christian sense or morality. Sexual energy, in Stoker's view, has great potential for evil."*

The interesting aspect of his novel is that he is able to sin with sexuality in a moralizing way. He writes incredibly vivid and sensual scenes, but still includes the themes of Christian redemption and the triumph of purity.

Enough similarities exist to assume that Vlad the Impaler, and the vampire myths of Eastern Europe, must have had a significant influence in the creation of *Dracula*. But it is becoming widely accepted that Stoker's own Dublin background, coupled with Irish folklore and mythology, that were perhaps the real creative source.

Most people do not realize that Stoker spent the first 30 years of his life in Dublin, and the influence of that city, along with other Irish influences, was enormous.

Only now is he being properly honored in the country of his birth via numerous Bram Stoker festivals and literary associations. Regardless, this Dublin author succeeded in creating the most terrifying, and most popular, creature in literary history, following in the lesser known footsteps of other Irish Gothic writers such as Charles Robert Maturin and Joseph Sheridan La Fanu.

The end of Stoker's life was rather depressing. Stoker's great-nephew, Daniel Farson, claimed that Stoker's wife became frigid around 1877, driving Stoker to other women including prostitutes. This would explain why Stoker had the reputation as a womanizer.

Through one of his dalliances Stoker contracted syphilis, probably in Paris, where many writers before him would seek discreet pleasure.

That particular episode of his life occurred about the time *Dracula* was written, and may have played some part in the sexual implications in the novel. Much of Bram's writing about that time exhibited signs of guilt and sexual frustration. This was in conflict with his conservative sexual mores.

Stoker wrote eighteen books before he died of syphilis in 1912, near poverty. He wrote other tomes about vampires, but nothing compared to the success of *Dracula*, which remains unsurpassed in its ability to shock.

It is the best-known horror tale of all time and has had a tremendous impact on the creative arts, having inspired or influenced 700 films and numerous television shows. *Dracula* has not been out of print since 1897, and has been translated into every major language (including Irish).

The final words of Count Dracula would come to embody the baneful character who would long outlive its creator: *"You think to baffle me, you - with your pale faces all in a row, like sheep in a butcher's. You shall be sorry yet, each one of you! You think you have left me without a place to rest, but I have more. My revenge is just begun! I spread it over centuries, and TIME IS ON MY SIDE."*

Dracula remains the biggest selling novel in the world, and the only book to outsell the Bible.

The Great Famine

"Ireland is in your hands,
in your power. If you do not save her,
she cannot save herself..."

- Daniel O'Connell to the British House of Commons,
1847

Whether it is referred to as The Great Hunger, The Great Famine, The Irish Holocaust, The Potato Famine, or An Gorta Mor ("The Bad Life"), the result was the same; one million Irish needlessly starved to death from 1845 to 1847 while the British government exported enough food to feed them all.

Some historians call it the greatest genocide in modern history. Those less critical of England said it was just a colossal miscalculation on their part as to the enormity and complexity of the potato crop blight and subsequent food shortage.

That 'miscalculation' devastated the population and fueled the already simmering hatred for England. It also forced a million Irish to immigrate to the US and Canada in to escape starvation and a continued life of degradation.

To understand the Great Famine one must first understand how the Irish came to be dependent on one foodstuff as their main sustenance. It's a long, sad story involving religious suppression and maltreatment.

The subjugation of the Irish began with Penal Laws in 1690s designed to repress the native Irish. These laws targeted Irish education, religion, and property rights. They were designed to keep the people poor and powerless.

They first decreed that no Irish Catholic could own a gun, pistol, or sword. Over the next 30 years the Penal Laws of the 17th Century would include the following:

The Irish Catholic was forbidden the exercise of religion
- forbidden to receive an education
- forbidden to enter a profession
- forbidden to hold public office
- forbidden to engage in trade or commerce
- forbidden to live in a corporate town or within five miles thereof
- forbidden to own a horse of greater value than five pounds
- forbidden to purchase land
- forbidden to lease land
- forbidden to accept a mortgage on land in security for a loan
- forbidden to vote
- forbidden to keep any arms for his protection
- forbidden to hold a life annuity
- forbidden to buy land from a Protestant
- forbidden to receive a gift of land from a Protestant
- forbidden to inherit land from a Protestant
- forbidden to inherit anything from a Protestant
- forbidden to rent any land that was worth more than thirty shillings a year
- forbidden to reap from his land any profit exceeding a third of the rent
- forbidden to be a guardian to a child
- forbidden, when dying, to leave an infant children under Catholic guardianship
- forbidden to attend Catholic worship
- forced by law to attend Protestant worship
- forbidden to educate his child
- forbidden to send his child to a Catholic teacher
- forbidden to allow a Catholic teacher to come to his child
- forbidden to send his child abroad to receive education

Edmund Burke, an Irish-born Protestant who became a British Member of Parliament (MP), described the Penal laws as *"well fitted for the oppression, impoverishment and degradation of a people, and the debasement in them of human nature itself, as ever proceeded from the perverted ingenuity of man."* The Lord Chancellor stated, *"The law does not suppose any such person to exist as an Irish Roman Catholic."*

The Act of Union came next in 1800 which resulted in Ireland's economy being absorbed by Britain. Although free trade now existed between the two countries, England used Ireland as a dumping ground for its surplus goods. Rapid industrialization in Britain brought the collapse of the Irish linen and woolen industries in the countryside with their less efficient handlooms.

By 1835, according to the British "Poor Enquiry'" survey, 75% of Irish laborers had no steady employment and begging became commonplace.

As conditions worsened, the French sociologist, Gustave de Beaumont, visited Ireland in 1835 and stated the following: *"I have seen the Indian in his forests, and the Negro in his chains, and thought, as I contemplated their pitiable condition, that I saw the very extreme of human wretchedness; but I did not then know the condition of unfortunate Ireland...In all countries, more or less, paupers may be discovered; but an entire nation of paupers is what was never seen until it was shown in Ireland."*

By the mid-1800s, a number of English politicians thought Ireland needed to be dragged into the modern world. A rather remarkable observation considering it was the English government who placed the Irish in that position. Regardless, the industrious British considered their rural Irish neighbors almost stone-age. They referred to them as "bog-trotters" and found their Irish Gaelic customs and language annoying, if not offensive.

To the English, an Irishman was lazy, shiftless, and totally lacking in the virtues of hard work and self-reliance. English newspapers depicted the Irish with ape-like features often behaving like petulant children. English reformers hoped to remake the Irish in their own image and in doing so end Ireland's cycle of poverty which they were certain was caused by bad moral character.

English reformers watched in dismay as Ireland's population doubled to over 8 million just before the Famine. Bountiful harvests meant the people were generally well fed and could raise large families, but unfortunately, there were very few job opportunities. The English found this wholly irresponsible. But at this point is history they weren't sure what to do about their primitive neighbors.

And then something terrible happened to the Irish. Their main food source failed in 1845 and the Irish began to starve. The English saw it as divine intervention and an answer to the Irish dilemma.

At first, the potato seemed a blessing from above. It thrived in the damp Irish climate, was easy to grow and produced a high yield per acre. In the period from 1780 to 1845, it helped double the Irish population from 4 to 8 million.

However, with this population explosion came an increased demand for land. The only solution was to divide the available parcels into ever smaller plots for each succeeding generation. Soon, the diminished size of these plots dictated the planting of potatoes as it was the only crop that could produce a sufficient yield of food on such limited acreage.

By 1840, at least 1/3 of Ireland's population was almost entirely dependent on the potato for its sustenance. Such a dependency can be disastrous if that main food staple were to vanish. And then the worst case scenario happened. The potato crop began to fail.

The potato blight began quite mysteriously in September 1845 as leafs on potato plants suddenly turned black and curled, then rotted. The cause was an airborne fungus (*Phytophthora Infestans*) originally transported in the holds of ships traveling from North America to England.

The infected plants fermented while providing the nourishment the fungus needed to live, emitting a nauseous stench as they blackened and withered. There had been crop failures in the past due to weather and other diseases, but this strange new failure was unlike anything ever seen. Potatoes dug out of the ground at first looked edible, but shriveled and rotted within days. The potatoes had been attacked by the same fungus that had destroyed the plant leaves above ground.

At first, the disease devastated the potato crops in both France and Holland. Then it struck Ireland in September 1845 and promptly destroyed 40% of the country's potato crop. In 1846, nearly 100% of the crop was lost. 1847 was much the same, except Ireland experienced a very harsh winter making that year beyond miserable for the poor Irish.

The crops fared no better from 1848-49. These losses were catastrophic to the people who lived in rural Ireland because of their complete dependence on the potato.

By October 1845, news of the blight had reached London. British Prime Minister, Sir Robert Peel, quickly established a Scientific Commission to examine the problem. After briefly studying the situation, the Commission issued a gloomy report that over half of Ireland's potato crop might perish due to "wet rot."

However, the British government did very little to mitigate the Irish starvation. Their assistance was limited by noninterventionist policies over human and social needs.

The dominant economic theory in mid-nineteenth century Britain was called "laissez-faire" (meaning: "let it be"). This policy held it was not the government's job to provide aid for its citizens, or to interfere with the free market of goods or trade. In short, they did nothing.

To his credit, Sir Robert Peel actually put his career on the line to push through assistance for the Irish, but he was constantly thwarted by the laissez-faire policies of the day. Peel did manage, unbeknownst to his own government, to order Indian corn from the Americas to be delivered to Ireland. This corn was only a last resort for the sufferers; it was difficult to grind and cook, not nearly as filling as potatoes, and it lacked vitamin C. It ran out quickly and was not replaced.

British public opinion was the Irish had brought this disaster upon themselves, so why should England bail them out. This was interesting as a similar potato crop disease occurred previously in Scotland, yet resulted in few casualties. That is because the English government, and local landowners, rallied to provide aid to avoid mass starvation. Historians believe it was because the Scots were Protestants...the Irish were not.

The Great Hunger in Ireland led to the greatest loss of life in Western Europe in the 100 years between the Napoleonic Wars and World War I. Entire villages perished. Cholera, deadly fevers, dysentery, scurvy and typhus swept the population.

People perished in such great numbers it was impossible to record them nor have enough coffins for burials. "Trap coffins," which were made with a trap door in the bottom, were used for the trip to the cemetery. Once there, the coffin was placed over the grave and the trap door opened to drop the body into it, leaving the coffin ready for the next victim.

A number of historians will argue the term "famine" is inappropriate and does not represent what they refer to as "genocide." While the fungus did eliminate the potato as a food source, the Irish were busy growing a number of other crops - more than enough to feed themselves.

Unfortunately, those crops were being removed at gunpoint by English soldiers garrisoned in Ireland. In 1847, 4,000 ships carrying £17,000,000 worth of foodstuffs; 10,000 head of cattle; and 4,000 horses and ponies sailed from Ireland to England. That same year 500,000 Irish people died of starvation and hunger-related diseases.

Tenants who were unable to pay the landlords found themselves evicted and their homes destroyed. There was no food, and now there was no shelter. Many of the homeless simply lay down by the roadside and waited to die. Those caught stealing food risked arrest and transportation to penal colonies in Australia. The British philosophy became obvious: starve them out, or ship them out.

It's true the British government did offer some minimal relief efforts. But those efforts were limited to soup kitchens, poorhouses, and public works projects. All failed miserably because they were too few and very poorly managed.

A number Irish Catholics refused to enter the soup kitchens because there was often one stipulation: those "taking the soup" had to denounce the Pope and join the Protestant church. Those who did sup were denounced as "soupers" and forever shunned by their former fellow Catholics.

The main voluntary attempts to deal with the crisis, especially in the west of Ireland, were undertaken by The Religious Society of Friends (Quakers) whose organizers included William E. Foster and James Tuke.

Philadelphia merchant, John Wanamaker, headed the Relief Committee and also contributed to the Friends' effort from this country. Eight ships filled with provisions sailed from Philadelphia. Others who contributed to the relief efforts included the Choctaw Indian Nation (who sent a very small, but very welcomed donation) and The Society of the Friendly Sons of Saint Patrick of Philadelphia. But all of these were merely drops in a very large bucket.

In adhering to laissez-faire, the British government also did not interfere with the English-controlled export business in Irish-grown grains.

Throughout the Famine years, large quantities of native-grown wheat, barley, oats and oatmeal sailed out of places such as Limerick and Waterford for England, even though local Irish were dying of starvation.

Irish farmers, desperate for cash, routinely sold the grain to the British in order to pay the rent on their farms and thus avoid eviction.

In the first year of the Famine, deaths from starvation were kept down due to the imports of Indian corn and survival of about half the original potato crop.

The poorer Irish survived the first year by selling off their livestock and pawning their meager possessions whenever necessary to buy food. Some borrowed money at high interest from petty money-lenders, known as *Gombeen* men. That term would be associated with any shopkeeper or merchant who exploited the starving during the Famine by selling much needed food and goods on credit at outrageous interest rates. They also fell behind on their rents.

On June 29, 1846, the British government announced the resignation of British Prime Minister Sir Robert Peel, Peel's Conservative government had lost political favor over the repeal of the Corn Laws which he had forced through Parliament.

Peel's departure paved the way for the extremely indifferent Charles Trevelyan who took full control of the Famine policy under the new Liberal government.

The Liberals, known as Whigs, were led by Lord John Russell, and were staunch believers in the principle of laissez-faire. Sir Robert Peel was the only hope the Irish had and the British government had forced him out.

Once he had taken control, Trevelyan ordered the closing of the food depots in Ireland that had been selling "Peel's" Indian corn. He also rejected a shipload of Indian corn already headed for Ireland. His reasoning, as he explained in a letter, was to prevent the Irish from becoming "habitually dependent" on the British government. His openly stated desire was to make "Irish property support Irish poverty."

Prior to replacing Sir Robert Peel, Charles Trevelyan had foreshadowed his deadly policy after a visit to Ireland. He said there were at least a one to two million people "too many" in Ireland and the eight million current residents could not possibly survive. *"Protestant and Catholic will freely fall and the land will be for the survivors....The real evil with which we have to contend is not the physical evil of the Famine but the moral evil of the selfish, perverse and turbulent character of the people."* Shortly after, he would be placed in charge of a policy that brought about that exact situation.

The Irish watched with increasing anger as boatloads of home-grown oats and grain departed from their shores for shipment to England. Food riots erupted in ports such as Youghal near Cork where peasants tried unsuccessfully to confiscate a boatload of oats.

At Dungarvan in County Waterford, British troops were pelted with stones. They responded by firing into the crowd killing two and wounding several others. British naval ships were then assigned to escort the food-laden riverboats as they sailed by the starving Irish watching silently from shore.

As the Famine worsened, and the Irish became more agitated, the British responded by sending in more troops. "Would to God the Government would send us food instead of soldiers," a starving resident of County Mayo once lamented.

In order to survive, the Irish in the countryside began to live off wild blackberries, nettles, turnips, old cabbage leaves, edible seaweed, shellfish, roots, roadside weeds, and even green grass. They found the best eating grass in the graveyards - and better yet - the grass growing on the newest graves were the most succulent.

The Irish sold their livestock and pawned everything they owned, including their clothing, to pay rent to avoid eviction. Food prices rose to the point it was unaffordable. Corn meal sold for three pennies a pound; three times what it had been a year earlier. As a result, children sometimes went unfed so that parents could stay healthy enough to keep working for the desperately needed cash.

Fish, although plentiful along the West Coast of Ireland, remained out of reach in waters too deep and dangerous for the 'currachs,' small cowhide-covered fishing boats. Starving fishermen pawned their nets and tackle to buy food for their families.

A first-hand investigation of the overall situation was conducted by William Forster, a member of the Quaker community in England. He was acting on behalf of the recently formed Central Relief Committee of the Society of Friends, with branches in Dublin and London. The children, Forster observed, had become *"like skeletons, their features sharpened with hunger and their limbs wasted, so that little was left but bones, their hands and arms, in particular, being much emaciated, and the happy expression of infancy gone from their faces, leaving behind the anxious look of premature old age."*

Nicholas Cummins, the magistrate of Cork, visited the hardest-hit coastal district of Skibbereen. *"I entered some of the hovels,"* he wrote, *"and the scenes which presented themselves were such as no tongue or pen can convey the slightest idea of. In the first, six famished and ghastly skeletons, to all appearances dead, were huddled in a corner on some filthy straw, their sole covering what seemed a ragged horsecloth, their wretched legs hanging about, naked above the knees. I approached with horror, and found by a low moaning they were alive -- they were in fever, four children, a woman and what had once been a man. It is impossible to go through the detail. Suffice it to say, that in a few minutes I was surrounded by at least 200 such phantoms, such frightful spectres as no words can describe, [suffering] either from famine or from fever. Their demoniac yells are still ringing in my ears, and their horrible images are fixed upon my brain."*

Holding her dead child, a mother begs for enough money to get a coffin. The dead were buried without coffins just a few inches below the soil, to be gnawed at by rats and dogs.

In some cabins the dead remained indoors for days as the living were too weak to move the bodies outside. In other places, unmarked hillside graves came into use as huge trenches were dug and bodies dumped in, then covered with quicklime.

Highly contagious 'Black Fever,' as typhus was nicknamed since it blackened the skin, is spread by body lice and was carried from town to town by beggars and homeless paupers. Numerous doctors, priests, nuns, and kind-hearted persons who attended to the sick in their lice-infested dwellings also succumbed.

Rural Irish, known for their hospitality and kindness to strangers, never refused to let a beggar or homeless family spend the night. In doing so, they often unknowingly contracted typhus. At times, entire homeless families, ravaged by fever, simply laid down along the roadside and died, succumbing to what was called, 'Road Fever.'

During the Famine period, an estimated half-million Irish were evicted from their cottages. Unscrupulous landlords used two methods to remove their penniless tenants.

The first involved applying for a legal judgment against the male head of a family owing back-rent. After the local barrister pronounced judgment, the man would be thrown in jail and his wife and children dumped out on the streets. A 'notice to appear' was usually enough to cause most pauper families to flee and they were handed out by the hundreds.

The second method was for the landlord to simply pay to send pauper families overseas to British North America. Landlords would first make phony promises of money, food and clothing, then pack the half-naked people in overcrowded British sailing ships, poorly built and often unseaworthy, that became known as "coffin ships."

The first coffin ships headed for Quebec, Canada. The three thousand mile journey, depending on winds and the captain's skill, could take from 40 days to three months.

Upon arrival in the Saint Lawrence River, the ships were supposed to be inspected for disease and any sick passengers removed to quarantine facilities on Grosse Isle, a small island thirty miles downstream from Quebec City.

But in the spring of 1847, shipload after shipload of fevered Irish arrived, quickly overwhelming the small medical inspection facility, which only had 150 beds. By June, 40 vessels containing 14,000 Irish immigrants waited in a line extending two miles down the St. Lawrence. It took up to five days to see a doctor, many of whom were becoming ill from contact with the typhus-infected passengers.

By the summer, the line of ships had grown several miles long. A fifteen-day general quarantine was then imposed for all of the waiting ships. Many healthy Irish thus succumbed to typhus as they were forced to remain in their lice-infested holds. With so many dead on board the waiting ships, hundreds of bodies were simply dumped overboard into the St. Lawrence.

Many families were told by their landlords that once they arrived in Canada, an agent would meet them and pay out between two and five pounds depending on the size of the family. But no agents were ever found. Promises of money, food and clothing had been utterly false. Landlords knew that once the paupers arrived in Canada there was virtually no way for them to ever return to Ireland and make a claim. Thus they had promised them anything just to get rid of them.

Others, half-alive, were placed in small boats and then deposited on the beach at Grosse Isle, left to crawl to the hospital on their hands and knees if they could manage.

Thousands of Irish, ill with typhus and dysentery, eventually wound up in hastily constructed wooden fever sheds. These makeshift hospitals, badly understaffed and unsanitary, simply became places to die, with corpses piled "like cordwood" in nearby mass graves. Those who couldn't get into the hospital died along the roadsides. In one case, an orphaned Irish boy walking along the road with other boys sat down for a moment under a tree to rest and promptly died on the spot.

The quarantine efforts were soon abandoned and the Irish were sent on to their next destination without any medical inspection or treatment. From Grosse Isle, the Irish were given free passage up the St. Lawrence to Montreal and cities such as Kingston and Toronto. The crowded open-aired river barges used to transport them exposed the fair-skinned Irish to all-day-long summer sun causing many painful sunburns. At night, they

laid down close to each other to ward off the chilly air, spreading
more lice and fever.

Montreal received the biggest influx of Irish during this time.
Many of those arriving were quite ill from typhus and long-term
malnutrition. Montreal's limited medical facilities at Point St.
Charles were quickly overwhelmed.

Homeless Irish wandered the countryside begging for help
as temperatures dropped and the cold Canadian winter set in.
But they were shunned everywhere by Canadians afraid of
contracting fever.

Of the 100,000 Irish that sailed to British North America
in 1847, an estimated one out of five died from disease and
malnutrition, including over five thousand at Grosse Isle.

Those who could not leave Ireland were left with the problem
of what to do with the dead who decaying lay all around. There
were not enough coffins to hold the dead, even if the poor had
money to pay for them. Stories abounded of entire families dying,
or of mothers losing all their children and carrying the bodies to
the cemetery on their backs, one by one. Visitors reported seeing
dead bodies stacked in ditches and dogs devouring corpses in
the fields; to their horror, they also observed people killing and
eating those same dogs.

The Irish, for their part, were not about to simply sit still
and die. The whole population of the starving country began to
move about. Cities, villages and entire districts were abandoned.
Western Ireland was nearly depleted of its population.

Among country folk, the centuries-old communal way of
life with its traditional emphasis on neighborly sharing, now
collapsed. It was replaced by a survival mentality in which,
every person fended for themselves. Family bonds disintegrated
as starving parents deserted their children and children likewise
deserted their parents.

One way to limit immigration to the US was to make it
unaffordable. Ports along the eastern seaboard of the U.S.

required a bond to be posted by the captain of a ship guaranteeing that his passengers would not become wards of the city.

Passenger fares to the U.S. in 1847 were up to three times higher than fares to Canada. The British government intentionally kept fares to Quebec low to encourage the Irish to populate Canada and also to discourage them from immigrating to England.

America in the 1840s was a nation of about 23 million inhabitants, mainly Protestant. Many of the Puritan descendants viewed the growing influx of Roman Catholic Irish with increasing dismay.

The Irish, for their part, were not about to simply sit still and die. The whole population of the starving country began to move about. Cities, villages and entire districts were abandoned. Western Ireland was nearly depleted of its population.

The 1841 census of Ireland conducted by the British revealed a population of 10,897,449. This figure includes the correction factor established by that year's official partial recount; the first incorrect count was 8.6 million which for political reasons is used today to mask the true number of deaths in Ireland during those years.

By the 1851 census the population in Ireland was only 6,552,385. It is generally accepted that one million people emigrated during the Famine. Therefore several million had starved and are buried in mass graves all over Ireland. Based on the true number that were conducted by the British government and are documented online, at least 3 million people in Ireland died during the famine years, 1847-1851.

The exports of Irish food and livestock were at an all-time high during those years, again according to written released British records. Britain was exporting enough food out of Ireland to feed a population of at least 30 million people.

The famine did much to foster a feeling of unity among the Irish against the English. Dedication to the Catholic Church increased and priests grew more powerful. Irish politicians began pushing the tenant agenda in Parliament, and their efforts formed the start of Ireland's independence movement.

On St. Patrick's Day, 1858, a former Young Ireland leader named James Stephens founded the Irish Republican Brotherhood. Around the same time, another rebel named Jeremiah O'Donovan Rossa founded a similar Phoenix Society in Skibbereen. These movements spread rapidly during the late 1850s and laid the groundwork that would lead to an Irish republic.

The Irish used to say, "God gave us the potato blight, but the English gave us the famine." There is some truth to this statement. When the Famine occurred, according to author Tim Pat Coogan, the English not only did very little, but they discouraged others from helping as well. And then sixty years England was shocked when the Irish would dare ask for their independence.

Los San Patricios
The Irish Soldiers of Mexico

"Sergeant, buck him and gag him, our officers cry,
For each trifling offense which they happen to spy,
Till with bucking and gagging of Dick, Pat and Bill,
Faith, the Mexican's ranks they have helped to fill."

- An anonymous Irish solider in the U.S. Army, 1846

There is probably no story more compelling, and yet little known, than the San Patricios Battalion of Mexico. There is a reason. History is written by the victors. So it is not surprising that the Irish soldiers of the Mexican army would become a rather negative footnote in American history.

Only recently have historians taken the time to ferret out the true story behind the men who would desert the U.S. military and join the Mexican army to take up arms against the United States.

Only now, as America strives for political correctness, do we understand the war with Mexico was truly an act of aggressiveness carried out solely to expand the southwestern territory available for slavery. It was the perfect example of manifest destiny. But in school we were taught a different version. It was instilled in us that Texans desired "freedom," much like our colonial ancestors, and they were willing to fight and die to attain this liberty. While no one doubts the fighting spirit of the Texans, unfortunately, like too many other wars, it had everything to do with increasing territory and little to do with throwing off the yoke of oppression.

Even Ulysses S. Grant, who served as an officer in the U.S. army during the Mexican war, would state in his personal memoirs that he would, *"regard the war which resulted as one of the most unjust ever waged by a stronger nation against a weaker nation. It was an instance of a republic following the bad example of European monarchies, in not considering justice in their desire to acquire additional territory, Even if annexation itself could be justified, the manner in which the subsequent war was forced upon Mexico cannot...To us it was an empire and of incalculable value; but it might have been obtained by other means. The Southern rebellion was largely the outgrowth of the Mexican war. Nations, like individuals, are punished for their transgressions. We got our punishment in the most sanguinary and expensive war of modern times."*

Historians were also quick to ignore the fact that the invading U.S. army deliberately targeted Catholic cathedrals, churches, and convents in Mexico; and U.S. soldiers often "brutally" interrupted Masses, processions and other religious services.

In 1846, Mexico was in a state of disarray, as various bandits and warlords roamed the land fighting for control. At the same time, Texans declared their independence from Mexico.

Seizing the opportunity, U. S. President James K. Polk sent troops to the disputed border to prepare for an invasion, hoping to gain control of the Santa Fe trades routes as well as the Pacific coast. That move led to armed confrontations, and then all out war.

At the same time, thousands of young Irish men were fleeing famine and British persecution in Ireland. In America, they were promised citizenship for their entire family, and a chance to fight England along the Canadian border, if they enlisted in the U.S. army.

With no other option available, many Irish immigrants joined the army, but were instead sent south to Mexico to fight in a territorial war. They quickly discovered, however, they would suffer discrimination far worse than when they were in Ireland.

In the mid-1840s, the anti-foreigner, anti-Catholic movement known as "Nativism" was in full force. A decade earlier, influential New York businessmen had formed the "Protestant Association" to preserve America from "Popery in this land of ours." It published newspapers, pamphlets, and such books as *"Awful Disclosures"* and *"The Secrets of Nunneries"* where they described orgies and ritual sacrifice of infants by crazed clerics. When a rumor spread that Ursuline nuns were molesting Protestant pupils in Charleston, Mass., a riot erupted in which the convent was burned to the ground.

In Philadelphia, in May 1845, a mob of several thousand armed with clubs, knives, pistols, and torches, in one night burned down three Catholic churches, two rectories, two convents, and 200 Irish homes.

The media also ran numerous hate-mongering depictions showing the Irish as having ape-like features and portraying them as unintelligent, drunk, and *"seditiously loyal to the pope."*

Because of this anti-immigrant fervor, Irish-Catholic soldiers were often singled out for harsh punishment by the Anglo-Protestant officers, and were often referred to as "Dutchies," "Micks," or "Potato-heads." Protestant soldiers committing the same infractions were dealt with much less severely. If caught intoxicated, some poor Catholic souls were literally branded with a "D" for drunkard. Others were "bucked and gagged" which involved hog-tying a soldier for hours with a rag stuffed in his mouth. Some were flogged until they collapsed, and then placed in the solitary confinement that consisted of a hole covered by a wooden door. Others were secured by the thumbs to a tree branch, or tied astride a wooden horse in the blazing heat all day. A few were even bound and tossed into a pond.

On top of the physical punishment, they were also forced to attend Protestant church services. As far as the U.S. army officer corps was concerned, to be Irish *and* Catholic was to be considered one of the lowest forms of life. For this reason, the desertion rate among these Irish-Catholic troops was high.

When some of the first Irish deserters reached the Mexican border, they were shocked to see these strange people worshiping as they did. The deserters also informed the Mexican government of the unfair treatment they endured as Catholic Irishmen.

Seizing the opportunity, Mexican generals quickly showered the American camps with thousands of leaflets, targeting the Irish, and emphasizing their shared Catholicism. They even offered a $10 bonus and 320-acre tracts of land to each new recruit. *"Irishmen! Listen to the words of your brothers, hear the accents of a Catholic people. Is religion no longer the strongest of human bonds? Can you fight by the side of those who put fire to your temples in Boston and Philadelphia? Did you witness such dreadful crimes and sacrileges without making a solemn vow to our lord? If you are Catholic, the same as we, if you follow the doctrines of Our Savior, why are you sword in hand murdering your brethren? Why are you antagonistic to those who defend their country and your own God? Are Catholic Irishmen to be the destroyers of Catholic temples, the murderers of Catholic priests, and the founders of heretical rites in this pious nation? Come over to us; you will be received under the laws of that truly Christian hospitality and good faith which Irish guests are entitled to expect and obtain from a Catholic nation. May Mexicans and Irishmen, united by the sacred tie of religion and benevolence, form only one people!* For many of the Irish, the offer of land, and individual respect, was quite tempting.

Approximately 4,000 U.S. soldiers deserted during the Mexican War, but only a small percentage joined the Mexican military forces. Enough did, however, so they were allowed to form a new battalion called "The San Patricios," named after the patron saint of Ireland, St. Patrick. Known deserters made up only one-third of the new battalion.

The majority were European and Mexican citizens, not citizens of the U.S, and many weren't even Catholic. Of the 120 known members, 40 were born in Ireland, and 18 were born in the U.S., Canada, or Great Britain, but had Irish surnames. But, for every O'Connor, there was a Schmidt. For every Kelley, there was a De Groot. In fact, Irish-born soldiers made up only 39% of the San Patricios. 21% were born in the U.S. 13% in Germany, Scotland 7%, Mexico 7%, England 4%, and the remaining soldiers were from Great Britain, Canada, France, Italy, Poland, and Spanish Florida.

Although the battalion was not entirely Irish-Catholic in composition, it did have a significant number of both categories, so the Mexicans would call this unique unit by various Irish names. Unofficially, they were the *Irish Volunteers*, or *Los Colorados* (The Red Guards) because of their red hair and ruddy complexions, or the *San Patricios Guards*. Officially, they were known as the *San Patricios Company*, an artillery unit.

In mid-1847, the Mexican Department of War reassigned the men as infantrymen and merged the San Patricios companies into the Foreign Legion (Legion Extraniera) which was referred to by some as the *Legion of Strangers*.

In 1848, the unit was expanded and the *St. Patrick's Battalion* was formed. Eventually they would number close to 300. A newspaper reporter from New Orleans described their flag as *"green silk, and on one side is a harp, surmounted by the Mexican coat of arms, with a scroll on which is painted, 'Libertad por la Republica Mexicana' ('Liberty for the Mexican Republic'). Underneath the harp is the motto 'Erin go Bragh.' St. Patrick adorned the front."* They carried a banner which was inscribed "Erin Go Bragh" with the image of St. Patrick.

Irishmen held the leadership positions, including a Sergeant John Reilly, who would later take credit for organizing the San Patricios. Reilly was a tall, broad-shouldered, blue-eyed, Galway man who hailed from the seaside town of Cliften. He stood six feet, one and three-fourths inches high, had dark hair, and a ruddy complexion.

He was married in Ireland and had a son (based on his letters). He was also a former soldier in the British army, probably joining at a military post in Ireland in the 1830s. He was a non-commissioned officer, and may have been in the Royal Artillery unit. He was probably stationed in British North America, perhaps New Brunswick, Newfoundland, or Quebec, from whence he deserted and fled south to Michigan.

Between 1843 - 1845 Reilly worked as a laborer in Mackinac County, Michigan near the Canadian-U.S. border. He was employed by Charles M. O'Malley from Co. Mayo, Ireland. O'Malley later recalled that, *"Reilly worked in my employ on and off for the space of two years, with whom I had more trouble than all the other men who worked for me."*

On September 4, 1845, Reilly went to nearby Fort Mackinac and enlisted with the regulars. He once wrote he would *"again attain my former rank or die."* He was assigned to the 5th Infantry and sent to Corpus Christi two days later. As part of Zachary Taylor's Army of Occupation, Reilly and 4,000 other infantrymen marched to the Rio Grande where they established camp opposite the Mexican town of Matamoros.

During the last three weeks of March, 1846, Reilly, along with most of Taylor's army, marched about 170 miles across uninhabited Texas prairie from the Nueces River to the Rio Grande, where they established a camp on the left bank of the river, opposite Matamoros.

On Sunday, April 12, 1846, Reilly received permission to hear Catholic mass in Matamoros. He convinced his Captain that a priest was holding mass on the Texas side of the river, but Riley crossed the Rio Grande into Mexico and never returned. After just seven months in the U.S. Army, Reilly had again deserted.

Just prior to the outbreak of war, the Rio Grande was only 200 yards wide at the point where the U.S. army camped. The Irish could see the religious ceremonies and hear the church bells. They were also enticed by the lovely senoritias and by the promise of exceptional treatment by the Mexican government including the granting of land.

With the combination of brutal military discipline, sickness and disease, discrimination, harassment, religious and ideological beliefs, the lure of women and alcohol, and tired of being used a cannon fodder for the U.S. Army, the Irish would began to desert.

But the Irish weren't the only ones. As mentioned earlier, many other foreign-born soldiers fled as well, and together with the Irish they would form the new San Patricio Battalion. The first thing the deserters did was don new uniforms. The Mexican military uniforms were much more colorful than Yankee duds. So the new recruits in the Mexican army exchanged their blue wool American garments for new military attire that was a darker shade of blue.

Artillery officers and enlisted men wore turkey-blue cloth coats, which had crimson collars, cuffs and piping. Their stand-up collars were emblazoned with a yellow exploding bomb, and two dozen brass buttons on the uniform were stamped with the bomb design. The most dramatic change was the hat.

For all ranks the new hat was a black leather shanko, about eight inches tall, topped with a red pompon. In the field, the officers wore a blue kepi (a visored cap with a round flat top sloping downwards toward the front). Enlisted men wore dark blue cloth barracks caps, piped in crimson, with a red tassel hanging in front. One can imagine the Irish thought themselves quite snappy-looking.

Lieutenant Reilly, and other American turncoats, gained their first Mexican War battle experience at the town of Matamoros on the Rio Grande. Beginning at daylight on May 3, 1846, they assisted Mexican artillerymen in bombarding the American garrison across the river at Fort Texas. General Zachary Taylor later reported, *"It is known that some of our deserters were employed against and actually served guns in the cannonade and bombardment..."*

Taylor then marched the bulk of his men toward the mouth of the river to secure additional supplies. Seeing the American forces split, Mexican General Arista crossed the Rio Grande about 12 miles below Matamoros, where he hoped to cut the American supply line.

The two armies clashed on May 8, near a water hole called Palo Alto. Arista had 3,700 men against Taylor's 2,290. The fiercely contested battled lasted from 2:00 p.m. until dusk. Eventually effective and mobile American artillery pounded the Mexican army causing them to withdraw.

The Mexicans fought a strong defensive position in an ancient river bed called "Resaca de la Palma," but were unable to stop the U.S. advance. They soon retreated in disorder back across the Rio Grande into Mexico.

The San Patricios would distinguish themselves later at the battles of Monterry, Cerro Gordo, Buena Vista, and finally, at Churubusco. It was during the battle of Monterrey that several captured Mexican officers told the Americans about the newly formed San Patricio battalion. The American army had been aware of their desertion problem, and they knew a few of their own had gone over to the other side. But they didn't realize the deserters had actually organized into a battalion.

The capture and occupation of Monterrey had been costly for the Americans. As the days went by, morale slipped and the desertion situation became even more of a concern. Fifty regular soldiers in the First Regiment of Ohio Volunteers had already deserted. According to a major in the Ohio outfit, *"these the enemy joyfully received and speedily enrolled in their ranks, where they served with courage and fidelity they had never exhibited in ours."* The never-ending stream of deserters allowed the San Patricios to continue to grow despite casualties.

As the battles raged on, several of the San Patricios would be captured. But with a relatively steady flow of new recruits - attributable to the Mexican army's enticement tactics - the Irish battalion remained strong. That is, until the Battle of Churubusco on August 20, 1847, when the bulk of the St. Patricios would be captured after running out of ammunition.

During the battle, the Mexican army tried to surrender three times, but each time the San Patricios pulled down the white flag, preferring to fight to the death.

While the Mexican army assumed they would be given quarter, the San Patricios knew capture meant execution.

Approximately one-third of the battalion was killed, a few lucky ones escaped.

Seventy unlucky soldiers were captured, placed on trial, convicted of desertion and condemned to death. General Winfield Scott ordered capital punishment for 50, but pardoned five, and reduced the sentence of fifteen others. After his capture, Reilly wrote to the British government: *"In the months of April 1846, listening only to the advice of my conscience, for the liberty of a people which had had war brought on them by the most unjust aggression, I separated myself from the North American forces."*

Reilly's death sentence was set aside because he had actually deserted prior to the U.S. declaring war on Mexico on May 13, 1846. Instead of being executed, he and 14 others were given 50 lashes and a hot-iron brand was burned on their cheek with the two-inch letter "D" for deserter. The officer in charge of the branding determined that Reilly's brand was not applied adequately, so he ordered a second brand burned on the other cheek. Reilly was then sentenced to prison.

The army constructed a scaffold in San Jacinto Plaza, and under it were placed eight mule-drawn wagons, supporting two prisoners standing at the end of each wagon.

Still dressed in their Mexican uniforms, 16 San Patricios were hanged and buried nearby. Two days later, Colonel William Harney, a brutal and inhumane soldier, executed the remaining 34 with unusual cruelty.

Harney decided to coordinate the execution with the American assault on Chapultepec Castle. The battle for this Mexican fortress atop a hill was clearly visible two miles away, and the San Patricios were forced to watch for hours. This included Francis O'Conner, who had lost both legs and was only hours away from death. Harney ordered O'Connor dragged from the field hospital and propped up on the gallows along with his fellow San Patricios.

As the Mexican tri-color was finally lowered, and the Stars and Stripes were raised, the trap door was sprung and the 34 San

Patricios dropped to their death. This would be the largest mass execution ever carried out in U.S. military history.

A Mexican newspaper at the time condemned the *"savage outrages"* heaped upon the condemned San Patricios: *"Mexicans, these are the men that call us barbarians and tell us that they have come to civilize us. These men who have sacked our homes, taken our daughters, camped in our holy burial places, covered themselves in blasphemous uproar with the ornaments of our altars – and have gotten drunk from our sacred chalices."*

The U.S. would eventually win the war and add 870,000 square miles of territory encompassing what are now California, Arizona, New Mexico, Texas, and parts of Utah and Colorado. The mass executions didn't completely deter desertions. Many of the surviving San Patricios who escaped capture continued to fight in the last engagements around Mexico City. In the ensuing months they would welcome additional recruits who deserted from the U.S. Army.

Mexican historians depict the account of the San Patricios as a romantic tale of gallant Catholic Irishmen whose conscience and religious persuasion obliged them to switch allegiance in the midst of the Mexican War. Like many aspects of history, once you *peel the onion*, you find the real truth. The members of the San Patricios were naïve and bewildered young men from varied national and religious backgrounds, many of whom were tempted by alcohol and opportunism.

Nearly all of the San Patricios had been privates in the U.S. Army, where several of them were troublemakers. Many had deserted several times, usually resulting in capture and confinement to the guardhouse. Some would even escape the guardhouse to join the Mexican army.

John Reilly was eventually released from prison and remained in Mexico. He rejoined the Mexican army, and for the next two years he served in Veracruz and Puebla. He was involved in an aborted coup d'etat of the Mexican government in July 1848.

The last record of him was in 1850 when he was honorably discharged out of the Mexican army along with $1,224 in back pay.

It was at this point that fact and fiction begin to collide. Most historians believe he returned to Ireland, but since he had a habit of spelling his name many different ways (Riley, Reilly, O'Reilly), he has been very difficult to track. Variation in patronymic spelling was common in Ireland, especially in Co. Galway, where the Gaelic language persisted. Even the Mexican government spelled it differently (Juan Reyle, Reley, Reely, Reiley). This was further complicated by the fact that neither Reilly nor many of his fellow soldiers spoke or wrote grammatically-correct English.

Reilly's return to the "Old Sod" is based on strong circumstantial evidence including a letter he wrote from prison to the British Minister in Mexico asking for his assistance in returning to his home country. However, there is no record of him arriving in Ireland.

According to author Robert Ryal Miller, in his book, *Shamrock and Sword*, Reilly seems to have disappeared into the same historical mists in which he first emerged.

The Molly Maguires
& the *Ancient Order of Hibernians*

"The name of a Molly Maguire being attached to a man's name is sufficient to hang him."

- Frank Gowen, Coal Baron & Molly Maguire Antagonist

Historians still argue over how to treat the legend of the Molly Maguires of the Pennsylvania coal region. They have either been portrayed as heroes of the American Labor movement, or as Irish-Catholic terrorists persecuting law-abiding citizens. Both perspectives contain some element of truth, but both overlook the many complexities involved, including the most often asked question: did they ever really exist?

In the mid-19th century, Irish Catholics immigrants who escaped the famine were treated with disdain by the mostly Protestant population in Philadelphia. They were referred to as a *"massive lump in the community, undigested, indigestible."* Riots frequently broke out between Protestants and the Catholic newcomers. The worst riot occurred in Philadelphia on May 6, 1844 when two Catholic churches were burned and 16 people lost their lives.

Between 1846 and 1854, 44% of all immigrants to the United States came from Ireland. At the same time, anthracite mining in eastern Pennsylvania was growing at an incredible rate. Irish, Welsh and English immigrants flooded into Eastern Pennsylvania (previously dominated by German and English farmers) lured by the prospect of employment in the expanding coal industry. These new immigrants brought with them different customs, experiences, and beliefs that often caused violent ethnic conflicts, particularly between the Irish and the Welsh.

Although they shared a common Celtic heritage, the Irish and Welsh found themselves separated by differences in religion, prior mining experience (the Welsh were miners, but the Irish were primarily farmers), and potential for advancement in the mining industry. Each of the skilled Welsh miners was assigned several unskilled laborers to help with digging and moving supplies ...and that role fell to the Irish.

The mining system that existed at the time was very much controlled by the mine owner. Not only did he own the mine, but he would almost always own the coal patch, which including the miner's homes and the company stores. The stores sold items (including work tools and dynamite which the miners were forced to buy) priced at least 20% higher than in private stores.

If the owner thought his men were purchasing supplies elsewhere, he would threaten them with their jobs. Because of the inflated supply costs, it was not uncommon for the Irish laborers to end a pay period in debt to the owner.

Keeping the miners in debt helped avert any threat of a strike as well as workers who might leave to join another company. Very quickly the Irish realized they had merely exchanged the poor economic situation in Ireland for the economic coal mine trap in Pennsylvania.

Any Irishman who dared speak out against the unfair conditions found himself unemployed and blacklisted from the growing cartel of mine owners. The terrible conditions led many of the miners to join a fledgling organization called the Workingmens' Benevolent Association (WBA), a trade union that fought for better conditions in the mines. Founded in 1868 by John Siney, a native of Ireland, the WBA utilized strikes as a tool to gain better working conditions.

Occasionally the workers' frustration got out of control and several of the mine bosses were subjected to violence. The mine owners were determined to smash the meddling union at any cost.

In 1870, the mine owners begrudgingly agreed to recognize the WBA as the legitimate representative of the miners. But the resulting conflict between workers and owners sparked sporadic violence against the owners.

Due to the number of Irish Catholic miners immigrating to the coal-mining region of Pennsylvania, it wasn't long before divisions of the Ancient Order of Hibernians (AOH) began to appear in the various mining towns.

The AOH was originally founded in New York City in 1836 due to its enormous Irish population. The main purpose of the AOH in New York was to guard the Irish people, and their churches, from violent anti-Catholic gangs. The AOH also helped the newly arrived Irish find jobs and places to live.

The second AOH chapter in PA was founded in Hecksherville, (Schuylkill County). The Pennsylvania AOH served the Irish mining population by organizing fundraisers to operate their own social welfare programs which provided death benefits for widows and children, sick pay for those unable to work, and funds during periods of unemployment.

The Hibernians also kept alive the Irish culture and tradition, as well as the teachings of the Roman Catholic Church. It was the only beacon of hope for the Irish who had been thrust into a dismal and oppressive economic situation. In essence, the goal of the AOH was the same as the WBA. The two organizations flourished and their ranks began to swell.

It is alleged that inside the individual AOH divisions in Pennsylvania there existed a sub-division of radical Irish-Catholics called the *Molly Maguires*.

It should be noted that at this point in history the facts become somewhat blurry. Historians agree on two theories: 1) not all of the local AOH chapters were Mollies, and, 2) all of the Mollies who were eventually convicted were members of the AOH. What is known about the American Mollies in Philadelphia is they apparently worked within the legal organization of the Ancient Order of Hibernians.

According to author Peter A. Weisman, the Molly/AOH organization was highly intelligent in its format. There was a division for each village, each with its own "body master" (president), treasurer, secretary, and outstanding members (brethren).

The body divisions would meet to discuss societal events, terrorist acts, and other issues. People who were attempting to undermine the Mollies were fingered and brought into the body's discussion. Decisions were then made as to proper action.

For example, if a brother had a problem with a supervisor who had fired him for appearing drunk at work, or cheated him out of the proper pay for a carload of coal, the body would listen to the case (both for and against) and vote according.

If murder were decided upon, a crippling bashing, or even a lesser beating, the job would be assigned to another body across the county. The men in the local chapter would be advised of the time and location so they could secure their own alibis. The imported Mollies would then perform the task, and then return to their hometown. Even if the task were performed in the middle of the day, no one would recognize the men who came from another town.

The local Mollies would then respond in kind when needed. In this way, the organization was able to create an anarchic martial law in which no one dared defy them for close to twenty years.

The growing power of the WBA, the AOH, and the violent pressure from the Molly Maguires, allowed Irish men to become elected officials. They in turn secured positions for their Irish-Catholic associates.

The Irish miners were beginning to stand on their own and become less subject to the whims of the dictatorial mine owners. This did not set well with the mine owners who obviously felt threatened. They saw their profits dwindling as the Irish became more emancipated, and it had to stop.

Over the years, the Pennsylvania Irish would gain a reputation for being hot-headed drunks. Whether that was accurate is another matter, but publisher Benjamin Bannan capitalized on this stereotype by ending editions of his *Miner's Journal* with amusing stories detailing with the silly, drunken antics of local Irishmen.

Threatened by the soaring population of mostly Democratic Irish-Catholics in Schuykill County, staunch Republicans like Bannan were seeking ways to keep the Irish in their place. The journal also suggested the local "Irish" authorities were doing nothing to curb the rampant disorderliness and violence committed by the Irish on honest citizens.

Franklin B. Gowen, the son of an immigrant Irish Protestant father, was among those accused of being too soft on the Irish during his term as Schuykill County District Attorney. Gowen was also the President of the Philadelphia and Reading Coal and Iron Company and would figure prominently in the history of the Molly Maguires.

It should be noted the Irish were not entirely innocent. They did their share of fighting, justified or otherwise. And they themselves didn't like emigrants, Catholic or non-Catholic, especially from southern and eastern Europe who they viewed as competition for jobs. It was this violent image that would help turn local townsfolk against the Irish, whom Bannan was credited with dubbing, the "Molly Maguires."

There is no evidence that the men who acted out against the Pennsylvania mine owners actually called themselves, Molly Maguires. Bannan brought the name to the American public and used it for all things he found unsavory about the Irish. The name remains somewhat of an enigma.

The most common tale concerns an Irish woman named "Molly Maguire" who led a revolt of poor farmers in secret violent attacks against absentee landlord's rent collectors. They were much like the "Whiteboys" who defended the downtrodden Catholics 100 years earlier. But Bannan kept the name alive through his various articles entitled, "A Molly on the Rampage," and "Molly Beating."

Later Gowen would testify in a legislative hearing in 1871 the area was under attack by a group of men called the "Molly Maguires."

It wasn't long before every crime committed in the area was blamed on the Mollies, and that included approximately fifty murders in Schuylkill County between 1863 and 1867.

Only a handful could actually be attributed to the Mollies, but Gowen pinned all of the murders on the Mollies, whom he called *"the incarnate fiends who rule the County."* It was Gowen who would eventually orchestrate a plot to trap the Mollies.

Frustrated by the Mollies, the coal barons turned to Alan Pinkerton, of the famous Pinkerton Detective Agency, who assigned the job of infiltrating the Mollie structure to a tough, out-going, Irish-Catholic detective named James McParlan. Pinkerton wanted an Irishman, and a Catholic, *"...as only this class of person can find admission to the Mollie Maguires."*

In truth, McParlan was actually hired by Frank Gowen who saw the Mollies as a threat to his growing wealth. Gowen knew how to manipulate the law. His plan was to destroy the labor unions by creating a myth that the Mollies and the Unions were synonymous.

In late October 1873, McParlan, now calling himself, "James McKenna," set out on a five-year mission to become a Molly Maguire. During those years he would report to Captain Robert J. Linden of Philadelphia. Only Pinkerton, Linden and Gowen knew his real identity.

McParlan eventually made his way into the AOH/Mollie organization and gained their respect...and all along he reported the Mollie's criminal activity to Linden. He even took part in many of the activities, but later claimed to have faked drunkenness to avoid being involved in the more heinous acts.

Born in 1844 in County Armagh, McParlan came to the United States in 1867. He made his way to Chicago, where he tackled odd jobs including entertainer in a German beer garden. He joined the Pinkerton Detective Agency in 1871 and went undercover to expose pilferers on the streetcars of Chicago.

McParlan was a slight, bespeckled man with an outgoing personality, a good sense of humor, and a knack for quickly ingratiating himself to those he met. What he lacked in experience, he made up for in other ways. He was an excellent boxer, but also a rough-and-tumble brawler; a nimble dancer of Irish jigs; a sweet-voiced tenor; a sophisticated ladies' man; and someone who could drink "unbelievable large quantities of whiskey and retain his faculties."

McParlan convinced the local Irish that he was wanted in Chicago for murder and counterfeiting, and even managed to get himself beat up and arrested by the local private constabulary. The theatrics were impressive. He put all of these talents to work and soon became accepted by the Irish community as James McKenna.

McParlan (McKenna) was accepted into the AOH on April 14, 1874, and rose high in the organization over the next two years, largely because he was literate and the majority of the Irish were not. He became secretary, and later president of the Shenandoah lodge. He also became a trusted advisor on many delicate issues…and he kept a record of all of them, including those acts of terror he was able to stop, those he could not, and those in which he partook.

McParlan reported the Mollies to be made up of Irishmen, noting some had been *"mix-bred in the evolution of mongrel America,"* but most were full-blooded Irish Catholics. He stated the group used violence and terrorism to combat the conditions of the mines, *"inflicting horror on police, supervisors, owners, blowing up railroad cars full of coal, organizing riots, sending out threats to everyone who spoke out against them."*

Based on the coal baron's smear campaign against the Irish, they were successful in swaying public opinion by characterizing the Mollies as mindless, heartless terrorists. They were also able to create enough speculation for the general public to believe the Molly Maguires, the WBA, and the AOH, were basically the same organization.

Fueled by economic problems in the 1870s - plus a decision by the WBA to strike in December of 1874 – was the catalyst for widespread violence that swept across the coal region. The result was miners and their families were facing starvation.

In a desperation move on the part of the miners, they reluctantly returned to work in July 1875, but had to disband the WBA as one of the conditions. With the WBA's back broken, the coal barons then set their sights on the AOH, which had become the defacto Irish-Catholic union in the area.

Through the well-choreographed newspaper articles, which blamed any and all violence on the Mollies, the Catholic Church suddenly found itself in an uncomfortable position regarding its relationship to the Ancient Order of Hibernians. If they did not denounce the Mollies (who were part of the AOH) they would be looked upon as condoning the violence.

In a controversial move, the Catholic Church excommunicated all of the Molly Maguires. Since the Catholic Church had separated themselves from the Mollies, the national AOH organization in 1877, under pressure from the Bishop of the Diocese of Philadelphia, were obligated to cut off the divisions in the counties of Northumberland, Columbia, Schuykill, and Carbon.

All that was left now was for the coal barons to deliver the final blow...the rounding up of the Mollies. When the arrests commenced, the Mollies knew they had an informer in their midst and AOH county (Schuylkill) delegate "Black Jack" Kehoe suspected McParlan.

When word was leaked to McParlan, he immediately requested a meeting ostensibly to defend himself, but mostly to buy himself time. The meeting was a ploy. McParlan had planned to use the meeting ruse to gather all of the Mollies together for a mass arrest. Kehoe had his own agenda. He never planned to have a meeting either, but would kill McParlan as soon as he saw him.

In the annals of the fight for Irish freedom, an informer is considered the lowest form of life. McParlan was aware of this, and he knew he had pushed his luck to the very brink. On March

7, 1876, he left the region on an early morning train bound for Philadelphia.

The trial of the accused Mollies was a foregone conclusion. All potential Irish-Catholic jurors were dismissed. The jury was made up of mostly German immigrants, some of whom readily confessed their limited knowledge of English made it difficult to follow the proceedings. Motions for a change of venue were denied.

Those that controlled the private coal police also controlled the courts. The prosecution team was headed not by the district attorney, but by attorneys on the mine and railroad payroll.

The judge presiding over the Mollie's trials was Cyrus L. Pershing, who in 1875 had lost the Pennsylvania race for governor to Republican John F. Hartranft (who had been voted into office by a pressing Irish vote spearheaded by the Mollies). Previously, he was the presiding Judge of Schuylkill County in 1872, where he returned after the defeat against Hartranft. His bias against the Mollies was obvious during the trial.

In an interesting twist, Coal baron Frank Gowen, the mastermind of the plan to bring down the Mollies, acted as State Prosecutor in some of the cases. His relentless determination to exterminate the Mollies can be summed up in his most famous quote, *"The name of a Molly Maguire being attached to a man's name is sufficient to hang him."*

McParlan would testify against the Mollies in 1876 and 1877 and identify John Kehoe's "Hibernian House," where Kehoe would preside over the legitimate AOH meetings, as the gathering place for the Mollies. McParlan would reveal, in detail, the criminal activities of the Mollies over the past five years.

At the end of the court proceedings, writer Francis P. Dewees summed up the era of the Molly Maguires as *"a reign of blood... they held communities terror bound, and wantonly defied the law, destroyed property and sported human life."* To no one's surprise, the Mollies were found guilty of murder and sentenced to death.

The first of four Mollies to be hung on June 21, 1877 were Alex Campbell, president of the Lansford AOH and a prominent tavern owner, who was found guilty for masterminding the murders of mine bosses James P. Jones and Morgan Powell in 1871. Proclaiming his innocence, Campbell placed his handprint on the cell wall of the Carbon County jail on his way to the gallows. It remains there to this day.

Next were Edward Kelly and Michael Doyle who were convicted, along with Campbell, of the 1875 murder Jones. Doyle was followed by John "Yellow Jack" Donohue who was found guilty of the murder of Powell. The priests asked the four men to kneel and all were given absolution. After the priests left the platform, the sheriff and his deputy removed the chains and slipped the ropes and hoods over their necks. The trapdoor was sprung, and the men fell to their death.

Thomas Duffy, James Carroll, James Roarity, James Boyle, Thomas Munley, and Hugh McGheehan were hung the same day in Pottsville. Ten more would be hung in the following eighteen months under similar charges, including John "Black Jack" Kehoe, dubbed the *"King of the Mollies,"* who was convicted of the stoning death of Frank W. J. Langdon in 1862. Thomas Munley and William Uren were hung for the murder of Thomas Sanger, a foreman. James Kerrigan, bodymaster of the Tamaqua AOH, saved his neck by turning state's evidence, earning the nickname, "Squealer." And finally, James Roarity was hung for the murder of Benjamin F. Yost.

When all was done, 20 men were found guilty of murder and were sentenced to death. Ten of them were hanged on June 21, 1877, which became known as "The Day of The Rope."

Some Molly Maguires were probably innocent of the crimes, specifically Alexander Campbell who was never proved to be connected with any crime, but was convicted solely on the testimony of "Squealer" Kerrigan.

Over the years, revisionist historians have referred to Franklin B. Gowen as selfish and elitist. Some even consider him *"disgusting."* He was the most important player in the Molly tragedy, and the one who connived to destroy them at all cost, regardless of guilt or innocence. Perhaps his guilt was too much to bear. Years later Gowen committed suicide in a Washington D.C. hotel room.

There are many accounts written about the Mollies, but McParlan, the one who was closest to whole affair, never set down a full record of his adventures. His only claim to fame was in 1914 when his exploits became the plot of the last Sherlock Holmes novel entitled, *Valley of Fear,* written by Sir Arthur Conan Doyle.

McParlan would stay on with the Pinkerton agency and end up running their west coast operation. But despite his successful career, McParlan would become a hopeless alcoholic. He died in obscurity in Denver, Colorado in 1919.

Controversy has surrounded the Molly Maguire story from the beginning. Most agree they were murderers, but how many were involved, and whether the guilty and the accused were one in the same remains a question. The execution of the Mollies ended the first wave of violence in the Pennsylvania coal region. However, the battle between mine owners and mine workers would continue. Finally, in 1890, the United Mine Workers of America was founded and ultimately improved the lives of the miners.

A century after the Maguires were executed, Pennsylvania Governor Milton J. Shapp granted "Black Jack" Kehoe a posthumous pardon, prompted by several of Kehoe's relatives and members of the Pennsylvania Labor History Society. The governor wrote, *"...it is impossible for us to imagine the plight of the 19th century miners in Pennsylvania's anthracite region."* It was John Kehoe's popularity among the miners that led Gowen *"to fear, despise and ultimately destroy him. We can be proud of the men known as the Molly Maguires, because they defiantly faced allegations which attempted to make trade unionism a criminal conspiracy."*

Confederate "Irish Brigades"

"Give it to them now, boys!
Now's the time!
Give it to them!

- The orders of Irish Confederate Col. Robert McMillan, upon seeing the Union Irish Brigade at Fredericksburg.

Even the most uninformed American has heard of the Federal Army's famous "Irish Brigade." Ever since the PBS series "The Civil War" peaked America's interest in the "War Between the States," information on the Union Irish Brigade appeared more frequently in books and paintings. If the average American couldn't relate to the Civil War, they could certainly relate to the Irish.

The Irish Brigade is usually shown resplendent in their blue uniforms, sprigs of boxwood in their kepis, and the green and gold flag of Erin fluttering behind them, as they charge headlong in to the history books screaming "Faugh A Ballagh!" (Irish Gaelic for "Clear the way!")

But little is known of the approximately 40,000 Irish immigrants who fought for the Confederacy, or of the 45 Irish units that served in General Lee's Army of Northern Virginia.

Clear the Confederate Way, written by Kelly J. O'Grady (Park Ranger-Interpreter for the Fredericksburg-Spotsylvania National Military Park) is a story never before told. It is primarily a military study of all of the CSA Irish units, but offers more than one-dimensional military narratives.

The story focuses on the mostly Catholic, Gaelic Southerners, not the Ulster Protestants of the 17th and 18th century who, "were already fully assimilated Americans by the middle of the 19th century" according to O'Grady. It proves that the Irish played a significant part in the building of the South, as well as defending their new "country" from the army of Northern aggression.

Most of the Irish who immigrated to America in the 19th century were farmers, and many were escaping the ravages of An Gorta Mor (The Great Hunger). The Irish who settled in the North were forced into the urban squalor of the ghettos, which was tragically dysfunctional for former country people. Transversely, the Irish who settled in the South (and the West) stayed true to their agricultural roots. At the time of the Civil War the Irish were the largest immigrant group in the American South and the largest immigrant group in the Confederate armies.

When analyzing the motives of any Southern soldier, the question of slavery usually surfaces. Why would good Irish Catholics support a Confederacy that defended slavery? O'Grady answers the question in a very forthright manner. *"...I don't believe the Irish in the North, the average Catholic immigrant, were clamoring to fight in the Yankee army for any intellectual reason, for Union or against slavery. There was little that northern allegiance held for them except employment at fairly good wages."* In fact, since the Irish competed with free Blacks at the bottom of the social order, many Irish were fiercely anti-Negro, and they frequently rioted against Blacks in Northern cities and continued to do so during the war.

The Southern Irish saw it differently, according to O'Grady. They viewed the South as a surrogate Ireland; an agricultural society fighting for its way of life against an Anglo-Protestant industrial state (much like England).

As far as the issue of slavery, O'Grady contents that it wasn't really an issue to the average Irish immigrant who had himself lived in virtual bondage in Ireland. With regards to the Catholic Church's position on slavery, the Southern Bishops considered slavery an ancient and accepted legal and economic system that was dying of its own accord in western societies. Maintaining social order, teaching slaves the Gospel and meeting their immediate humanitarian needs were deemed more important at the time.

While the Federal Irish could not understand why their fellow countrymen could fight for the pro-slavery Confederacy, the Southern Irish rebels could not comprehend why the Federal Irish could fight for a Cromweillian, English-style government. The rebels believed they followed the true path of the Irish patriots, and viewed the Federal Irish as part of a British force fighting for the North. One Confederate Sergeant wrote that the Northern Irish were so well equipped that even the lice they carried were stamped with the gold letters, R.I.B., for Royal Irish Brigade! What was often wholehearted support for the Confederacy by the Southern Irish, contrasts with Northern Irish reticence for the Union cause.

A common misconception about the South is they were a purely Anglo-Saxon culture. The opening lines to the secessionist anthem, "The Bonnie Blue Flag," reinforces the Southern belief in a native born brotherhood.

> *"We are a band of brothers,*
> *And native to the soil,*
> *Fighting for our liberty,*
> *With treasure, blood and toil."*

Most people do not realize is that Irishman and vocalist, Harry McCarthy, wrote those lyrics to match the tune of an old Irish song called, "The Jaunting Car."

In raw numbers, many more Irishmen took up the Union banner. Pulitzer Prize winning historian, James M. McPherson, noted the Irish were the most under-represented immigrant group in Northern armies. In short, O'Grady contends that Southern Irishmen may have been better Confederates than Northern Irishmen were Federals.

O'Grady also dispels the myth the Federal Irish Brigade's service in the war won the Irish of the North a place in American society. In truth, the brigade - and its first leader Thomas Francis Meagher - were often denigrated and despised by other officers in the army. Not unlike the African-Americans of the Tuskegee Airman who did their part in World War II, but still returned to a segregated and unappreciative America.

O'Grady explained in an interview that it was, *"...as if the brigade was an Irish ghetto of the Army of the Potomac, segregated and ridiculed, as the Irish had been back in northern civilian life."*

Records have shown that Confederate accounts of the Irish in Southern ranks sometimes relate merry and mischievous anecdotes. Whereas Union reports regarding the Irish are full of vehement bigotry. The New York and Boston Irish communities certainly created powerful political and social organizations after the war, but it was in spite of their war service, not because of it.

The south was much more accepting of the Irish in their communities before and after the war. Richmond, Virginia elected its first Catholic mayor in 1873, many years before an Irish mayor was elected in New York or Boston.

To any detractors that might challenge O'Grady's opinion regarding the authenticity of the Confederate Irish, he said one need check no further than any 19th century southern cemetery. There one can find the Irish names and note their Confederate allegiances. The most unyielding proof can be found in Catholic cemeteries where there are Celtic crosses emblazoned with C.S.A. units; Irish soldiers' tombstones flying the battle flag; or straightforward monuments erected to the memory of all Catholic Confederate Soldiers, most of whom were Irish.

In his research, O'Grady often saw a mirror image of the Irish on both sides. The green flags, the shamrocks, the "Faugh A Ballaughs," and "Erin Go Braghs," all those distinctly Irish symbols and slogan can be found in regiments in both the North and South. He even discovered Irish soldiers with the same name fighting on both sides in the same battle.

O'Grady explains that the origin of the phrase "Faugh A Ballaugh" (which means, "Clear The Way") and has always be attributed to charging Yankee Irish Brigades.

It actually originated with Irish regiments fighting in the British army during the Napoleonic wars. The Yankee Irish expropriated it during the Civil War, but Richmond's Montgomery Guard, an Irish Confederate unit, probably used it first in the war on July 18, 1861 at Bull Run. O'Grady explains that an Irish skirmish line, commanded by Co. Limerick native, Captain John Dooley, literally cleared the way for James Longstreet's brigade in the first great battle of the war.

Truth be known, there were no official "Irish Brigades" in the Army of Northern Virginia, although two companies from New Orleans dubbed themselves the "Irish Brigade."

In the organization of the Confederate armies, the Irish units were integrated with other Confederate units. On the Union side, General George McClellan wanted to do the same with the Irish regiments. However, the politicians overruled what was a very egalitarian idea on his part. McClellan thought units segregated by nationality went against the very idea of the Union they were fighting for. If the general had his way, the Federal Irish Brigade might never have been formed.

In the South, Irish communities, often Catholic parishes, formed Hibernian units which were assigned to regiments for brigades as any other company or unit would have been.

The largest single unit of Irish troops in Lee's army was the 6th Louisiana Volunteers. This unit was involved in the thick of the fighting in the East in virtually every battle. Its hard service included Stonewall Jackson's Valley Campaign, The Seven Days, Second Manassas, Sharpesburg, Fredericksburg, Chancellorsville, and Gettysburg.

The 8th Alabama "Emerald Guard," Company I, consisted of 104 Irish-born soldiers out of a total of 109 men. They wore dark green uniforms and their banner was a Confederate First National flag ("stars and bars") on one side with a full-length figure of George Washington in the center. The reverse was green, with a harp surrounded by a wreath of shamrocks, and the slogan "Erin Go Braugh" ("Ireland Forever") and "Faugh A Ballagh."

Company I, along with other companies of the 8th Alabama, won its first laurels on the fiercely contested field of Williamsburg, losing approximately 100 men. At Seven Pines the 8th was again under deadly fire and its loss was 32 killed, 80 wounded, and 32 missing. The 8th Alabama, and the Emerald Guard unit, continued to be utilized in subsequent engagements, each time losing more men.

The Emerald Guard even engaged Thomas Francis Meagher's Federal Irish brigade during one particular assault.

Other Irish units included: Emmet Guards, Company G, 17th Virginia; Irish Volunteers, Company K, 1st South Carolina; Jeff Davis Guards, Company H, 11th Virginia Regiment; Virginia Hibernians, Company B, 27th Virginia; Emmet Guards, Company D, 1st Louisiana; Sarsfield Rangers, Company C, 7th Louisiana.

One of the more colorful Confederate officers was General Joseph Finegan, a short, stumpy native of Clones, Ireland. He was described as a *"born fighter, of hot Irish blood,"* by his Irish-Confederate contemporaries, who often observed him riding his horse back and forth in front of him men during battle.

Finegan was a political general, in that he had no prior military experience, and used his connections to secure an appointment as a brigadier general. Later he would be named commander of the Department of Florida for Confederate forces. But unlike a number of political generals - whose lack of military experience was detrimental to the Southern cause - Finegan was a hellcat.

His rapid rise through the confederate ranks was remarkable for an Irish immigrant. As department commander, Finegan used his organizational skills to raise and train men, as well as gather the necessary equipment.

By early 1864 he had amassed a force of 5,200 Confederates which he planned to use if the Federals invaded the State of Florida. His plan would be tested on February 7th when Union Brigader General Truman Seymour landed at Jacksonville with the 10th Corps consisting of 5,100 men, and moved inland.

Abandoning his original defensive tactic, Finegan advanced on the Federals. He did this without adequate knowledge of the enemy's strength and without good communication with his subordinates.

On February 20, Finegan engaged the advancing Federal army at Olustee. Eyewitnesses recall Finegan and his son under heavy fire. The younger Finegan had been assigned to his father's staff. What seemed like a safe way to protect his son turned distressing as the son *"plunged into the thick of the fray."* His anxious father yelled to the boy, *"Finegan me B'ye, go to the rear, me B'ye! Ye know ye are ye mither's darlin."*

Finigan's offensive tactic proved successful. Union forces, including a vanguard of the 7th New Hampshire and the 8th U.S. Colored Infantry, were routed. The Confederates had captured six guns, 1,600 small arms, and 150,000 rounds of ammunition. Later, Finegan was criticized for not pursuing the fleeing Federal forces. None the less, his victory captured the attention of Robert E. lee who tapped him for brigade command in Virginia during the summer of 1864.

O'Grady points out that he does not claim that the Confederate Irish were present in great enough numbers to sway the outcome of a particular battle. However, he does state that 19 companies of Irishmen accompanied Stonewall Jackson in the 1862 Shenandoah Valley campaign, which made up 10% Jackson's fighting force.

The book puts the Southern Irish troops on the battlefield in every major battle in the Eastern Theatre, so that the reader can decide if their presence made a difference. During his research, O'Grady discovered that Confederate accounts of battles show that Confederate Irish soldiers are frequently on the front lines, and quite often were color bearers. Many of the Irish brigades were actually "Color Companies," which was a post of honor.

Grady explores an interesting, and somewhat controversial, theory in his book regarding post war history. He opines that with the Union victory, Irish nationalists in America, North and South, closed ranks to tout the Irish Brigade's loyal service to the winning side. They did this hoping to garner more support from the American people for Irish independence or home rule.

Southern Irishmen could have become a symbol of successful Irish rebellion, a role model for their homeland, if the Confederacy had actually won. But politically, it made sense to use the Irish Brigade's high profile service as the icon of Irish participation in the war.

While the Irish in the big Northern cities remained segregated in their own enclaves, Southern Irish became more assimilated into the mainstream population after the war.

There is some evidence of post-war Southern Irish complicity with what was a cynical political rehabilitation scheme. Therefore, Irish Confederates left little in the written record about their Southern loyalty, even when they were well placed to do so. Intentionally or otherwise, it's not so much that they lost their *Irishness* in a larger culture, explained O'Grady, *"but that the Irish culture blended with southern society so well that few saw a reason to point out the difference."*

Over time, according to O'Grady, the Irish assimilated so well that many people today do not realize there were ever any Irish people present in the South.

In his memoirs, Capt. John Keely ('Andrew' Jackson Guards, Company B, 19th Georgia Regiment) told the story of how members of the brigade visited him at his hospital window after his leg was shattered at Bentonville in March 1865. *"Good bye, Capt Keely, give us Irish soldiers always, you stayed with us as long as you could, and we won't forget you,"* he was told. His own company broke ranks to shake his hand, with one soldier saying: *"The honor of old Ireland...should never be tarnished."*

The 69th New York
The Premier Irish Brigade

Raise that green flag proudly, let it wave on high,
"Liberty and Union" be your battle cry;
"Faugh-A-Ballagh" shout from your center to your flanks,
And carry death and terror wild into the foeman's ranks."

- Song composed "by an Irishman"
at a 69th New York fund-raiser, New York, 1861

From earliest times, Irish warriors, Irish mercenaries and Irish swordsmen found employment abroad. There were Irish soldiers at Calais and Agincourt in the 14th century and Irish mercenaries in Germany in the early 16th century.

From the late 16th century on, with the collapse of the Gaelic order, thousands of Irishmen (nicknamed "The Wild Geese") found employment in the Spanish, French and other armies. In medieval times, Irish mercenaries were in demand in Europe because of their willingness to endure hardship.

The fall of the Gaelic order did not mean the end of a Gaelic or military tradition: rather it marked its transfer to foreign lands. As the centuries passed, the Irish would find employment in England, and eventually make their way to the United States where they would fight in the American Civil War.

It would be no stretch to consider this migration the continuation of the Irish fighting tradition. The lure of stable employment was also a draw…something difficult to obtain for the primarily country Irish in the northern American cities.

A perfect example was Thomas Francis Meagher whom the British Crown had banished to Tasmania for his activities on behalf of Irish independence. He later escaped and made his way to America, joining the 69th New York State Militia at the beginning of the Civil War.

Like most volunteers, Meagher thought the Southern Rebellion would last only a few months. Therefore, the 69th started out as a "90-day regiment" and first saw action at First Bull Run under the command of Colonel Michael Cocoran.

At the end of the 90-days enlistment period, Meagher returned with his regiment to New York. Shortly after his return, and realizing the war would last much longer than anticipated, Meagher began raising a unit of Irish volunteers for a three-year enlistment from New York, Boston and Philadelphia. This unit would eventually become the 69th (the nucleus of the Irish Brigade) and the 63rd, and 88th New York Voluntary Infantry Regiments, primarily consisting of Irish recruits. In February 1862 President Lincoln appointed Meagher brigadier general of the Irish Volunteers.

The officers and men of the Irish Brigade were among the most unusual in the Union army. A surprisingly large number had combat experience in the papal service of St. Patrick, and Austrian and British services. A single unit contained seven lawyers who enlisted as privates.

Elizabeth Meagher, wife of Thomas, had the honor of resenting the new flag to the 69th which she personally embroidered. On the green base were harps and sunbursts and the motto "No Retreat." The regiments that followed after the 69th also received flags from members of the women's Committee.

In December 1861, the New York regiments took up winter quarters near Alexandria, Virginia, where they were assigned to General Sumner's division of the Army of the Potomac. Years later, survivors would recall 14 year old Johnny Flaherty of Boston entertaining on the violin while his father, *"livened the festivities by playing an Irish tune on the war pipes."*

The canteen, which hardly ever seemed to contain water, was eagerly passed around. Private Bill Dooley remarked, *"It is as well to keep up our spirits by pouring spirits down, for sure, there's no knowing where we'll be this night twelve months."* Conversely, Chaplin Dillon succeeded in convincing a large number of the 63rd N.Y. to take the oath of abstinence against the use of alcohol. Those who did not abstain quickly scrambled for the whiskey rations of the new teetotalers.

In between battles against the Confederacy there was always plenty of Irish rebel plotting afoot. Many of the men were members of the Fenian Brotherhood, a group of Irishman dedicated to the overthrow of the British in occupied Ireland.

Dr. Lawrence Reynolds, the surgeon of the 63rd N.Y., as well as the Brigade's poet laureate, was the head of the Army of the Potomac Fenian Circle. Meetings were held regularly on the first Sunday of every month in the brigade's hospital tent. It seemed that nearly all of the officers in Meagher's Irish Brigade were Fenians by late 1862.

The 69th Irish Brigade saw its first action in the Peninsula campaign. During the Battle of Fair Oaks, the Irish Brigade conducted a fierce bayonet charge earning the praise of army commander McClellan.

At Gaine's Mill they supported Fitz John Porter, and later engaged in vicious hand-to-hand combat at Savage Station and Malvern Hill. The Irish brigade was beginning to earn a ferocious reputation.

On more than one occasion, a Union General was known to ask, "where are my green flags?" And after the Seven Days battles, Confederate General Robert E. Lee asked a subordinate about the fluttering green flag. When informed about the regiment, Lee remarked,, "Ah yes, that Fighting 69th."

The various engagements had taken a toll on the Irish and many of Meagher's men were dead, wounded, or seriously ill, including the death of Lieutenant Temple Emmet who succumbed to malaria. Emmet was a popular young staff officer, and the grandnephew of one of Ireland's greatest martyrs, Robert Emmet. Realizing his ranks were depleting, Meagher received permission from General McClellan to secure new recruits in New York.

The next battle for the reformed Irish Brigade was Antietam. The brigade was located in the Union center and attacked the

Confederates in the now famous, "Sunken Road." With Meagher at their head yelling, "boys, raise the colors and follow me!" the Irish moved against the waiting rebel forces. A rail fence separating the Irish from the Confederates quickly disintegrated due to enemy fire. The shaken Irish brigade continued the attack. The Irish color bearers fell so often in the battle that an aide to McClellan stated, "the day is lost, general – the Irish fly." A second or so later, the aide corrected himself, "no, no their flags are up, they are charging."

Meagher had been carried from the field unconscious, thrown from his wounded horse. Col. Patrick Kelly had been shot through the jaw, but would survive and remain with the 88th New York. The Irish lost over 500 officers and men, killed or wounded. The 69th sustained a staggering casualty rate of 61.8%, while the 63rd lost 59.2%.

The brigade recuperated from its staggering ordeal and was later joined by the 116th Pennsylvania to help fill the ranks.

In December 1862, enroute to Fredericksburg, the Irish Brigade passed the house of slain Confederate General Turner Ashby. An older woman rushed out of the house and ran in to the middle of their ranks. Hysterical, she began screaming, and invoked the curse of God on them for taking her son's life. This was no doubt unnerving to the more superstitious Irish soldier.

Prior to crossing a pontoon bridge into Fredericksburg, the command shook out their colors. The nearby 14th Brooklyn (84th N.Y.) cheered the marching Irishmen, as the band of Hawkins' Zouaves (9th N.Y.) struck up the brigade's marching tune, "Garry Owen." The Irish Brigade now marched with sprigs of green in their caps, a bright green battle flag, with gold harps and the Gaelic words "Riamh Nar dhruid O sbairn lan" ("Never retreat from the clash of spears").

Sadly, the Irish brigade would do just that…and quite soon. The brigade marched toward a stone wall where the Confederates were waiting. The Irish waved their hats at the 8th Ohio Infantry as they headed toward the wall. One member of the Ohio said,

"they pass to our left, poor glorious fellows… a half-laughing, half-murderous look in his eye. They reached a point within a stone's throw of the stone wall. No further. They try to go beyond, but are slaughtered. Nothing could advance farther and live."
The soldier from Ohio was quite accurate. When the Rebels opened fire, the federal line staggered, and the Irish began to fall by the dozens. The day was a complete disaster for the Irish.
The first and only attack of the day had failed. The next day Meagher wrote in his journal: "Of the 2,200 men I led into action the day before, 218 now appeared on that ground that morning." That same morning General Winfield Hancock saw three Irishmen standing alone. *"Close up with your company!"* he ordered. *"General, we are our company,"* one of them replied.
To add insult to injury, the 69th believed they had lost their national standard…for the first time in the Brigade's history. Devastated, they conducted a search of the battlefield. They eventually located the color-sergeant, who was dead and propped up against a tree with his hands clasped upon his chest. Upon further examination, they found the Stars and Stripes wrapped around his body.
Despite grievous defeat, the Irish Brigade could still claim they never lost a flag. But the fact remained that for the first time in the history of the Irish brigade they were forced to retreat. That indignity was almost too much too bear. When asked about the Irish Brigade years later, Confederate General Lee remarked, *"Never were men so brave."*
Meagher had become very unpopular with other high-ranking officers by his constant political speeches and activities, and for his defeat at Fredricksburg. He once referred to Union Generals as merely "political generals." It was also generally believed he regarded the brigade more as an independent symbol of Irish glory than an effective unit of the army.
When Meagher requested he again be allowed to recruit for his depleted brigade, he was refused. In fact, there was a proposal to abolish the Irish Brigade altogether and distribute the units among other commands.

Meagher could not bear this indignity. He resigned his commission in disgust on May 19, 1863. When he departed, he left behind a decimated unit. They had suffered heavy casualties in their many engagements. The battles at Fair Oak's, Gaines's Mill, White Oak Swamp, Glendale, Malvern Hill, Antietam, Fredericksburg, and Chancellorsville had reduced the ranks to one-half of a regiment.

Forty-two year old Galway native, Colonel Patrick Kelly, of the 88th New York, had been given command of what was left of Meagher's brigade. After a month of recuperating, the Irish Brigade, now attached to the 1st Division of the II Corps, headed north with the Army of the Potomac in an effort to intersect General Lee's Confederate Army of Northern Virginia. The Federals believed Lee was heading for a small Pennsylvania town called Gettysburg.

On July 2, 7:00 am, after marching for several hours, the Irish Brigade arrived behind Cemetery Ridge. They were placed on the crest of the ridge, about one half-mile south of Evergreen Cemetery.

The battle of Gettysburg had actually begun the previous day when two Confederate corps had attacked two smaller Union corps northwest of Gettysburg. During the night of July 1-2, the Confederates took up positions parallel to the Federal positions, while additional Union troops (including the Irish Brigade) had been hurried toward Gettysburg to reinforce and extend the Union line southward. From their position on Cemetery Ridge, the Irishmen could look west and see the Confederate positions on Seminary Ridge about a mile away.

At 10:00 am, off to the left of the Irish Brigade's position, the sound of picket fire began. The sound intensified, and soon artillery shells were falling nearby with ear-shattering explosions.

Catholic chaplain, Father Corby, assigned to the 88th New York of the Irish Brigade, knew the unit would soon to march in to battle. So he climbed a large rock in front of the Brigade and prepared to give the Catholic rite of General Absolution to the

530 men. As artillery shells continued to fall on Cemetery Ridge, Father Corby urged the men to do their duty well, and warned the Church would *"refuse Christian burial to the soldier who turns his back upon the foe or deserts the flag."* Then the men fell to their knees as the priest stretched out his hand and uttered the Latin words of Absolution. This event had become one of the most celebrated events in the history of the Irish Brigade.

Soon thereafter, Sickles' III Core began their march toward the Emmitsburg Road, but was soon forced back by Confederate Lieutenant General James Longstreet's assault. Wave after wave of Rebel troops would join the attack.

As the Confederates pushed the Federals back toward the critical position of little Round Top, the Irish Brigade was ordered to their feet, and marched southward in four parallel columns, each four abreast and 35 men long. Other brigades joined the Irish. They moved along the west face of Cemetery Ridge towards the fighting at Devil's Den, which was in the process of being over run by the Confederates. A gaping hole had been opened in the vicinity of the Wheatfield. To avoid a total collapse of the Federal line, Caldwell's II Corp Yankees (which included the Irish Brigade) were ordered to plug the gap. While shells exploded around them, the Irish Brigade entered Trostle's woods and moved to the north end of the Wheatfield.

The Irish formed a single, two-rank battle line with the 63rd N.Y. on the left, followed by the 88th, 69th, 28th, and 116th. The Irish formed the center of the north edge of the Wheatfield. Kelly then began the Irish Brigade's advance. At the same time, the Confederates of Kershaw's South Carolinian Brigade were advancing north towards the Wheatfield. The Rebels scrambled through the trees and rocky terrain at a point called "Stoney Hill," which was an extension of Devil's Den. The two armies were on a collision course.

The Irish Brigade continued their advance in the chest-high wheat, but was still 200 yards away by the time the Rebels gained the top of Stoney Hill. The Confederates poured brisk fire into the Irish as the advanced, but it had little effect. The Irish were able to return fire with deadly accuracy. Because of the position of the Rebels, they had to lean over the boulders to fire downward, exposing them to Irish lead. After firing several volleys, the South Carolinians wavered, and Kelly gave the order for the Irish to charge up Stony Hill. Once the Irish crested the top, they were chest to chest with the enemy. According to author Kevin O'Beirne, in his article, _In to the Wheatfield_, *"at the top, hand-to-hand combat ensued amongst the rocks in the woods in a whirling melee as officers fired pistols at targets less than ten feet away, and bayonets and musket butts were used with effect."*

Soon the Confederates began to give way. The effect of the Irish Brigade's fire had been devastating. One Federal soldier later remembered the crest of the hill was covered with dead Confederates. Most had been struck in the head or chest. Lieutenant Charles Grainger of the 88th New York related a humorous incident, *"A captured Confederate colonel was sitting comfortably sheltered behind a rock and laughing until tears rolled down his cheeks, while a private of the 88th and one of the 69th had dropped their muskets and were hammering on each other in order to decide which took the prisoner."* Although wounded in the elbow, Grainger himself led the captured Rebel away while the two men continued to pummel each other.

The Irish continued to advance and pushed the Carolinians southward over the top of the Stoney Hill and down the other side. Having done that, they found themselves under fire from not only the retreating Carolinians, but from the 50th Georgia as well. They had to fall back down Stony Hill on their way to an area north of little Round Top. To accomplish this, the Irish Brigade had to run a deadly gauntlet back through the Wheatfield while being fired upon by the Rebels on three sides. It was dreadful.

The survivors finally made it through Trostle's woods, and kept going past Little Round Top, and then reformed on the

Taneytown Pike in the back of Cemetery Ridge. The trip through the Wheatfield to Stony Hill, and then back again, had virtually destroyed the tiny brigade.

For the most part, the Irish Brigade's involvement at Gettysburg was over. They would be ordered to build breastworks from stone and rails, and then use them for shelter when the Confederate artillery pounded the Federals in the moments preceding Pickett's Charge.

There would be more fighting ahead for the semi-reformed Irish Brigade for the next two years. Under Kelly's command, they would fight at Bristoe Station, Auburn, and in the Mine Run campaign.

In early 1864, bolstered by new recruits, the Brigade saw action in the Overland and Petersburg campaigns. Sadly, Colonel Kelly would be killed at Petersburg on June 16, 1864.

On May 3, 1864, the Irish Brigade moved out of its winter encampment with 10 field officers. Within six weeks six of these officers would be dead and the other four seriously wounded. Its losses were so great that it finally disappeared in the consolidated brigade.

Despite their decimation, and eventual disbanding, the Irish Brigade never lost a flag.

Myles Keogh
The Irish Dragoon

"Everywhere we saw the enemy.
Do not fear for me, dearest mother,
I am prepared."

- Letter Myles Keogh to his mother during the Papal War, 1860

Myles Keogh was the quintessential 18th century Irish military figure: young, handsome, heroic, brave, and yet quite sensitive. In the words of Union General Jacob Cox, *"he was born a soldier."* His short but adventurous life can be broken down into three distinct military phases:

1) Fighting for the Pope,
2) Fighting to preserve the Union,
3) Fighting for George Armstrong Custer.

Fighting was the common denominator.

He was born Myles Walter Keogh on March 25, 1840 at Orchard House, Leighlin Bridge, Co. Carlow, Ireland. He was raised a pious Catholic.

His grandfather, Thomas Kehoe, had also been an army captain who fought on the side of the defeated Catholics at the Battle of the Boyne in 1690. His Uncle, Patrick Keogh, had been executed by the English at Carlow Town following the Wexford Rebellion of 1798. His father, John Keogh, was a Captain in the Fifth Royal Irish Lancers.

Myles mother, the former Margarete Blanchfield, was from a prosperous landholding family whose ancestral seat was

Rathgarvan, near Cliften, in Co. Kilkenny. She was a cultured woman who was often called "the Belle of the Army." The Blanchfield family estates had been confiscated by the English under Cromwell, and part of them, including Rathgarvan, was returned in the late 17th century. The eventual return of the lands to the Blanchfields afforded Keogh was a more affluent upbringing than the normal Irish boys of the 1840-1850s.

When famine struck Ireland in the 1840s, the Keogh family (which included Myles and his 12 brothers and sisters) were not directly affected by the potato blight, but they were touched by the typhoid fever which accompanied the famine.

Myles contracted typhoid, but survived. His brothers James and John, and his sister, Julia, died during this time, presumably of typhoid. So even though the Keogh family lived fairly well due to John's position with the Lancers, the family never lost their distrust for the English. They had taken their land once; it was always possible they would do it again. His maternal aunt, Mary Blanchfield, willed the family estate to Myles, but he rejected the life of a gentleman farmer to seek adventure in the military.

In 1856, at the age of 16, Keogh entered St. Patrick's College at Carlow, Ireland. Sometime in the spring of 1860, after attending for almost four years, he withdrew. Not only was the life of a country gentlemen not to his liking, but neither were scholastics.

Historians believe he followed the career path, and lifestyle, of the fictional character in his favorite book, *Charles O'Malley, The Irish Dragoon.* O'Malley, an Irish orphan, had left college to join the cavalry. O'Malley was a dashing young officer who loved danger almost as much as he loved being Irish: *"There's nothing like being an Irishman. In what other part of the habitable globe can you cram so much adventure into one year? Where can you be so often in love, in liquor, or in debt; and where can you get so merrily out of the three? Where are promises to marry and promises to pay treated with the same gentleman-*

like forbearance; and where, when you have lost your heart and your fortune, are people found so ready to comfort you in your reverses?

So at age 20, Keogh left Ireland with his two friends, Daniel Keily of County Waterford, and Joseph O'Keffee of County Cork. They had planned to join the French Foreign Legion, but joined the Papal Army instead.

In March 1860, Keogh heeded the call from Pope Pius IX to help preserve the sovereignty of the Papal States that were threatened with annexation by the armies of Piedmont-Sardinia. The 40-year struggle for control of the Italian peninsula was coming to a head, and the Pope was desperate.

Many Italians, sympathetic to the Piedmont-backed revolutionary forces of Giuseppe Garibaldi, viewed the continued existence of the Papal holdings as an impediment to a united Italy. Garibaldi was a soldier, revolutionary, and a self-proclaimed enemy of Roman Catholic priests. He called the priesthood *"that emanation from hell, the pestilent scum of humanity, the very scourge of God."*

On the other hand, Papal soldiers, including Keogh, saw themselves as religious crusaders, and modeled their uniforms after those worn in the Crusades.

In an effort to protect the Pope's territory, and to thwart Garibaldi, Catholic volunteers were recruited from through out Europe, including 1,400 young men from Ireland. England, sympathetic to Garibaldi and his Italian revolutionary patriots, tried to dissuade the Irish from joining the Papal Army by reminding them that foreign military service was a misdemeanor. That had never stopped the Irish before, and it didn't work this time. The Irish were placed in a special battalion – The Battalion of Saint Patrick.

In July 1860 Keogh was appointed lieutenant in a four-company battalion garrisoned in the Adriatic port city of Ancona. The outnumbered papal defenders put up a spirited defense, but the main body of the 18,000 man Papal army was eventually defeated in the Battle of Castelfidardo, and Ancona was attacked by land and sea. Keogh was among the 80 who survived to reach Anacona, where they surrendered on September 28. The Papal War was over, and Keogh's first military experience had lasted all but six weeks.

After a brief stint in prison in Genoa, Keogh and 45 Irish comrades traveled to Rome at the invitation of Pope Pius IX, where they joined the Papal Guard as the green-uniformed, "Company of Saint Patrick." Keogh was also awarded two medals for valor; the "Medaglia Pro Petri Sede," for fighting in the battles of Castelfidardo and Ancona, and the "Ordine di San Gregorio" (Order of St. Gregory the Great), a particular mark of papal approval for having *"distinguished himself in a sortie."*

With the battle to unite Italy now over, and Papal guard duty growing rather dull, Keogh, now 22 years old, looked elsewhere for his next military adventure. Soon his interests turned to the American Civil War, where the Union was ardently seeking experienced European officers.

Therefore in February 1862, Keogh resigned his commission in the Company of Saint Patrick. With his senior officer and friend, Daniel J. Keily, Keogh boarded a steamer for Manhattan where they rendezvoused with fellow papal comrade, Joseph O'Keeffe. The three adventurers were able to tap into family connections and gain an audience with Abraham Lincoln in the White House.

After expressing their desires to fight for the Union, Lincoln saw the three were given captains ranks and assigned to the staff of Irish-born Brigadier General James Shields of County Tyrone. Shields - a good friend of President Lincoln - was preparing his forces to confront the Confederate army of Stonewall Jackson in the Shenandoah Valley. Jackson was desperately trying to link up with General Robert E. Lee's forces near Richmond. On June 6, Shields told one of is generals, *"I will send you all the cavalry I have if you can burn the bridge and tear up the railroad, but there are few. I will send Captain Keogh to lead them."* This would be Keogh's first cavalry experience.

During the battle Keogh exhibited great bravery under fire. His friend, Keily, suffered a severe head wound and was carried from the field (Keily eventually recovered and was transferred to the 2nd Louisiana Cavalry where he would become it's commander). Keogh won several commendations for bravery in the Valley Campaign and was making quite an impression on seniors Union officers. But there was a dark side to the dashing soldier. He was known to be moody, overly emotional, and a heavy drinker. He was even described by some as a brutal officer who frequently amused himself by beating up hapless enlisted men.

Shields was later recalled to Washington, and Keogh and O'Keffee were transferred to the staff of cavalry Brigadier General John Buford, who was considered the finest cavalry General on both sides of the war. Buford often referred to the two as his *"Irish twins,"* and described them as *"dashing, gallant and daring soldiers."* Army of the Potomac Commander, George McClellan, was equally impressed, describing Keogh as *"a most gentleman-like man, of soldierly appearance"* who had a remarkable record *"for the short time he had been in the army."*

Within the first few weeks of his new assignment, Keogh fought in the second Battle of Bull Run. He would later fight in the Fredericksburg and Chancellorville campaigns, as well as Brandy Station, one of the Civil War's true cavalry saber encounters. Keogh and O'Keffee were briefly assigned to the staff of General George B. McClellan, who knew them by their reputation, and wanted them by his side. Under McClellan, Keogh fought in the battle of Antietam in the hills of western Maryland.

For some reason, Keogh grew very fond of McClellan, and looked to him as a surrogate father. But despite the victory at

Antietam, President Lincoln removed McClellan from command for not pursuing General Lee back to Virginia when he had the rebels on the run. He was replaced with Ambrose Burnside. Keogh was quite saddened by McClellan's leaving. According to author, Edward S. Luce, after McClellan's departure, Keogh sat down in a railroad station, and with tears streaming down his face, he buried his head in his arms and cried.

At the end of the Civil War, Captain Myles Keogh had been assigned to one of four regiments charged with protecting the frontier against hostile Indians. The conflict with the Indians was heightened when a group of militiamen committed a dreadful attack on an Indian camp. This brutal act would help set the stage for an historic encounter in South Dakota between a coalition of Native American tribes and the U.S. Cavalry. The charge would be ignited by the arrogance of one officer in particular, Lieutenant Colonel George Custer.

In November 1864, a band of Cheyenne and Arapaho Indians, under Chief Black Kettle, was attacked and slaughtered at Sand Creek by Colorado militia. The horror was indescribable as women and children were shot down and mutilated. Black Kettle and his wife (who sustained eight bullet wounds) were able to escape. They vowed revenge. When news of the slaughter spread among the Indian tribes, two thousand Cheyenne, Sioux, and Arapaho warriors moved eastward, killing, burning, and looting. To combat the Indian attacks, the 7th Cavalry was organized at Fort Riley, Kansas on November 16, 1866, and Myles Keogh was given command of "I" Company. Keogh's oftentimes arrogant and occasionally brutal behavior reflected on "I" Company, and they were referred to as "The Wild I." Lieutenant Colonel George Armstrong Custer, the assistant commander, was leading a division of the 7th Cav which included 10 – 15 fifteen regiments.

The 7th took up posts across the Kansas and Colorado Territory. Keogh's I company was billeted at Fort Wallace in Western Kansas, and helped to protect the Butterfield Overland Stage route and railroad construction crews.

In the Fall of 1866, the Cheyenne leader, Roman Nose, came to Fort Wallace and delivered an ultimatum to the Butterfield Stage Company, *"Stop running or we will wipe you out!"*

The stages did not stop, and the first of many battles began on March 26, 1867 when the Cheyennes attacked the Goose Creek stage section, eleven miles west of Fort Wallace.

For the next three months, I Company was in the center of the war with the Cheyennes. After 26 separate Indian attacks, Keogh became frustrated with fighting a defensive battle. He wanted to chase them down and wipe them out, and so he complained to district headquarters, *"...if the Indians are not followed up to their village and killed, then it is useless to expect peace or rest on this route,"* Keogh explained. His commanders thought otherwise, and he was subsequently reprimanded for sharing his opinion.

Eventually, after several more years of fighting, General Phillip Sheridan decided to increase pressure on the Indians, and his plan began with a three-way winter attack. One force would move east from New Mexico, another southeast from Colorado, and the largest force, a battalion of infantry and eleven companies of the 7th Cavalry would move south from Fort Dodge, Kansas. At the same time, Black Kettle was establishing his winter camp of fifty-one lodges in a valley on the Washita River. Other bands of Cheyennes, Arapahoes, Kiowas, and Commanches camped downstream from Black Kettle.

On the morning of November 23rd, Custer's command moved out of Camp Supply. Custer ordered the regimental band to play the Irish ditty, 'Garryowen,' as they rode out in the snow. Keogh had introduced the song, a favorite of the 5th Royal Lancers, when they were stationed in Garryowen (a suburb of Limerick), to Custer. Custer loved it, and the tune became the favorite of the 7th.

After searching for Black Kettle's camp, Custer's Osage scouts finally smelled a campfire and heard a baby's cry. They had discovered the Indians. The troops advanced cautiously.

Custer spoke with his officers, and then divided his command into four parts to attack from four sides at once. Custer knew nothing of the strength of the Indian camp...he didn't even know who the Indians were. He had left his supply train far back on the trail, and he held back no reserves. He didn't care. He was itching to attack.

Custer ordered a complicated 4-sided attack over ground he had never seen before. Author Charles L. Convis called the plan, *"...daring...reckless...glorious...stupid, it was pure Custer."* The Indians had no sentries. They had not expected an attack in the cold, deep snow.

At daybreak, the regimental band struck up, Garryowen, the signal for the attack...and the cavalry charged. Second Lieutenant Frank Gibson of A Company wrote later, *"there was no hope for escape for the surrounded savages."* Black Kettle, his wife and son, were killed instantly. The fighting was quick, and at the end, between ten and twenty warriors were killed, and twice as many women and children. Several white captives were freed, and many items found in the Indian camp linked the warriors to raids on farms in Kansas that had resulted in the deaths of 90 settlers. This was Custer's first big fight with the Indians. His second, and last, one would come eight years later.

For the next eight years Keogh remained in command of "The Wild I." While Custer dealt with a chronic frontier desertion problem, the 7th Cavalry continued to battle the Indians until March 14, 1871 when I company was sent from Kansas to Louisville, Kentucky to help fight illegal distillers and control the growing Ku Klux Klan organization.

Historians have studied letters written by Custer to his wife, Libby, and from Keogh to his own relatives and friends, to try to ascertain the relationship between the two men. Custer once mentioned to Libby that he found Keogh's behavior *"rather absurd"* when Keogh asked Custer to *"send a handsome collection of flowers to Miss Hf...He must think I'm made of money,"* said Custer.

Author Charles Convis believes the comment by Custer, in itself, points out the fundamental difference between the two men. While Keogh battled bouts of depression, he was primarily seen as a jovial fellow who fit the Irish stereotype of the day: emotional, poetic, romantic, a drinker. He had no political aspirations, nor was he terribly interested in rising in the ranks (he spent 14 years as a Captain). On the other hand, Custer was a non-drinker (he gave it up during the Civil War), became the youngest major-general in the army's history, and once aspired to be president.

In the spring of 1876, General Sheridan planned a three-column attack against hostile Sioux and Cheyennes, converging on the headwaters of the Powder, Tongue, and Rosebud Rivers, all tributaries of Yellowstone. Custer had fallen out of favor with Washington, and command of the third column, the 7th Cavalry, was given to General Terry. With tears in his eyes, Custer pleaded with Terry to allow him to lead a regiment into battle. *"I appeal to you as a soldier to spare me the humiliation of seeing my regiment march to meet the enemy and I not share its danger."*

Custer was eventually allowed to join the 7th, but he would be under Terry's command. As the 7th's regimental band played *Garryowen* and *The Girl I left Behind Me*, the column marched out of Fort Lincoln at 5:00 a.m. on May 17.

The story of the battle of The Little Big Horn has been told ad naseum. It is doubtful there is any American alive who cannot tell the tale of the tragic outcome.

Believing he was attacking the end of an Indian encampment, and seeking the element of surprise, Colonel Custer led his regiment right smack into the middle of 4,000 warriors…five to eight times as many as he had originally estimated. Custer and his men fought bravely, despite being caught in a giant hornet's nest. But in the end they were totally annihilated.

Since Custer and his entire command were wiped out, the tale of their final moments on earth were told by the only survivors, the Indians. Fearing reprisal, Gall was reticent at first to tell the story. He later acquiesced.

According to Gall, Custer led his command along the ridge, parallel to, and about one-mile from, the river. Custer had planned to attack the Indians on one side, while Reno attacked from the other side. When Reno retreated, Gall, who had been fighting Reno, led most of his Hunkpapas across the river and attacked Custer from the south while Crazy Horse led his Oglalas around to attack from the north. Gall's warriors crept up a ravine and stampeded the horses of Companies L and I. The fleeing horses carried the reserve ammunition of the two companies.

Then the Indians on foot drew the soldiers' fire while Gall organized his mounted warriors. As the Indians charged they basically overran L Company and about half of I Company. Several Indian accounts suggest that Keogh remained mounted until very near the end of the battle in order to move quickly and maintain an organized defense.

During the final minutes of the battle, Keogh divided his time between F Company and the remnant of his own company. This was probably accurate as his body was surrounded by both F Company and I Company men. The troops in Keogh's battalion were repeatedly charged by mounted warriors, but it appeared most of them were killed by dismounted warriors firing from bushes and thickets.

Many of the men were shot through the side or back, suggesting they were exposed to fire from nearby, hidden Indians. A clump of cherry bushes near where Keogh and his sergeants fell was probably used to conceal the killers of the sergeants.

When Gall attacked, Custer ordered Calhoun's Company L and Keogh's I to dismount. Company F, under Lieutenant Reily, dismounted next. Thus, Keogh's three-company battalion stretched out along the ridge to defend themselves against Gall, while the two-company battalion rode on to face Crazy Horse. Gall's report continued: *"The first two companies (Keogh's and Calhoun's) dismounted and fought on foot. They never broke, but retired step by step until forced back to the ridge upon which all finally died. They were shot down in line where they stood. Keogh's company rallied and were all killed in a bunch. When Reno attempted to find Custer by throwing out a skirmish line, Custer and all who were with him were dead. When the skirmishers reached a high point overlooking Custer's field, the Indians were galloping around and over the wounded, dying, and dead, popping bullets and arrows into them. When Reno made his attack at the upper end, he killed my two wives and three children, which made my heart bad. I then fought with the hatchet.*" Apparently Gall's wives and children were digging turnips at the time of the attack.

Historians have compared the different Indian versions of what they believed to be Keogh's final moments. Despite some slight differences, noted historian Charles Kuhlman is convinced the Indians identified Keogh wearing a buckskin shirt and a broad brimmed hat as the bravest soldier they ever fought.

The Indians reported that a mounted officer was charging back and forth, exhorting his men to an organized resistance, and on one occasion, protecting his men by turning his horse broadside to the Indian's fire. The Indians reported this officer was eventually killed.

A description of the officer was given by Chief Red Horse in 1877: "*Among the soldiers was an officer who rode a horse with four white feet. The Indians fought a great many tribes of people and very brave ones, too, but they all say that this man was the bravest man they ever met. He alone saved his a command a number of times.*" Two Moons, a Cheyenne Chief, described the officer in 1898: "*Then the Sioux rode up the ridge on all sides, riding very fast. The Cheyennes went up the left way. Then the shooting was quick, quick. Pop – pop – pop very fast. Some of the soldiers were down on their knees, some standing. Officers all in front. The smoke was like a great cloud, and everywhere the Sioux went the dust rose like smoke. We circled all around him – swirling like water around a stone. We shoot, we ride fast, we shoot again. Soldiers drop, and horses fall on them. Soldiers in line drop, but one man rides up and down the line – all the time shouting. He was a brave man."*

Years after the battle one of Gibbon's scouts named Will Logan insisted he had found Captain Keogh's body just outside a triangle of three war ponies. Logan described Keogh's death as it was described to him by various Indians. Apparently Keogh was the last to fall. He stood alone, facing the charge: *"pow-pow-pow-pow-pow-pow...came six lightening pistol shots from the triangle and six red warriors died in the air...Like the flame of a coal blazed in his eyes. His teeth glistened like a fighting grizzley."*

Historian David H. Miller, relying on interviews with seventy-one Indian survivors of the battle, also thought Keogh was fighting to get back to Custer when he was killed. He had this to say: *"Among the bravest of the soldiers was a big man with a stubby black beard and long mustaches which curled up at the ends. Several Cheyennes, including Turkey Legs, had ridden him down toward the end of the fight. He acted much as leader of the soldiers might have been expected to act, although the white metal bars he wore had little meaning to the Indians – they assumed the captain's insignia was some sort of personal medicine. His body lay among those part-way down the slope, near the barricade of dead horses. Amazingly, he seemed to come to life right before their eyes. He propped himself up on one elbow and looked around as though he had just arrived from another world. Looking about with a wild expression on his face, almost like that of a madman, he gripped a pistol in his right hand. A courageous Sioux warrior ran forward, grabbed the revolver out of the white man's hand, then turned it on him and shot him through the head. The Cheyennes mustered up enough courage after that to strike and stab him until there were all sure he was dead. He was the last man of Custer's company to be killed on the ridge."*

Apparently Keogh's body was not mutilated, for when the Indians stripped the body they discovered a tiny *Angus Dei* hanging around his neck. It has been theorized that the Indians believed this medal contained powerful medicine that would bring harm to anyone who further disturbed its wearer. Since Keogh's body was not mutilated, and his horse, Comanche survived the battle, military personnel were able to match the wounds on Keogh's body to that of his horse.

Keogh had apparently been shot while mounted having had his knee shattered by gunshot. Keogh could not have remained mounted after such a wound. This is confirmed by "Little Soldier," one of Gall's warriors who recalled seeing Keogh kneeling between Comanche's front legs and continuing to fire his carbine from under the horse's chest.

When Keogh was shot in the head, his hand still gripped the reins. Little Soldier said he was in need of a horse, but no Indian would go near a horse whose deceased owner still held the reins. That has been offered as another reason why his body wasn't molested by the Indians. He lay naked except for his socks, with a Catholic *Agnus Dei* medal around his neck kept inside of a small leather pouch.

The Indians took his custom-made English pistol, which surfaced in Canada about a year later. The brave who claimed ownership would not sell. At least four other items belonging to Keogh were eventually recovered: his watch, gauntlets, a photo of himself wearing his *Pro Petri Sede* medal, and a blood-spattered photograph of a young woman.

Like Custer, Keogh had never before been seriously wounded. He had survived the Papal War, the Civil War, numerous skirmishes with Indians, the Ku Klux Klan and Moonshiners. He even had two horses shot out from under him. Perhaps, like Custer, he was beginning to feel invincible. And invincibility, coupled with an attitude of superiority, can make for a deadly combination.

The Fenian Invasion of Canada

"We are the Fenian Brotherhood,
skilled in the arts of war,
And we're going to fight for Ireland,
the land we adore,
Many battles we have won,
along with the boys in blue,
And we'll go and capture Canada,
for we've nothing else to do."

- Fenian Soldier's Song

Whether one considers it a brave raid or a foolish invasion, the Battle of Ridgeway, which pitted a rag-tag Irish-American Army against the might of the British Empire, left a permanent mark on the history of Canada and the United States.

The political structure in Ireland was very weak in the 18th century due to poor harvests and petty church grievances. The late 18th to late 19th centuries saw a series of tumultuous events: 1) reform movements began, 2) the Commercial Propositions for Free Trade failed, 3) the Irish witnessed the results of the French Revolution, and, 4) the radical society of United Irishmen sought complete independence from Great Britain by initiating a number of revolts.

In 1845, the potato fungus, brought by ships from America, spread like wildfire throughout Europe all but destroying Ireland's principal food source. The Irish peasantry was completely dependent on the potato as their main dietary stable.

The next year (1846) the fungus returned. There was no fungus in 1847, but the prior two years had depleted any reserve supply. Then in 1848 it returned with a vengeance. Over 2 million people died of starvation and disease.

The Great Famine (*An Gorta Mor*) changed Ireland forever. The most drastic effect was the rapid declination of the population through death and emigration.

In just three years, the population decreased by two million. The Irish blamed the British government for not interceding. Most British politicians saw it as "God's will" and so they did nothing.

Those who remained in Ireland and survived The Great Hunger encountered another hardship: Landlord Harassment.

By 1879, in response to the poor treatment of tenants by landlords, the Land League was formed to protect tenants and boycott production. Unfortunately, this resulted in landlords declaring war on Irish tenants who were harassed and evicted at will. They were forced to live wherever and however they could. When visiting Ireland during this time, Sir Walter Scott said of Ireland's masses, *"people live in cabins that would scare serve for pigsties in Scotland."*

Angry and frustrated over years of oppression and abuse, many of the Irish were drawn to a political faction called the "Young Irelanders." Headed by John Mitchell and several others, the Young Irelanders represented a militant stance to completely sever ties with Great Britain. They were responsible for raising patriotic sympathies and enraged the British government by initiating countless uprisings. In short, they wanted a revolution.

As many Irish men and women immigrated to the United States seeking a better life, they took with them the influence of the "Young Irelanders."

During October of 1858, a ceremony in New York's Tammany Hall marked the birth of a new American revolutionary movement conceived by two Young Ireland exiles, "Captain" James Stephens and John O'Mahoney.

O'Mahoney had been injured during the 1848 Irish revolution and was captured and exiled to the U.S. by the British. Both men found enough anti-English sentiment in the U.S. to convince them a successful revolt among Irish-Americans was entirely possible. O'Mahoney envisioned an army of Irish-Americans returning to Ireland and forcing out the British.

O'Mahoney first step was to spearhead an American "Fenian" organization. This would be an off shoot of the "Irish Republican Brotherhood" which originated in Ireland in 1858. The IRB was a secret oath-bound society dedicated to armed revolution. He reported to Stephens who would run the IRB in Ireland. In essence, the American Fenians would be an auxiliary to the IRB in Ireland.

The name "Fenian" was chosen by O'Mahoney as it, *"... represented the yearning for nationhood embodied in an ancient ideal."* It is the Anglican version of the Gaelic *"Na Fianna,"* a term which refers to the ancient protectors of the Ard Ri (High King).

According to legend, Fiona MacCumhail (Finn McCool) was the commander of the "Fianna," a military-like band of noble men-at-arms that sprung up from the earth of Ireland to defend her in time of peril.

As the Fianna assured Ireland's independence in pre-Christian times, O'Mahoney envisioned the Fenian Brotherhood battling for Irish independence.

At first, Irish-Americans were slow to support O'Mahoney. But eventually he raised enough men to form the 99th New York State Militia (The "Phoenix Regiment") and became its colonel.

By November 1858, forty military units in various states would be established. Among these were Corcoran's Irish Legion, the O'Mahoney Guards of San Francisco, CA, and the Emmett Guards from Richmond, Boston, and Philadelphia. Thousands of young Irishmen joined these units and eagerly awaited their encounter with the British Empire.

Unfortunately, by 1860, the American Civil War interrupted O'Mahoney's plans for an armed insurrection. Stephens, still in Ireland, hoped the Fenians would stay out of the War Between the States. No such luck. The American Fenians were adamant about their participation…on both sides.

O'Mahoney, realizing an opportunity, used the civil war to recruit new members and gain also valuable wartime experience, primarily in the Union Army. From 1860 to 1865 the Fenian ranks began to swell.

In October of 1865, at the end of the Civil War, a convention was held in Philadelphia to resume the task of organizing an uprising to free Ireland.

County Cork-born William Randall Roberts of New York advocated an invasion of Canada, hoping to use it as a bargaining chip for Ireland's freedom. O'Mahoney, on the other hand, lobbied for an actual armed invasion of Ireland. The Fenian Senate sided with Roberts and he was elected Chief Executive of the Senate, and was appointed Secretary of War.

County Cork-born Major-General "Fighting" Tom Sweeney (of Mexican War and Civil War fame) was charged with developing a plan to secure an independent territory for Ireland where an *"Irish Republic in exile"* would be established and then be used as a bargaining chip to free Ireland. They patterned their plan after what had recently occurred in Texas by the United States.

If the Fenians were successful, they would enter into negotiations with the British Empire to exchange Canada for Ireland's independence. Since O'Mahoney strongly disagreed with the plan, he subsequently lost his dictatorship over the IRB. The man who conceived the IRB had been summarily sacked.

The plan involved a five-pronged attack that would strike north across the border from Chicago, IL; Milwaukee, WI; Buffalo, NY; Vermont; and along the Saint Lawrence River. The Fenians even envisioned the Irish Navy sweeping Lake Huron, Lake Erie and Lake Ontario.

Irish privateers were to prey upon British shipping, close the St. Lawrence River, and cut off British access to Quebec. However, the Irish Navy at the time only consisted of five sailing vessels, a tug, and two steamer transports, all docked in Chicago. Hardly an intimidating fleet.

Less idealistic Fenians saw this entire plan as rather ridiculous. However, they reckoned the attack could precipitate war between the U.S. and Great Britain, or at least cause enough of a ruckus to force the British Empire to reinforce Canada with a large number of regular troops. Hopefully this reinforcement would include soldiers currently stationed in Ireland. Either of those circumstances would create a favorable climate for an armed uprising in Ireland.

On May 31, former Union Cavalry officer, Brigadier General John O'Neil, was designated to command the invasion. Without any written instructions, or a map of the Canadian countryside, O'Neil assembled his force of 800 soldiers. Given the fact that the 35 year-old O'Neil was a General, he was poorly mounted. He moved about Fort Erie on an *"anemic nag."* The reins were made of clothesline; the saddle was of an *"antique pattern."*

On May 22, he mobilized the men of his 13th Tennessee Fenian Regiment and headed toward Cleveland, Ohio by train. Once he Louisville, Kentucky, he was joined by Colonel Owen Starr and the 17th Kentucky Fenian Regiment. The two regiments, with a combined strength of 342, proceeded on to Buffalo, NY, where the other Fenians were to gather.

When O'Neil and Starr's regiments arrived in Buffalo, they were broken up into smaller groups and taken into the homes of the local Irish-Americans in the community. The Tennessee and Kentucky troops, combined with the 18th Ohio Fenian Regiment and the 7th New York Fenian Regiment, swelled the total Irish-American army to over 1,000.

A Buffalo newspaperman, visiting the Fenian camp, said the soldiers were a rag-tag group. He reported some soldiers wore artillery jackets and others wore sober black broadcloth dress coats. He also reported, *"there was a decided preference for green"* and that he found two green Fenian flags flying over the camp.

The Fenian volunteers were mostly young men in their 20s; former Union and Confederate soldiers united in a common

Irish cause. Many wore black felt hats or the fancier stovepipes. They were fairly well behaved, only a few brawlers fell into police hands.

It wasn't long before the sudden gathering of strangers would cause concern among local Buffalo officials. The Irish were hardly discreet. The Mayor of Buffalo telegraphed a warning to the mayors of Toronto and Hamilton, Ontario, and Buffalo police were ordered to remain on duty all night. The U.S. Marshall was also notified, and the U.S. warship "Michigan" was put on alert.

A Major "Durr," stationed at Fort Porter; after being informed of the Fenian presence; informed Buffalo officials he had only 50 regulars and, *"little war material on hand."*

At that particular juncture, the Fenians were far better supplied than the U.S. Army. Local press reported, *"Five wagon loads of ammunition for their use had rolled into town while Paddy O'Day's* (a local tavern) *was packed to the rafters with boxes of muskets, pistols, and other war equipment."*

More and more Fenians poured into Buffalo from Nashville, Louisville, Cincinnati, Indianapolis, Columbus and other western areas. It was reported they were drilling in O'Day's cellar.

The Fenian hierarchy had established a centralized command structure and a clandestine system of logistics, which was financed by donations from Irish-American communities.

Nothing the Fenians did was a secret. Their complex mobilization efforts were freely discussed in the Irish-American communities, and British informers easily infiltrated the Fenian ranks. Correspondence from the British Embassy in Washington notified authorities in Canada of virtually every Fenian move. This was no clandestine operation.

So as early as March 1866, 10,000 Canadian militia volunteers had been stationed at the border in anticipation of an assault they figured would occur on St. Patrick's Day. Many of those militia units were armed with outdated and poorly maintained weapons, and also lacked basic field equipment. Among the other shortages was a dearth of trained leaders. Social status was the only qualification for leadership in the militia, and that has been the downfall of many armies throughout history.

On April 10, 1866, O'Mahoney, the ousted IRB founder, was looking to reassert his leadership. He assembled his own force of several hundred Irish-American volunteers at Eastport, Maine. Determined to beat O'Neil into Canada, he had intended to capture Campo Bello Island, New Brunswick, situated at the mouth of the St. Croix in the entrance to Passamaquoddy Bay.

However, tipped off by informers, the British dispatched a gunboat to the island and deployed a regiment of regulars. American gunboats were also sent to intercede.

The Fenians were caught by surprise, but no clash occurred. The Fenians were forced to leave with their tail between their legs. Even though it was an embarrassment, it had one bright spot. The British, believing this was the main raid they had been waiting for, assumed the Fenian threat was over. They were so sure, that many of the Canadian militia units were withdrawn from their positions and demobilized leaving the Canadian border nearly defenseless.

At midnight, O'Neil's small army, ready to take on the British Empire, marched to Lower Black Rock on the Niagara River, about three miles from Buffalo. One in four Fenian soldiers must have had second thoughts during the march, as 200 soldiers simply vanished into the night. By 3:30 a.m. O'Neil's army, now reduced to approximately 500, boarded four canal boats to be ferried across the Niagara River.

At 4:00 a.m. Col. Starr planted the Irish flag on British soil, thus giving the Irish a temporary moral victory. General O'Neil then issued orders to cut all telegraph wires from Ft. Eire and to destroy the railroad bridge leading to Port Colborne. They also burned two bridges at French Creek and Miller's Point on their way to Chippewa.

However, hearing that a British force of 5,000 was heading for the Fenian camp, O'Neil changed direction and headed towards Ridgeway along the Limestone Ridge Road. By daylight on June 2, the Irish army advanced to within three miles of Ridgeway (about six miles west of the Niagara River).

Col. Starr then sent out advance skirmishers who encountered a mounted British patrol, which forced Starr and his men back. O'Neil ordered his men to stand their ground and form a battalion parallel to the enemy. The 500 or so Irish volunteers then engaged the 850-man British force composed of the 2nd Militia Battalion, Queen's Own Rifles (QOR), the red-coated 13th Battalion Hamilton Infantry, and the York and Caledonia rifle companies, all led by 42-year old businessman, Lt. Col. Alfred Booker.

Booker was actually caught by surprise even though his intelligence said the Fenians were close by. He was sure they were much farther away.

For more than an hour the Fenians and the British-Canadians exchanged fire from behind rocks and trees. Eventually the British began to run low on ammunition. General O'Neil perceived the enemy was trying to turn their flanks, and he ordered his men to fall back about approximately 100 yards.

The British, believing the Fenians to be in full retreat, began a rapid pursuit. The Irish waited until the British had reached a point close to their line, and then poured volley fire into their ranks. Caught unaware by the Fenian fire, and fearing a cavalry charge (even though only a few Fenian officers rode horses) the British formed "squares" in an effort to protect themselves from a cavalry charge. The Irish then concentrated their fire on the solid, exposed enemy mass in the middle of the road. The British became disoriented, then demoralized. That's when O'Neil ordered a bayonet charge. The British broke rank and ran. The Irish chased the enemy for three miles at which time the British threw away their guns and knapsacks and *"everything that was likely to retard their speed."*

It was now the British who were in full retreat. The undisciplined Fenians eventually abandoned their pursuit of the enemy in favor of collecting battlefield mementos. Twelve

British soldiers were captured; about 30 were wounded and a dozen lay dead.

Even though the Fenians had achieved a momentary victory, their position was precarious. O'Neil had received the news that Colonel George Peacock and his 1,700 troops, which included the British 16th and 17th regiments and a six-gun field battery, were on their way. O'Neil had to flee to Ft. Erie and seek reinforcements from the United States. Without them, he would risk annihilation.

Once he arrived at Fort Erie, he quickly realized the anticipated reinforcements didn't arrive, having met severe resistance on the U.S. side. His had been the only mobile force as no other Fenian regiments had entered Upper Canada. He was all alone.

By the evening of June 2, O'Neil was surrounded by 5,000 British troops. Wounded Irishmen were quickly placed aboard wagons and several were left with Canadian citizens who promised to care for them. The dead were buried and the retreat began.

Captain Hamilton crossed the Niagra and informed O'Neil that arrangements had been made for him and his men to cross back over the river into the United States. O'Neil and his men boarded a scow barge across the Niagara River at 2:00 a.m. on the morning of June 3, 1866.

As the scow approached the American side, it was hailed by the American warship, USS Harrison, which fired a warning shot across their bow from its 12-pound pivot gun. If the Fenian scow did not "heave-to" it would be sunk. General O'Neil had no choice but to surrender, *"because we respected the authority of the United States in defense of which many of us had fought and bled during the late war."*

The Fenian troops were kept aboard the scow for four days, unprotected from torrential downpours, until they were discharged on their own recognizance for a later appearance to face charges of violating the neutrality laws.

On June 6, not yet resigned to defeat, General Spear crossed into Lower Canada. Brigadier Michael C. Murphy advanced 15 miles into Lower Canada before being driven back. Spear led his 2,000 men from St. Albans to Frelighsburgh, St. Armand, Slab City, and East Stanbridge, plundering along the way.

On Friday, June 8, Colonel Michael Scanlan's Fenian regiment defeated the British forces at Pigeon Hill. On June 9, with the U.S. having seized their supplies, General Spear retreated back to the U.S.

Lt. Col. Livingston of the U.S. 3rd Artillery Regiment gave the British permission to cross the border to capture the retreating Fenians. Some of the Irish-Americans were run through with British sabers while Livingston watched and did nothing. A Vermont woman was accidentally shot and killed by a British soldier while standing on her door-step. U.S. citizens were outraged, and Livingston was severely reprimanded for allowing a violation of U.S. sovereignty.

Many Fenian prisoners were tried in Toronto and 22 were sentenced to death. Corporal John O'Neil and his officers faced charges of violations of the neutrality laws at the Erie County Courthouse in New York. They were found guilty and sentenced. However, when the political smoke cleared, they were released.

On the June 15, 1886, 5,166 Fenian troops were paroled in Buffalo, NY. Another chapter in the fight for Irish independence was over.

The rising of the Fenians in Montreal failed due to the strength of the regular British forces who were joined by 10,000 militia and three warships in the harbor.

The British lost 16 men (two later dying from wounds and two from heatstroke) and 74 wounded. The Fenians captured six enemy soldiers from the Queens Own Rifles, Caledona Rifles, 13th Battalion, York Rifles, and the 2nd Battalion. The Fenians lost only five men (two later dying from wounds) and recorded only 17 wounded.

Despite the failure of the campaign, the Fenians, *"fought magnificently,"* according to a battlefront correspondent from the Buffalo Morning Express. The reporter also exclaimed, *"The forces on both sides fought with great bravery and showed admirable stuff."* In the face of defeat, The Irish had a moral victory.

O'Neil, the hero of the Battle of Ridgeway, was later elected President of the Senate of the Irish Republican Brotherhood.

In 1870, still dreaming of a free and independent Ireland, O'Neil and Spear made one last attempt to *conquer* Canada. They instigated an uprising in Manitoba with a band of 40 hard core Irish-Americans and Metis (Canadians of French and Indian ancestry). This uncoordinated action, not sanctioned by Fenian leadership, was suppressed in short order by U.S. and Canadian authorities, but not before he seized the town of Pembina on the Red River.

Also not one to quit, in 1881 Fenians under William B. O'Donohue crossed the border from the U.S. and seized the Hudson's Bay Company post at Pembina, Manitoba. They were followed in short order by U.S. troops and arrested.

Finally, the Fenian war on British Canada was over. After working as a land speculator, Former General O'Neil retired to a small town on the Elkhorn Rover in Nebraska, which bears his name. He died at Omaha, Nebraska on January 7, 1878.

British Canada initially disregarded the Battle of Ridgeway as much ado about nothing. Secretly, it scared them to death. Many historians believe the Fenian raid was the catalyst for the creation of the Dominion of Canada in 1867 which allowed the British to withdraw their forces.

The Canadians then assumed responsibility for their own defense by recruiting and training a 40,000 member militia force. No longer would they depend on inexperienced college gentlemen to defend their nation.

Irish-Americans have celebrated the victory at the Battle of Ridgeway ever since; insignificant though it was. They especially reveled in the routing of the "Queen's Own Rifles," commanded by Colonel Alfred Booker. For many years after the encounter, the following song would be sung by groups of proud Fenians:

The Queen's Own Regiment was their name,
From Fair Toronto town they came.
To put the Irish all to shame –
The Queen's and Colonel Booker.

What fury fills each loyal mind!
No volunteer would stay behind.
They flung their red rag to the wind –
"Hurray, my boys!" said Booker.

Now helter skelter Ohio,
See how they play that "heel and toe!"
See how they run from their Irish foe-
The Queen's and Colonel Booker!"

Ned Kelly
Australian Bushranger

*"Mind you,
die like a Kelly, Ned!*

**- Ellen Kelly to her son, Ned, on the eve of his
execution, November 11, 1880**

In 1840, a young gamekeeper name John "Red" Kelly was
employed by Lord Ormond, a wealthy aristocrat who owned
the estate of Killarney. A farmer who lived in the Golden Vale
of Tipperary complained to the police that two pigs had been
stolen from his farm, each valued at ten shillings. The police
investigated the matter and soon arrested Kelly on suspicion of
theft.

Like many Irish "criminals" before him, on January 1, 1841,
21 year-old John Kelly was found guilty by a jury and sentenced
to seven years via transportation to Australia, the world's largest
British penal colony.

After spending the first 7 months in a local jail (gaol), Kelly
was placed on board the convict ship, "Prince Regent." Shackled
and manacled hand and foot, Kelly and 182 other convicts were
bound for Van Dieman's Land (later known as *Tasmania*).

Few, if any, ever returned to Ireland. One year after John
Kelly was convicted of theft, the Prince Regent dropped anchor
in the Derwent River by the Port of Hobart.

After serving his seven-year sentence, Kelly was released
and found work doing odd jobs until he earned enough money to
buy passage to the Australian mainland.

He eventually found work as a bush carpenter in Melbourne,
the capital of the Port Phillip District. He also met an attractive
18 year-old named Ellen Quinn, the daughter of migrants from

Country Antrim, Ireland. The two fell in love, much to the chagrin of Ellen's parents who did not approve of the former convict.

Desperate, the young lovers escaped on horseback to Melbourne, just one step ahead of Ellen's furious parents, and were married on November 18, 1850 at St. Francis Roman Catholic Church.

In June 1855, Ellen gave birth to their first son, a boy named Edward, soon to be known to all of Australia as "Ned." The exact place and date of birth of Ned is not known, as was a common occurrence in the Australian frontier days.

Most historians believe he was born at Beveridge, Victoria in either 1854 or 1855. When Ned was born, he joined his older sister, Ann, who was born in 1853. Later, five more children arrived: Margaret (1857), James (1859), Daniel (1861), Catherine (1863), and Grace (1864).

In 1864, the Kellys moved from Beveridge (now Victoria) to Avenel, further inland, where they could continue their dairy farming. They were remembered as "poor strugglers," which was a term used to describe poor farmers of the time. Poor or not, "Red" Kelly had become a quiet, decent citizen, according to historians.

Sometime between 1864 and 1866 the Kelly children, along with many other children, were on their way to school. In doing so they would, each day, cross a river called "Hughes Creek." On this particular day a young boy named Richard Shelton slipped and fell into a deep waterhole. Shelton panicked, and began to drown, when Ned, age 10, dived in and saved the boy. The boy's parents, proprietors of the Royal Mail Hotel, presented Ned with a valuable "green silk sash, with a heavy bullion fringe." It would become his most prized possession for his entire life.

John "Red" Kelly died on December 27, 1866, leaving Ellen to support seven children. At age 11, Ned became the man of the family.

In 1867, Ellen moved the family from Avenel to Greta to be near her own family, the Quinns, who were squatters in that area.

In 1869 she moved again, this time to "Eleven Mile Creek," near Greta. It was at this time that Ned left school to help out the family. They eked out a living selling "sly grog" (illegal alcohol) and provided accommodations for passing carriers, hawkers, seasonal workers, and travelers of all sorts. The Kelly home was now an official public house, and Ned and his brothers were introduced to all sorts of scoundrels and riff-raff.

Ellen's brothers also played a largely influential, but ultimately detrimental, part in the lives of the Kelly boys. Known as a "wild lot," the uncles were expert horsemen who delighted in drinking and brawling and included some jail-time for cattle rustling and horse stealing.

Uncle Jimmy Quinn was constantly bragging about how he would "get even" with the policemen who had put them in jail. All of the uncles seemed determined to square things with the police who they felt had unjustly imprisoned them. This loathing of the local police did not go unnoticed by young Ned.

Ned's first run-in with the law occurred on October 14, 1869 when Ned was fourteen. A Chinese hawker named "Ah Fook" stopped at Mrs. Kelly's and asked for a drink of water. He could have gotten a drink from the nearby river, but historians believe he was actually an informer for the local police instructed to see if the Kelly's were selling illegal liquor.

Anne Kelly offered Ah Fook a drink from the creek, which he tasted and then spat out. He began to wave his arms furiously and shouted at Anne. Anne became frightened and told him to go away. Hearing the ruckus, Ned came running from the paddock. When he arrived he told Ah Fook to "clear out." Fook produced a bamboo stick and began waving it around. Ned wrestled the stick out of his hands and proceeded to whack Ah Fook several times on the shins and then chased him down the road.

The next morning, a local police sergeant arrived at Eleven-Mile Creek and arrested Ned for robbery and violence. Ah Fook claimed Ned had robbed him of ten shillings and threatened to beat him to death. Although this was untrue, young Ned was remanded, without bail, and locked up for fifteen days before the local magistrate eventually dismissed the charges.

In the eyes of the police, Ned was nothing more than a juvenile bushranger. As far as Ned was concerned, this episode just confirmed everything his uncles had said about the corrupt and abusive local police.

While still in his teens, Ned did many things to earn a few shillings for the family such as "ring-barking," breaking in horses, mustering cattle, fencing, and perhaps a little cattle rustling on the side. Ned was no saint.

The Kelly family was one of the many smaller farmers in the area who were constantly at odds with the big landowners who, at any time, could call on the police to protect their interests.

The Kellys, and their cousins the Quinns and Lloyds, used horses like currency, and regarded all unbranded strays as fair game. In the eyes of the law, that could be considered horse thievery.

The Kellys also viewed local police patrols as their natural enemies. When a local Superintendent named Nicholson, a Scotsman, took over the northeastern police district, he was told that Mrs. Kelly's house was a notorious meeting place for rogues and cattle-thieves.

In a report Superintendent Nicholson stated, *"the Kelly gang must be rooted out of the neighbourhood and sent to Pentridge Gaol, even on a paltry sentence. This would be a good way of taking the flashness out of them."* Thus began a cat and mouse game between the Kellys and the local police that would last for some time.

Harry Power was one of the most notorious bushrangers in Victoria who had the reputation of holding up stagecoaches single-handed. He was an acquaintance of Ned's uncle, Jack Lloyd, who suggested that 14 year-old Ned joined up with Potter and act as his lookout. His career as an outlaw had officially begun.

After committing more than 34 documented hold ups, Harry Power was finally apprehended when Ned's uncle Jack led authorities to his hideout. The temptation of the 500-pound reward was too much for Jack, who most likely shared the reward with his two brothers-in-law, John and James Quinn.

Power was convicted of, "robbery under arms" and sentenced to 15 years in jail. He was finally released in 1885. Harry's life ended ignominiously at Swan Hill on October 10, 1891 when he fell into the Murray River and drowned.

In 1870, Ned was arrested for assault and served three months in jail. In August 1871 he stole a horse and served three years. After his release in 1874 he returned home to find that his mother had remarried a man named George King, a very clever horse-thief. Ned had worked with King for a short time running stolen horse across the Murray River for sale in New South Wales. King gave Mrs. Kelly four children…and then he moved on.

Ned worked in sawmills for three years and pretty much stayed out of trouble. But he must have missed the outlaw life, for after three peaceful years he formed his first gang in late 1876 and began to focus on horse and cattle stealing. His gang included younger brother, Dan; sullen-tempered Steve Hart; cousin Tom Lloyd; and Joseph Byrne, a heroin addict and superb marksman.

By age 23, Ned had become an imposing figure. He was six-feet tall with an athletic build and a full, bushy, beard. He looked older than his years, and dressed well, but not in the flamboyant style popular with bushrangers of the time.

In October 1878, a trooper named Alexander Fitzpatrick had arrived at the Kelly home to serve a warrant for the arrest of Dan Kelly. Apparently, before arriving at the Kelly's, he had imbibed at a local tavern, and once at the Kelly's, he made a drunken pass at Ned's sister, Kate.

Dan Kelly, rushing to his sister's aid, knocked Fitzpatrick to the ground, and in the ensuing scuffle, the trooper injured his wrist.

Mrs. Kelly bandaged the trooper's wrist and invited him to supper in an effort to quell the situation. Her attempt to make peace didn't work. Fitzpatrick reported to his superiors that Dan Kelly had resisted arrest and that Ned had burst into the room and shot the trooper in his wrist. Ned was 400 miles away at the time. When police reinforcements arrived, Dan Kelly had disappeared into the bush.

Frustrated, the police then arrested Mrs. Kelly for the attempted murder of a police officer. She was sentenced to three years hard labor. A charge vehemently denied by the Kelly clan. As far as Ned was concerned, this was the final straw, and he returned swearing vengeance.

The police knew Ned was back in the area, so Ned and Dan vanished into the Wombat Ranges, 20 miles into the rough country near the town of Mansfield. There they met up with Steve Hart and Joe Byrne.

The police hunt intensified, and on October 1878, Police Sergeant Kennedy (accompanied by constables Lanigan, Scanlon, and McIntrye) rode out to engage the Kellys.

Unbeknownst to the constables, Ned had discovered their campout and when two of the troopers rode out on patrol, the Kelly gang emerged silently from the bush and *"ordered them to bail."* Lonigan jumped to his feet and drew his revolver, but Ned shot him dead. McIntyre immediately surrendered.

Suddenly Kennedy and Scanlon returned to the camp and opened fire on the outlaws. A gunfight followed, with the policemen dodging from tree to tree. Ned eventually killed both Kennedy and Scanlon, but during the ruckus McIntyre managed to escape on Kennedy's horse. The gang then covered the bodies of the troopers with blankets, broke camp, and rode out.

When McIntyre reached Mansfield he related the story of a cowardly ambush by the Kellys. The public reaction was outrage. Two hundred policemen were drafted into the area with instructions to bring in the Kelly gang dead or alive. Skilled "backtrackers" were also brought in from Queensland to ferret out the bushrangers.

The Kellys proved too elusive. In fact, they staged an amazingly daring bank raid in the township of Euroa on December 9, 1878. During the raid they seized the local railway station, imprisoned all there and stayed overnight. They would remain on the run for another two years, robbing the Bank of New South Wales in 1879, after first capturing the local police in Jerilderiea.

On June 27, 1880, the Kelly gang captured the railway station at Glenowan. They herded a small crowd of people into Mrs. Ann Jones's hotel near the station. With the police hot on their trail, Ned decided it was time to stand and fight.

Unafraid, the Kelly gang proceeded to sit and drink with the locals, and on Sunday they held a light-hearted "sports" meeting in the hotel yard. Ned even removed his guns and competed in a hop, step and jump event.

But at night, Ned and his boys were busy with a little project that involved exceptionally loud banging and clanging that could be heard echoing throughout the hotel.

Ned had planned to derail the Sunday train by destroying part of the track. He knew the train would be carrying police from Melbourne. However, the train didn't arrive until Monday, which allowed two local citizens, who had learned of the plan, to warn the train before it reached the damaged track. The police and backtrackers de-trained and swarmed into the town.

Befuddled from too much drink and not enough sleep, the Kelly gang was caught off-guard. But Ned was ready. In a backroom of the hotel he and his men had constructed homemade armor made from ploughshares, including a cylindrical helmet, a breastplate with apron, and a backplate laced with leather thongs. That was the reason for all of the hammering. The armor weighted 90 pounds.

At 3:00 a.m., under the command of Superintendent Hare, the police surrounded the hotel and took up firing positions. *"I would like a word with you,"* Hare shouted to Ned. *"I have nothing to say to you,"* replied Ned as he raised his gun and shot Hare in the wrist.

With that, the rest of the Kelly gang came lumbering out of the hotel, weighed down by their homemade armor, and began firing their weapons. Hare quickly retreated to the local post office.

As the bullets clanged off Ned's armor, he escaped to the north side of the hotel, but not before he was wounded in the foot, hand, and forearm. The arm wound was most serious as it prevented Ned from using his Spencer repeating rifle, which must be supported by the left arm.

Joe Byrne and Dan Kelly - bullets ricocheting off their armor - were forced to retreat back into the hotel. Ned, bleeding freely, staggered into the stockyard and tried to mount a horse. But the weight of 97 lbs of steel made it impossible, so he lumbered his way into the woods towards his tethered grey mare. He tried to unfasten his armor, but his injured hands made it impossible, as he could not undo the bolts. He was able to remove his helmet, but was unable to load his rifle due to injuries. He decided to lie hidden in the bush, so he untethered his mare and let her go.

Sometime before dawn, Ned returned to the hotel to find the body of Joe Byrne. Confused, he ran back into the woods where he collapsed due to a loss of blood. When he awakened, he decided to again return to the hotel to rescue his brother, Dan, and Steve Hart.

As the sun rose, out of the woods stepped Ned, still clad in his dented armor, walking slowly towards the police line. A railway guard named Jessee Dowsett spotted Ned and began firing at his legs. Another constable followed suit, and big Ned Kelly tumbled to the ground.

Within minutes the police had surrounded the strange figure of Ned Kelly. They had to cut the thongs to free him from his armor. On his person, Ned was carrying the green silk sash from his childhood. He had so many wounds the police were certain he would not survive. His face was a mask of blood.

The police carried him into the railway station. A Roman Catholic Priest named Father Matthew Gibney administered the last rites at the request of Ned's two sisters.

Father Gibney then returned to the hotel where the police had kept up a murderous fire, despite the sixty-two hostages inside. The police had set fire to the hotel in hopes of smoking out the rest of the gang. But when no one evacuated the hotel, Father Gibney agreed to enter the burning structure in hopes of saving the men. He quickly discovered that Dan Kelly, Steve Hart, and Joe Burne had been dead for quite sometime. It appeared to have been suicide, perhaps by poison, as the two men lay side by side, heads propped on folded blankets. Martin Cherry was rescued, but died later.

Twelve and a half hours after the gun-battle began, on June 28, 1880, the Kelly gang was no more. Ned was taken by the police to the Melbourne Gaol hospital and carefully nursed back to health. On October 28, 1880 he was put on trial.

He appeared before Sir Redmond Barry, the same man who sentenced his mother to three years imprisonment, and the one who swore he would see Ned Kelly hang. To no one's surprise, Judge Barry sentenced Ned to death by hanging.

When asked by Sir Redmond if he had any last words to say, Ned told him they would soon meet in a fairer court in the sky, and that he would see him there. Many people remembered those words when Sir Redmond suddenly became ill two days later and died soon afterwards.

Ned had become so popular that over 60,000 people signed a petition to have his sentence reprieved, but the Executive Council would not be swayed from executing the bushranger.

The day before his execution, his brothers and sisters were allowed to see him one last time. Then his mother was given a few minutes to say good-bye. Her last words to him were, *"mind you, die like a Kelly, Ned!"*

At 10:00 on November 11, 1880, Ned was taken to the gallows at the Old Melbourne Gaol. As the hangman adjusted the noose around his neck, Ned looked around him and said, *"Ah well, I guess it had to come to this."* A white cap was placed over his head and face. As it was pulled down over his eyes, Ned, with a sigh, spoke his last words, *"such is life."*

After being hanged, Kelly was left on the gallows for the required half hour before his body was taken down. A death mask was made, a minor autopsy was performed, and he was buried in the graveyard at the gaol, despite having requested that his body be left to his friends for burial in consecrated ground.

It has been said that his head was removed and used as a paperweight, but there is no strong evidence for this. Although it is true his head was removed for whatever reason. Nonetheless, the headless body was buried in an unmarked grave on the grounds of the Old Melbourne Gaol. It was later removed to Pentridge Prison's Cemetery.

Like most outlaws, Ned Kelly died young. He was expert with a "running-iron" on stolen unbranded stock, and was a deadly accurate shot with revolver or rifle. Surprisingly articulate for an uneducated person, he was fiercely loyal to his friends and family, and had a sardonic sense of humor.

To the last, his courage never deserted him, and to be *"as game as Ned Kelly"* came to mean, in Australian folk-language, a kind of reckless heroism.

The Irish Guards in WW1

"O'Leary came back from his killing...
as if he had been for a walk in the park."

**- Sergeant J. G. Lowry, describing the exploits of
Lance Corporal Michael O'Leary**

The telegram received in the Orderly Room of the Irish
Guards at 4:00 p.m., August 4, 1914, was succinct: *"Get on
with it."* With that, the Irish Guards joined the rest of the United
Kingdom and went to war against Germany. The "war to end all
wars" had begun for Great Britain.

The Irish Guards were a relatively new unit at the outbreak
of World War I. They were not officially formed until April 7,
1900 when Queen Victoria issued the following order: *"Her
Majesty the Queen having deemed it desirable to commemorate
the bravery shown by the Irish Regiments during the operations
in South Africa in the years 1899-1900 has been graciously
pleased that an Irish Regiment of Foot Guards be formed, to be
designated the 'Irish Guards.'"*

Immediately following the order from the Queen, the
British War office issued a letter that a new regiment would be
incorporated into the Brigade of Guards. Recruiting for the new
regiment began immediately in Ireland and Scotland. Irishmen
serving in other regiments of the British Army were offered a
bounty to transfer to the start-up regiment. The first recruit was
James O'Brien of Limerick.

The new regiment performed one of its first public events
at the funeral of Queen Victoria on February 2, 1901, and
received its first Colors on May 30, 1902. The King (Edward
VII), as Colonel-in-Chief, wore the uniform of the regiment
and addressed the regiment for the first time, asking them to
"emulate the proud example of your brothers of the Grenadier,

Coldstream and Scot Guards." On St. Patrick's Day, 1902, Her Majesty Queen Alexandra made a gift of shamrocks to the regiment. This became an annual event that continues to the present day.

The Irish Brigade would first see action in the "Boer War" in South Africa. Thirty-three brigade members were originally recruited as "marksmen." It was noted they had "no horsemanship skills" but quickly mastered the task.

The Guards encountered their only substantial action when their column was ambushed by a Boers commando unit inflicting heavy casualties. The Guards, although distinguishing themselves by covering the retreat of their comrades, lost five men. But their true test would come several years later in "The Great War."

At the start of Word War I in 1914, the Irish Guards were quartered at Wellington Barracks in London, and formed part of the 4th Guards Brigade. Commanded by Brigadier General R. Scott-Kerr, the brigade consisted of the 2nd Battalion Grenadier Guards, 2nd and 3rd Battalions Coldstream Guards, and the 1st and 2nd Battalion Irish Guards.

Once the War Office telegram was received by the Irish Guard headquarters, mobilization notices were sent to every Irish Guard reservist (1,322 men), many of whom were already serving with the Royal Irish Constabulary in Ireland.

By August 5th, the first of the reservists reported to Wellington Barracks. Once mobilization was completed, the Irish Guards were sent to Southhampton for training, and later boarded the S.S. Novara for Harve France, where they would remain for five grueling years in bloody combat with the German army.

There were many heroes in the Irish Guard during World War I. But two individuals stand out as the epitome of courage under fire. Here is their story:

Michael John O'Leary was 24 years old when he was sent to the front in November 1914. He was born in Gearagh, between Macroom and Inchigeela, in Co. Cork in 1890. Prior to joining the Guards, he spent some time in the Royal Canadian Mountain Police in Saskatchewan, where he became a Canadian citizen.

O'Leary was assigned to the 1st Battalion of the Irish Guard, already engaged in fierce trench warfare in the La Bassee district of France. By the end of January, the 1st Battalion was stationed near the La Bassee Brickfield, and was subject to constant withering fire from the Germans. On the last night of January, the German fire was particularly intense.

On that night it was decided the trenches were much too costly to hold. So prior to evacuating, the 1St Battalion was ordered to make a last ditch effort by charging the German position. Before advancing, they knelt in silent prayer with their Chaplain, Father Gwynn. The Irish knew many of them wouldn't be coming back.

Almost immediately, British artillery began a fierce bombardment of the German positions. The intent was not only to terrorize the German line, but also to break up the barbed wire entanglements in front of the German trenches. The sound of this intense bombardment could be heard 20 miles away. No. 2 Company of the Irish Guards was ordered to keep up "hot rifle-fire," which would keep the Germans pinned down if any of them decided to flee the bombardment, as well as convince the Germans to expect an attack from their direction. No. 1 Battalion, which included Michael O'Leary, was in a trench on the left of No. 2's trench.

Historians claim that O'Leary was actually "off duty" at the time, and thus was certainly within his right to not fight. But he chose to fight.

With a shout, No. 1 Battalion of the Irish Guards was ordered to charge. With bayonets fixed, they scrambled over the parapet and began a 150-yard dash toward the German position.

O'Leary was much faster than his comrades, and despite looking occasionally over his shoulder at his fellow soldiers, he soon left them behind. He encountered a railway bank, but cleared it effortlessly and continued toward the German line.

O'Leary then came to a small mound, were he paused to assess the situation. In front of him lay a German machine gun that was laying down heavy fire at the trench occupied by the No. 2 Battalion of the Irish Guards. No. 2 Battalion had successfully duped the Germans into believing they would be making the charge. The Germans hadn't noticed the charge made by No. 1 Battalion.

Suddenly, the Germans detected their motion and turned their machine gun on the advancing No. 1 Battalion. At this critical moment, O'Leary began firing his weapon at the German gun crew, and one by one they dropped until five of the Kiezer's finest lay dead around the gun.

The lad from Cork captured the gun and saved his comrades from certain annihilation. Undeterred, O'Leary spotted another barricade further on manned by five more German soldiers, and he headed in that direction. The Germans spotted him, but O'Leary was able to fire first and killed three. The two remaining Germans immediately surrendered.

O'Leary confessed later that his second exploit was a perilous one. He had lost his bayonet, and had to trust his marksmanship. His rifle was loaded with only 10 rounds, and 8 had found their mark. By the time the last two German soldiers surrendered to O'Leary he had no ammunition left.

In the aftermath, Sergeant O'Leary had killed eight Germans, captured a machine gun, taken two German prisoners, and secured two strong positions, from which the Germans could have inflicted heavy casualties. Lance-Corporal O'Leary was promoted to Sergeant, on the spot.

Company Quartermaster Sergeant J. G. Lowry of the Irish Guards explained what happened next: *"O'Leary came back from his killing as cool as if he had been for a walk in the park, accompanied by two prisoners he had taken. He probably saved the lives of the whole company. Had that machine gun got slewed round, No. 1 Company might have been nearly wiped out. We all quickly appreciated the value of O'Leary's sprinting and crack shooting, and when we were relieved that night, dog-tired as we were, O'Leary had his arm nearly shaken off by his comrades."*

Very quickly, the word of his O'Leary's deeds spread through out the Western world. He was immediately awarded the English "Victoria Cross," a plain bronze cross with the simple motto "For Valor," one of the most coveted military decorations in the world. He was also promoted to Lieutenant.

On the evening of Friday, February 19, 1915, the London newspapers carried the following headlines: *"How Michael O'Leary won the V.C.", "How Michael O'Leary V.C., Kills Eight Germans and Takes Two Barricades," "The Wonderful Story of Michael O'Leary."*

O'Leary was immediately sent back to England and Ireland to receive the accolades due a returning hero. He was cheered in Cork, as well as his native village of Inchigeela.

On July 10, 1915 tens of thousands of well-wishers turned out to greet him in London's Hyde Park. O'Leary drove from the Strand to the park in an open carriage, still wearing his war-stained uniform, and cheered along the way by his new admirers.

O'Leary would later become a military recruiter, whose specialty was recruiting the Irish. He would go on to achieve the rank of Major in the Irish Guards before leaving the military.

He died in North London on August 1, 1961 and is buried in Mill Hill Cemetery. His V.C. medal is on display at the Irish Guards Royal Head Quarters in London.

To his dying day, he never quite understood all of the fuss. *"Faith, a bit of a shindy is no great matter at all,"* he would say.

One can not overlook the irony of O'Leary, and the other Irish soldiers, fighting on the side of Britain, compared to what would transpire one year later when hundreds of Irish Volunteers would wage a short but intense war against the English in the streets of Dublin.

O'Leary simply did what the Irish have done for ages, he choose to earn a living fighting another man's war. That certainly does not take away the fact that he was a very brave fellow, and deserved the honors heaped upon him.

George Bernard Shaw was so impressed with his exploits that he based his play "O'Flaherty, V.C.", on the heroic deeds of Michael John O'Leary.

Father Francis M. Browne was born on 3 July, 1880 in Cork, Ireland to Brigid and James Browne. He attended Bower Convent in Athlone, Christian Brothers College in Cork, Belvedere College in Dublin, and Castlenock College in Co. Dublin.

He graduated in 1897 and toured Europe, joined by his brother, who presented him with a camera so Brown could record their travels.

In 1911 Browne began his theological studies at Milltown Park, Dublin. After being ordained on July 31, 1915, the 35-year-old Francis Browne traveled to London to join the Irish Guards as a Chaplain.

For the next five years he served with the Guards in France, Flanders, and Germany. During his service he saw the horrors of trench warfare, and the "meat grinder" called "The Great War."

As far as he was concerned, the war wasn't so great. He was wounded five times, once quite severely in the jaw. In April 1918, his lungs were severely damaged by mustard gas. Most people thought he should go home to rest, but he continued to serve. Like most Catholic chaplains in WWI, Browne was not afraid to perform his duties under the worst of circumstances.

His bravery so impressed Rudyard Kipling, whose son served in the Irish Guards, that Kipling was inspired to write about the brave Chaplin:

"The Huns had their revenge a few days later when the Battalion's billets and Headquarters at Poperinghe were suddenly, on April 11, shelled just as the Battalion was going into line at Ypres. The thing began almost with a jest. The regimental Chaplain was taking confessions, as is usual before going up, in Poperinghe church, when the building rocked to bursts of big stuff obviously drawing nearer. He turned to open the confessional slide, and smelt gas--chlorine beyond a doubt. While he groped

wildly for his gas helmet in the dusk, the pentinent reassured him: "It's all right, Father. I've been to Divisional Gas School today. That smell's off my clothes." Relieved, the Padre went on with his duties to an accompaniment of glass falling from the windows, and when he came out, found the porch filled with a small crowd who reported: "Lots of men hit in an ambulance down the road." Thither ran the Padre, to meet a man crazy with terror whom a shell-burst had flung across the street, half stripped and blackened from head to foot. He was given Absolution, became all of a sudden vehemently sick, and dropped into stupor. Next, on a stretcher, an Irish Guardsman crushed by a fallen wall, reported for the moment as "not serious." As the priest turned to go, for more wounded men were being borne up through the dusk, the lad was retaken by a violent hemorrhage. Supreme Unction at once was his need. Captain Woodhouse, R.A.M.C., the regimental doctor, appeared out of the darkness, wounded in the arm and shoulder, his uniform nearly ripped off him and very busy. He had been attending a wounded man in a house near headquarters when a shell burst at the door, mortally wounded the patient, killed one stretcher-bearer outright and seriously wounded two others. The Padre, dodging shells en route, dived into the cellars of the house where he was billeted, for Sacred Elements, went back to the wayside dressing station, found a man of the Buffs, unconscious, but evidently a Catholic (for he carried a scapular sewed in his tunic), anointed him, and--the visitation having passed like a thunderstorm--trudged into Ypres unworried by anything worse than casual machine-gun fire, and set himself to find some

Sufficiently large sound cellar for Battalion Mass next morning. The Battalion followed a little later and went underground in Ypres--Headquarters and a Company in the Carmelite Convent, two companies in the solid brick and earth ramparts that endure to this day, and one in the cellars of the Rue de Malines. Later his commanding officer, Colonel (later Field Marshal and Lord) Alexander said of Browne that he was 'the bravest man I ever met.' Father Browne received the Military Cross with Bar from the British Army, the Croix de Guerre from the French, and a personal decoration from the King of Belgium.

During the occupation of Cologne, Germany, Browne took many pictures of his fellow Guardsmen. He entitled the album "The Watch on the Rhine." It is still one of the prize possessions of the Irish Guards at their headquarters in Wellington Barracks, London.

Browne's photographic talent also secured him a place in history as early as 1912, when, as a guest of the O'Dell family, he boarded the R.M.S. Titanic at Southampton. He decided to take several rolls of pictures during his short cruise. The Titanic sailed for Cherbourg, France, and the next day Browne and Titanic arrived in Queenstown, Ireland. Browne disembarked with a handful of film that, unbeknownst to him at the time, would contain the last surviving photographs of the great liner before her fateful encounter with an iceberg.

Father Browne would eventually become the Superior of St. Xaver's Church in Dublin, but he continued to travel the world taking photographs, nearly 42,000 of them.

After 1929 he became a member of the "Retreats and Mission" staff of the Irish Jesuits, and preached all over Ireland until his death in 1960. His photographs are now in the archives of the Irish Jesuits in Dublin.

When he died, his obituary appeared in The Irish Guards Association Journal: *"everyone in the Battalion, officer or man, Catholic or Protestant, loved and respected Father Browne and he had a great influence for good. A great Christian, a brave and loveable man, we who knew him so well will always be grateful for his friendship and for the example that he set."*

As mentioned previously, Rudyard Kipling, had a son, John, who served in the Irish Guards. Tragically, John was killed while serving with the Guard during WWI. Contemplating his son's sacrifice, and those of the other Irish Guards, Kipling would again be inspired to put pen to paper and attempt to encapsulate the war on behalf of the Irish Guard. *"They were too near and too deeply steeped in the War that year's end to realize their losses. Their early dead, as men talked over the past in Cologne, seemed to belong to immensely remote ages. Even those of that very spring, of whom friends could still say, 'if so-and-so had only lived to see this!' stood as far removed as the shadowy great ones of the pre-bomb, pre-duckboard twilight, and, in some inexpressible fashion, they themselves appeared to themselves the only living people in an uncaring world."*

The Irish Guard still exists to this day and are currently on duty in Iraq, Afghanistan, and Cyprus. They are affectionately known world-wide as the "Micks."

Irish Gangs of New York

"The Plug Uglies were
for the most part gigantic Irishmen,
and included in their membership
some of the toughest characters of the Five Points."

- Herbert Ashbury, Gangs of New York

Criminal gangs have existed for thousands of years. The word "thug" dates back to India in 1200 AD and refers to a gang of criminals (Thugz) who roamed the country, pillaging and looting towns along their way. These Thugz had hierarchy, hand signs, and rituals.

Organized gangs would exist in many other countries as well. Even the oceans would give birth to the pirates, who were nothing more than a sea-faring gang of reprobates. So it is no surprise that gang activity would eventually infiltrate America's emerging cities where they could prey upon an endless supply of unfortunate victims, as well as each other.

During the first ten or fifteen years of its history "The Five Points" of New York was a fairly decent place. Named for the points created by the intersection of Orange, Cross, Anthony, Mulberry, and Little Water streets, the neighborhood would eventually be known as the center of vice and debauchery throughout the 19th century.

In the beginning, only one policeman, or "Leatherhead," was needed to preserve order. By 1820, a whole regiment of policemen wouldn't be able to route all of the gangsters and criminals from their dens and burrows.

During this time the district began to disintegrate and sink into the poorly drained swamp. It became unsafe for occupancy and the stench from vapors arising from the marshlands made the whole area a health hazard. The residents lived in windowless, teeming apartments unfit for habitation, according the historian, Tyler Anbinder. Alcoholism, violence, and prostitution were commonplace. Poverty was epidemic, and living conditions so intolerable the reforming sociologist, Jacob Riis, used the area as a case study for the *"wretched excesses of urban life."* A Swedish reporter visiting the Five Points once wrote, *"lower than to the Five Points it is not possible for human nature to sink."*

Those families that had the means quickly abandoned what was left of their dwellings for Manhattan Island, and their places were taken, for the most part, by freed Negro slaves and shanty Irish, who had swarmed into New York on the first great wave of immigration.

By 1840, the Five Points district had become the most dismal slum section in America. To some observers, it was worse than the Seven Dials and White Chapel districts of London, and those places were just awful. Charles Dickens visited the five Points in 1842 and wrote the following, *"Debauchery has made the very houses prematurely old. See how the rotten beams are tumbling down, and how the patched and broken windows seem to scowl dimly, like eyes that have been hurt in drunken frays. Many of these pigs live here. Do they ever wonder why their masters walk upright in lieu of going on all-fours? And why they talk instead of grunting?"*

In the depressing Five Points district, the Irish were overwhelmingly the majority. A census conducted by the Five Points House of Industry during the time of the Civil War (1860-1865) showed the number of Irish households at 3,435, while the next in number were the Italians with 416. There were 167 families of "Native American" stock. These were families who had been in the U.S. for several generations, and should not be confused with the term "Native-Americans" who are also referred to as "Indians." 73 other families claimed to be from England.

More than 3,000 people lived in Baxter Street from Chatham to Canal, a distance of less than half a mile. One lot in particular (25' X 100') held slums which sheltered 286 people. Around the Points and Paradise Square were 270 saloons, and many more speakeasies, dance halls, houses of prostitution, and "green grocers." Even the names of the saloons attested to their depravity: Suicide Hall, The Morgue, Hell's Gate, Cripples' Home, Tub of Blood, and Inferno.

The churches and welfare agencies professed great distress over the conditions at the Five Points, but nothing was done until the late 1830s when Presbyterian congregations sent missionaries into the area. But the population of the Points was principally Irish, and devoutly Catholic and the missionaries were viewed as "Protestant devils" and driven out of the area.

The original Five Points criminal gangs began in the tenements, saloons, and dance halls of the Paradise Square district, but their actual transformation into a criminal organization followed the opening of the cheap green-grocery speak-easies that sprang up around the Square.

The first speak-easy was established in 1825 by Rosanna Peers. Piles of decaying vegetables were displayed on racks outside the store, but in the back room Rosanna sold liquor at prices lower than the local saloons. This room became the haunt of thugs, pickpockets, murders, and thieves.

The gang known as the "Forty Thieves" was the first New York Irish gang with an acknowledged leadership structure. Organized by Edward Coleman in 1826, it was said to have formed in Rosanna's grocery store and often used the store as their meeting place.

The "Kerryonians," composed of natives of County Kerry, Ireland, was also a product of Rosanna's back room. This small gang seldom roamed beyond Center Street and did little fighting. Its members devoted themselves almost exclusively to hating the English. Other gangs such as the "Chichesters," "Roach Guards," "Plug Uglies," "Shirt Tails," and "Dead Rabbits" were organized and had their rendezvous in other grocery stores. In time, these grocery stores would become the meeting places for the worst scum of Manhattan.

The gangs called their members by code nicknames such as "Bloody" Bill, "Dirty Face" Jack, "Boiled Oysters" Malloy, "Pig" Donovan, "Eat-em-up" Jack McManus, Gyp the Blood, Eddie the Plague, and "Baboon" Dooley. Not to be outdone, the female consorts of these thugs took on names like "Red-Light" Lizzie, "Hell-Cat" Maggie and Jane "the Grabber." Many of the names used by present day gangs have their roots in this period.

Each Five Points gang had a unique style of dress that set them apart from the others. The Shirt Tails wore their shirts outside of their pants, like the Chinese immigrants of the day. The Roach Guards took their name from a Five Points liquor seller. Their battle uniform was a blue strip on their pantaloons. The Dead Rabbits adopted a red stripe on their pants, and when heading into battle, would carry an actual dead rabbit impaled on a pike. (It should be noted that in the slang of the period, a "dead rabbit" was a very rowdy, athletic fellow).

One of the more intriguing gangs was the Plug Uglies. Their named evolved from the enormous plug hats, which they stuffed with wool and leather and drew down over their ears to serve as helmets when they went into battle. According to author Herbert Asbury, in his book, The Gangs of New York, *"The Plug Uglies were for the most part gigantic Irishmen, and included in their membership some of the toughest characters of the Five Points."*

Other gangs would cringe when a giant Plug Ugly sauntered by. He usually carried a huge bludgeon in one hand, a brickbat in the other, a pistol sticking out from his pocket, and his tall hat jammed down over his ears, all but obscuring his callous eyes. He also wore heavy boots studded with great hobnails that he used to stomp his hapless foe. His main function was to seek rival gang members to pummel.

The Dead Rabbits and the Roach Guards spent most of their time hating each other, as the Rabbits were a disgruntled offshoot of the Guards. During one of the many heated Guard meetings, two factions began to argue over a particular issue. In the middle of all the shouting, someone threw a dead rabbit into the center of the room. One faction considered this an omen, and they broke off to form the Dead Rabbits.

Despite their mutual hatred, when it came to protecting their turf from the waterfront or Bowery gangs, they would fight together, supported by the Plug Uglies, Shirts Tails and Chichesters. When the Dead Rabbits did engage a Bowery gang, these two groups constituted some of the greatest gang conflicts of the early nineteenth century. According to Asbury, *"Sometimes the battles raged for two or three days without cessation, while the streets of the gang area were barricaded with carts and paving stones, and the gangsters blazed away at each other with musket and pistol, or engaged in close work with knives, brickbats, bludgeons, teeth, and fists."*

Not only would the gangster's style of dress set them apart, they would even develop their own language. Some of the verbiage was so peculiar and indecipherable that in 1859, George W. Matsell, Special Justice and Chief of the New York Police, collected and published a dictionary of the slang entitled, *Vocabulum, or The Rogue's Lexicon.*

It is obvious that some of the slang can be traced to Irish and/or English verbiage, but the majority of the slang remains a complete mystery. Here are some examples: *"Paddy Fitzpatrick had to snitchel the bloke's gigg."* (break the man's nose). *"Can't you kiddy the bloke?"* (can't you bribe the man?) *"No, he wears a Joseph's coat."* (he's straight and can't be bribed). Another example: *"He told Jack how he cracked a casa last night and fenced the swag. He also flimped a yack, and then pinched a swell of a spark fawney."* (He told Jack how he robbed a house, and then sold the stolen items. He also strong-armed a pocket-watch from a fellow, and then stole a diamond from a rich guy). Present day linguists are still baffled.

The Bowery Boys, also called Bowery B'Hoys because they were mostly Irish, didn't start out to be a gang of criminals. In the beginning, the typical Bowery Boy was most likely a butcher, mechanic, or a bouncer in a saloon. He was almost always a volunteer fireman, and often competed against other fire companies to be the first to reach a fire.

It was considered a disgrace to show up to a fire and find all of the hydrants in use. Often times the Bowery Boys would battle rival fire companies over the right to use a particular hydrant...often overlooking the reason they were called out in the first place.

The original Bowery Boy was a burly ruffian with his chin adorned by Uncle Sam style whiskers. On his head was a stovepipe hat, usually battered, and his trousers were tucked inside his boots. He constantly chewed tobacco, and usually whittled away on a wooden shingle with a knife...his most prized possession.

In the ensuing years, a Bowery Boy would become a rather dapper dresser, which led to his eventual downfall. It seems the Bowery Boys spent more time trying to look good rather than protecting their turf. Regardless, some of the most ferocious brawlers fought in the ranks of the Bowery Boys, including "Butcher" Bill Poole, who would eventually leave the mob to form his own gang of cutthroats. It was said that "Bill the Butcher" killed for sport.

The Bowery Boys were actually one of several Bowery gangs who patrolled the lower East Side. Other Bowery gangs of the early days were: "True Blue Americans," "American Guards," "O'Connell Guards," and "Atlantic Guards." Their membership was principally Irish, but they do not appear to be as criminal or ruthless as their peers in the Five Points.

The True Blue Americans were rather amusing and quite harmless. They wore stovepipe hats and long black frock coats, buttoned close under the chin that reached to their ankles and flapped and flopped when they walked. Their chief mission in life was to stand on a street corner and denounce England. According to the author, Herbert Asbury, *"like most of the sons of Erin who have come to this country, they never became so thoroughly Americanized that Ireland did not remain their principal vocal interest."*

Gang members weren't limited to the lads. Many women, some fierce beyond belief, were active participants in the gang wars. Hell-Cat Maggie was a member of the Dead Rabbits gang during the 1840s. She was said to have filed her teeth to points, and wore long artificial nails made of brass. Howling her banshee battle cry, Hell-Cat Maggie would rush head long into the fray, biting and clawing her foes into submission.

Sadie the Goat and Gallus Mag were voracious hellions as well. Sadie the Goat would walk up to unsuspecting men on the street and headbutt them. This would temporarily startle the victim so her minions could rob and assault the poor fellow.

Gallus Mag, a 6 foot Englishwoman who held court at a dank Water Street bar called the "Hole in the Wall," had a propensity for biting the ears off folks who rubbed her the wrong way. She kept her ear collection in a pickle jar on the bar for all to see.

For many years the Bowery Boys and the Dead Rabbits waged a bitter war over turf, and a week hardly passed in which the two gangs did not come to blows, either along the Bowery or on the battleground of Bunker Hill, north of Grand Street.

Other Bowery gangs including the American Guard, whose members prided themselves on their native born ancestry, usually supported the Bowery Boys. But, as mentioned previously, they often fought amongst themselves. Fueled by their abhorrence for Irish Catholic immigrants, The American Guards once challenged the O'Connell Guards during the summer of 1835.

At the time the O'Connell Guards were known as the *"particular champion of Tammany Hall,"* a powerful political machine. These gangs came to blows on the lower East Side at Grand and Crosby Streets, and spread as far as the Five Points when other gangs joined in. The Mayor and the Sheriff alerted every policeman in the city, and finally had to call in the army to quell the fighting.

Corrupt Tammany Hall politicians quickly learned they could control blocks of voters and elections by buying gang support. In time it would build its strength on the muscle of Irish gangs.

The Tammany Society was formed in New York City in 1786. Initially a social organization, it became increasingly political, and by the middle of the 19th century had become a significant force in city government. Although controlled by wealthy men, the organization attracted the support of the working classes and the immigrant population.

When Tammany was organized in New York in 1789, it represented middle-class opposition to the power of the "aristocratic" Federalist Party. Incorporated in 1805 as a benevolent body, the Society of Tammany became identified with the Democratic Party by means of identical leadership within both organizations. The makeup of the society was substantially altered in 1817 when Irish immigrants, protesting Tammany bigotry, forced their right to membership and benefits.

Over time, Tammany Hall would appeal to particular ethnic and religious minorities. Italians, Germans, and Poles all shared abject poverty right along side the Irish. By catering to these immigrants, Tammany Hall would gain its power.

The rival Native American party detested foreigners, especially those in elected office. They vigorously demanded the repeal of naturalization laws by which Tammany Hall had gained such an enormous following. Tammany Hall representatives would often dole out of gifts to the poor, and at the same time bribe rival political faction leaders. In time, the name "Tammany Hall" became synonymous with urban political corruption.

By 1855 it was estimated that New York contained at least 30,000 men who belonged to the various gangs, and who had vowed allegiance to the political leaders of Tammany Hall or their rivals, the Know Nothings or Native American party.

All of these political parties used the gangs as their personal enforcers. At every election, gangs employed by rival factions rioted at the polling places, smashing ballot boxes and assaulting honest citizens who attempted to cast their ballot, while the gang members themselves voted early…and often. As the gangs grew, so did the political power of the specific parties, and each of them had no respect for local authorities.

While the early gangsters of the Five Points and the Bowery were frequently thieves and, on occasion, murders, they were primarily brawlers and street fighters with their battles taking place in the open, and usually against each other.

The "Whyos" of Mulberry Bend, who came later, fought everyone. They were considered *the most ferocious criminals who ever stalked the streets of an American city."* One of them was more than a match for a Dead Rabbit or a Plug Ugly, and certainly would have wiped the floor with a Kerryonian.

The origin of the name is unknown, but it is believed to have arisen from a particular call used by the gangsters, which to an outsider sounded like the calling of an owl. The gang itself is believed to be an out-growth of the Chichesters of the old Five Points who, around 1880, apparently outlasted the Dead Rabbits, Shirt Tails, Plug Uglies, and an assortment of other gangs from Paradise Square.

They weren't entirely Irish, but unlike the earlier Irish gangs, the Whyos victimized anyone and everyone…not just the English. The Whyos extended their operations throughout the city, and made some of the most notorious raids along the lower West Side and in the Greenwich Village district. They fought many desperate battles with other gangs and with the police.

According to legend, the Whyos accepted no man as a member until he had committed a murder, or at least made an honest effort to do so. They also became entrepreneurs, often advertising, via a printed and distributed price-sheet, the cost of inflicting body harm for hire. The pioneer of this fee-for-service pummeling was Piker Ryan. When he was eventually arrested, the following price list was found in his pocket:

Punching	$2.00
Both eyes blacked	$4.00
Nose & jaw broke	$10.00
Jacked out	$15.00
(knocked out with blackjack)	
Ear chawed off	$15.00
Leg or arm broke	$19.00
Shot in leg	$25.00
Stab	$25.00
Doing the big job	$100 and up

At one time the Whyos were so powerful that most of the other gangs had to ask their permission to operate. But they weren't the only gangs to control the underbelly of Manhattan from 1880 to 1920. The Gophers (pronounced "Goofers") were so-named because of their propensity to hole up in basements and cellars. Their leader was "Mallet" Murphy whose moniker was bestowed due his usage of a mallet as a weapon.

Other Irish Gopher Chiefs were: "Newburg" Gallagher, Marty Brennan, "Stumpy" Malarkey, "Goo Goo" Knox, "One Lung" Curran, and "Happy Jack" Mulraney, who suffered from a facial rictus which gave him a permanent grin. He once killed a barkeep for laughing at him.

The 500 plus members were divided into companies under the Gophers banner: the Gorillas, the Rhodes Gang, the Parlor Mob, and the Battle Row Ladies Social and Athletic Club (also called the Lady Gophers, and led by the famous "Battle" Annie). Just like the Whyos, the Gophers openly advertised their rates for various assaults and murder.

By the 1890s, the Whyos and Gophers began to die out, as many of their members had either been killed or were doing time in prison. So, much like their predecessors, the Plug Uglies, Dead Rabbits, and Bowery Boys, the Whyos had run their course.

At the start of the 20th century Jewish organized crime pretty much took over the Five Points, pushing out the Irish. The Jewish gangs hired themselves out as enforcers and bullied both labor unions and management during the labor unrest of the 1900s.

The new influx of Italian immigrants in the early 1900s bred what became the most dominant, and most infamous, criminal organization in American crime.

Paul Kelly (a.k.a. Paolo Antonio Vacarelli) formed a mixed ethnic gang called "The Five Pointers." From this gang sprung its farm team, "The Five Point Juniors," whose most famous alumni were Meyer Lansky, Bugsy Siegel, and Lucky Luciano.

The most famous Five Points alumni was Al "Scarface" Capone who went down in history as orchestrating the infamous 1929 Saint Valentine's Day Massacre. Dressed as policeman and businessmen, Capone's "North Side Gang" executed six of Irish Bugsy Moran's men in a garage on the north side of Chicago.

This action was a result of the long-standing feud between Moran's Irish-American gang, and Capone's Italian gang, for control of organized crime in Chicago. As a result of the long-standing warfare, the Irish came up short and ceased to be the dominating criminal force in Chi-town. The Italians were now in charge.

Titanic
The Irish Connection

"For God's sake, let the girls past to the boats…"

- **Passenger, James Ferrell, pleading to Titanic crewmen**

The story of the Titanic has been told and retold ad nauseam in numerous books and on film. It has become the most tragic tale of the early 20th century, taking on almost a mythical proportion.

Historians will be quick to point out that in the top 10 shipping disasters of all time, the Titanic was no worse than many other sea tragedies.

Almost no one has heard of the *Sultana* whose boiler exploded in the Mississippi River killing 1,547 people in 1865. Or the *General Slocum* that burned in the New York East River in 1904 killing 1,021. The list continues: the *Lusitania* lost 1,198 lives; the Canadian *Empress of Ireland* lost 1,012; and when the *Mont Blanc*, loaded with munitions, exploded in the Halifax dock in 1917 it killed 1,963 and injured 9,000.

But with the possible exception of the *Lusitania*, few events haunt the western imagination more than the sinking of the *Titanic*. Perhaps it was the grander of the ship, the first true luxury liner, and its wealthy passengers that have allowed the ship to live in infamy. Even the name *Titanic* has become synonymous with disaster.

The *Titanic's* association to the Irish is obvious. It was built at the Harland and Wolff Shipyards in Belfast, Northern Ireland. This was an Irish-designed, Irish-made ship whose last port of call was Queenstown (Cobh) Ireland. The last photographs on board were taken by Father Francis Browne, an Irish-Catholic Jesuit priest who disembarked at Cork harbor, and whose photographs live on today. Many of the *Titanic's* crew was Irish, as were many of its passengers.

Thousands of Irish Catholics worked in the shipyard building the Titanic, yet two interesting myths evolved to the contrary. The Protestants claim that a vessel so complex and sophisticated could only have been built by Loyalists. The Catholics claim the vessel was doomed from the start because they were excluded from the shipyard, and that the ship's number spelled out "No Pope" in mirror writing. Obviously, neither stories were totally accurate, but some say there may have been some seeds of truth.

On Wednesday, April 10, 1912, Captain Edward Smith gave the signal for the White Star liner to sail on her maiden voyage from Southhampton to New York, with a stop in Queenstown (Cobh). At 10:40 p.m., Sunday, April 14, LookOut Frederick Fleet spotted an iceberg. Within 30 seconds the ship had impacted the berg, tearing a gash in the side of its hull. It was only a glancing blow, but it was enough to initiate its slow death.

The ship's designer, Thomas Andrews, calculated the amount of water it had taken on and knew the vessel was doomed to sink. After sending a mayday message, giving their coordinates as 153 km south of the Grand Banks of Newfoundland, Captain Smith gave the order to uncover the lifeboats and evacuate the passengers.

Many of the passengers refused to believe the ship was sinking. Because of this, the first lifeboat launched only contained 12 passengers. Its capacity was 40. However, once the vessel's stern began to rise slowly from the sea, only then did the passengers take the threat serious.

It wasn't long before the situation degenerated into pure chaos. There were only 20 lifeboats for the 2,207 passengers. Anyone can do the math. Once the lifeboats were launched, 1,600 were left on board, their fate sealed. Many jumped into the sea. Those whose necks weren't broken when the lifejackets were thrust upwards upon impact would freeze to death in the frigid waters. Many of the 3rd class passengers were locked in steerage and never had a chance.

Nearly nine decades have passed since the sinking of the great ocean liner. When historians and filmmakers retell the events of the disaster at sea, the focus is usually on the wealthier passengers such as John Jacob Astor, the Guggenheims, Straus', and "Unsinkable" Molly Brown. Little has been mentioned of the 3rd class passengers, many of who were from Ireland, who were left to fend for themselves.

Of the total number of passengers, approximately 123 were from Ireland (primarily from the parish of Addergoole in Co. Mayo and a small hamlet in South Galway) who had set sail from Cobh (Queenstown). The 63 males and 60 females had boarded the giant ship at Queenstown (Cobh), Co. Cork on April 11, 1912. Virtually all of them rode in steerage to save money, and most of them were friends or relatives.

As the ship sank, the first and second class passengers were allowed to board the lifeboats first. The 3rd class travelers had to wait their turn. In most cases their turn never came. By the time the steamer, *Carpathia,* arrived in answer to the mayday calls, the death toll had reached 1,500. Seventy-six of the 123 Irish passengers perished.

The following are the true stories of nine Irish travelers, one English Priest, and one fortunate girl who literally, "missed the boat."

Thomas Kilgannon, 22, born in the village of Currafarry, Co. Galway on April 2, 1890, Tom was a farm laborer in Ireland with few prospects for the future. His friend, Martin Gallagher, convinced him to immigrate to America, where he planned to meet his brother, John, in New York City. He boarded the Titanic at Queenstown as a third class passenger. As the ship was sinking, he assisted Margaret Mannion and Ellen Mockler into a lifeboat. He then handed his Aran woolen sweater to Margaret as she was descending in the lifeboat. Thomas' body, if recovered, was never identified. Margaret later returned Thomas' sweater to his family in Currafarry.

Ellen Mary Mockler, 23, was born in the village of Currafarry, Co. Galway. She traveled in a group from Caltra parish led by Martin Gallagher, and included Thomas Kilgannon, Tom Smyth, and Margaret Mannion. Ellen was rescued, along with Margaret Mannion, in Lifeboat 16, which Ellen later recalled as being only partially full. She stated that none of the crew was particularly helpful, and if not for the "three Irish men" she was traveling with she might not have been rescued.

In 1917 she was ordained into a Catholic order of nuns, the Sisters of Mercy Motherhouse, and moved to Worcester, Mass., where she took the name, Sister Mary Patricia. She taught in schools for many years. She often told her students how she remembered *"hearing chickens and hens"* as she headed up to the boat dock, and how she recalled her friend, Martin Gallagher, falling to his knees and reciting the rosary as she was lowered into the lifeboat. Sister Mary died in a nun's convent on April 1, 1984, her 95th birthday.

Martin Gallagher, 29, was born in the village of Currafarry, Co. Galway. He first immigrated to America in 1900 and lived in New York City. He was returning on the Titanic after visiting his family in Ireland. He bought his third class return ticket, as did the others from Caltra Parish, at Ryan's Travel Agency in Ballygar, Co. Galway. At the time of the collision, Martin was able to locate Ellen Mockler and Margaret Mannion and took them and several other Irish girls to Lifeboat 16. After seeing them safely in the boat, he stepped back on the deck. The last the girls saw of Martin, he was leading a group of Irishmen in the recitation of the Rosary on Titanic's sloping deck. His body, if recovered, was never identified.

James Farrell, 26, was from Aghnacliffe, Co. Longford. He boarded Titanic as a third class passenger bound for New York City. He was credited with escorting sisters Kate and Mary Murphy, Katie Gilnagh and Kate Mullen through a barricade to safety by insisting to crewmen blocking their passage, *"For God's sake let the girls past to the boats, at least!"* The crewmen complied, but locked the gate behind the girls, trapping the remaining steerage passengers. The rescue ship *MacKay Bennett* eventually recovered his body, and he was buried at sea on April 24, 1912.

Eugene Patrick Daly, 29, was from Athlone, Co. Westmeath, Ireland and was traveling to New York. He boarded the Titanic at Queenstown. As the Titanic steamed away from port, Daly played "Erin's Lament" on his Uileann pipes for his fellow passengers in steerage. After the collision, Daly and many other third class passengers were held below deck for what seemed a lifetime.

A final rush of men carrying weapons allowed Daly and the others to make it to the top deck. Daly then helped Maggie Daly and Bertha Mulvihill to the boat deck and to Lifeboat 15. It was Daly who later testified that, *"an officer pointed a revolver and said if any man tried to get in he would shoot him on the spot. I saw the officer shoot two men dead because they tried to get into the boat. Afterwards there was another shot, and I saw the officer himself lying on deck. They told me he shot himself..."*

Daly stated he jumped over the side but was able to climb aboard "an upturned collapsible raft." He watched as people were sucked down the *Titanic's* funnels "like flies." Daly stated later only the thickness of his overcoat saved him from freezing to death. For the rest of his life he never went anywhere without his overcoat. He eventually made a claim of $50 for his lost pipes.

During a recent excavation, a set of uileann pipes were recovered from the wreck.

Bridget "Delia" McDermott, 28, was born in Knockfarnaught, Lahardane, Co. Mayo. She lived with her parents in a thatched cottage in Addergoole Parish. She was planning a trip to visit her cousin in St. Louis, Missouri and had purchased a third class ticket. She was one of 14 people, led by Katherine McGowan, from Addergoole who were to travel on the *Titanic*.

One day before the trip she traveled to the town of Crossmolina to purchase some new clothes. She was happy to find herself a *"smart new hat."* The evening before she departed for Queenstown, a mysterious man in black approached her and her friends in Lahardane village. She felt a hand tap her on the shoulder. When she turned around she saw a little man whom she thought was a "traveler." As Bridget reached in her purse to give him a few pennies, he spoke, telling her he knew she was going on a long journey. *"There will be a tragedy, but you will be saved,"* said the wee man before disappearing. When Bridget asked her friends if they had seen the man, they replied they had not.

When the ship struck the iceberg, a Stewart knocked on her door and told her to get dressed and go top side, which she did. She initially secured one of the first spots in a lifeboat, but suddenly remembered she left her new hat in her cabin. She jumped out of the boat, fetched her hat, and then found a spot in a different lifeboat, but she had to jump 15' from a rope ladder into the boat. She was eventually rescued by the *Carpathia.*

Bertha Mulvihill, 24, was from Athlone, Co. Galway, but had previously immigrated to Rhode Island. She had returned to Athlone to attend a wedding and was traveling back to Rhode Island to make wedding plans of her own.

She boarded the Titanic at Queenstown as a 3rd class passenger along with her friend, Margaret "Maggie" Daly. Bertha and Maggie were "looked after" by Eugene Patrick Daly.

When the ship hit the iceberg she threw her coat over her nightdress and headed to the upper deck "with much difficulty," and secured a spot in Lifeboat 16. Sitting in the boat, she remembered she had left her picture of Irish Patriot Robert Emmet in her cabin. As she watched the Titanic go down, she said to herself, *"Good-bye, Robert."* Bertha and Maggie were eventually rescued by the *Carpathia.* Bertha's fiancé, Henry Noon, met her at the dock.

Father Thomas Byles, 42, was born in Yorkshire, England and raised in a protestant family, the son of Reverend Alfred Holden Byles. Many were shocked when he converted to Catholicism.

Father Byles was on board the Titanic enroute to New York to officiate at the wedding of his brother, William. When the ship struck the iceberg, Father Byles helped the third class passengers up the stairs and into lifeboats. Then he went to the "after-end" of the deck and heard over 100 confessions, and prayed the Rosary with those who were not able to find room in the boats. He was offered a seat in a lifeboat but refused.

Passengers who were lowered in lifeboats would later recall hearing the voice of Father Byles as he comforted the screaming passengers left behind.

Father Byles perished and his body was never recovered. His brother did not reschedule the wedding, but had another priest perform the ceremony. Following the wedding, the couple went home, changed in to mourning clothes, and then returned to the same church for a memorial mass for Father Byles.

Edward Ryan, 24, hailed from Croom, Co. Limerick and boarded the Titanic at Queenstown as a third class passenger. His destination was Troy, NY. On the night of the sinking Edward managed to sneak aboard Lifeboat 14 wearing a towel over his head. In a letter to his parents dated May 6, 1912 he stated, *"I stood on the Titanic and kept cool, although she was sinking fast. She had gone down about 40' by now. The last boat was about being rowed away when I thought in a second if I could only pass out (get in to the boat) I'd be alright. I had a towel round my neck. I just threw this over my head and left it hang in the back. I wore my waterproof overcoat. I then walked very stiff past the officers, who had declared they'd shoot the first man that dare pass out (get in to the boat). They didn't notice me. They thought I was a woman. I grasped a girl who was standing by in despair, and jumped with her 30' into the boat."*

It has been a matter of debate for years whether Edward intentionally passed himself off as a woman to gain a seat on the lifeboat.

Margaret Norton Rice, 40, was born in Westmeath, Ireland. She immigrated to Montreal, Quebec, Canada where she met and married William Rice when she was 19. Two of their five sons were born in Montreal.

In 1909 the family moved to Spokane, Washington, where William went to work for the Great Northern Railroad as a machinist. It was in Spokane where they would have three more sons. William was killed in a train accident, and Margaret used the substantial insurance settlement to return to Co. Athlone, Ireland with her five sons.

In 1912 she decided to move back to Spokane, and booked passage on the Titanic with her sons; Albert 10, George 9, Eric 7, Arthur 4, Eugene 2. After the collision, third class passenger Bertha Mulvihill recalled seeing Margaret Rice holding the youngest child, with the rest of the children clutching her skirt. The entire family perished. Margaret's body was recovered by the *MacKay-Bennett*. She was still holding her young son.

Josephine Agnus Connolly, 16, was born in 1896 in Kilcanavee, Kilmacthomas, Co. Waterford. One of the lucky ones, she was to have sailed on that fateful day, but last minute passport problems prevented her from boarding.

Her mother had insisted she go to America where she might continue her schooling past the 8th grade, which, in Ireland, was the mandatory end of a woman's education.

When Josephine, a devout Catholic, learned of the disaster, she truly believed God had saved her. With much trepidation, she eventually boarded the Olympic, sister ship to the Titanic, and made her way to New York. From there she traveled on to Oil City, Pennsylvania where her uncle, reneging on his promise to educate her, put her to work in his home.

After one year, Josephine escaped her servitude and made her way to Akron, Ohio where she found employment with Mina Miller, the mother-in-law of Thomas Alva Edison.

Josephine would eventually marry an Italian named Samuel Plazo, and together they would have seven children (and 35 grandchildren).

In the many years that followed the disaster, when someone would utter the once infamous phrase first coined by a White Star employee at Titanic's maiden voyage, "Not even *God* could sink the Titanic," Josephine would calmly reply, *"they never should have said that."*

Eamon de Valera
The Tall Fellow

"Just a line to say
a last good-bye.
I am to be shot for
my part in the Rebellion."

- DeValera in a letter to his friend, 1916

Edward de Valera was born in New York City on October 14, 1882 to Juan Vivion de Valera, a Spanish Cuban sugar planter, and Catharine Coll, a native of Bruree, Co. Limerick, Ireland. Juan Vivion de Valera was a musician who died at age 30, when Edward was only two years old.

According to author Tim Pat Coogan, Edward's mother wanted little to do with him. Five months after Juan's death, Catherine sent him to live with her uncle, Patrick Coll, in the family home in Knockmore, Bruree, Co. Limerick. This decision was made despite objections from Juan Vivion de Valera's father, who had traveled from Cuba to claim his grandson.

Catherine remained in America, became a domestic servant, and three years later married Charles Wheelwright, a coachman. They eventually had two children, Annie and Thomas. Even when she had a new home and family, she did not take Edward back.

On a typical evening in the house of his great-uncle, Edward would listen to long and impassioned arguments from visiting neighbors. He would hear discussions regarding such individuals as Charles Stewart Parnell, Healy, Gladstone, and Chamberlain. Eamon would also learn the Irish language from his grandmother, and from an old storyteller in Bruree.

Edward was encouraged by his great-uncle to read as much as possible. He read about Napoleon, the Scottish Chieftains, and the Spanish soldiers at Kinsale Bay (which strengthened his pride in his Spanish ancestry). He also learned about the great Irish warriors of old: Hugh O'Neill, Red Hugh, and Owen Roe. He was also bombarded with stories about English persecution of Irish people throughout the centuries.

Edward appeared to prefer life in boarding schools to living with his Mother's relatives. He attended Blackrock College in 1898, the centenary year of the "The Great Rising," and one of the more romantic periods in Irish history. The many centennial celebrations in Dublin did not go unnoticed by Edward; now called "Dev" by his friends.

He excelled in his studies, and was also a good athlete, often winning many running events. Some say he had a particular fondness for rugby. He was sometimes teased because of his tall, foreign appearance, but none-the-less, appeared to be well liked by his classmates. After he left Blackrock, he assumed a professorship position in mathematics and physics at Rockwell College, near Cashel. In 1904, while working at Rockwell, Edward graduated from Royal University with a degree in mathematical science at the age of 22.

The turning point for Dev was in 1908, when he joined the Gaelic League, Connaught Division. The Gaelic league was trying to rebuild Irish nationalism through teaching its members about the Irish language.

As Tim Pat Coogan writes, "everything else of importance which followed flowed from that decision: his marriage, involvement in revolution, and later, his political career." While others continued to debate the pro and cons of being a *Parnellite*, and drone on incessantly without any conclusion, de Valera chose the language classes and group discussions offered by the Gaelic League. What Sinn Fein was doing on the political side, the Gaelic League was doing in the cultural area.

Dev became so engrossed in the Irish culture that he enrolled as a student at the Leinster College of Irish. It was also about this time that he changed his name to the Gaelic version of Edward,

Eamon . While attending Leinster he met Janie O'Flanagan (Sinead ni Fhlannagain), a teacher and amateur stage actress. They were married in 1910 and would eventually have five sons and two daughters.

In 1913, the Ulster Volunteers were training in a blaze of publicity – drilling, parading, and forming corps of dispatch riders. The Irish Parliamentary leader, John Redmond, was not concerned about the armed Orangemen. However, Schoolmaster Padric Pearse, exclaimed, *"...personally, I think the Orangeman with a rifle (is) a much less ridiculous figure than a Nationalist without one."* This sentiment was echoed by fellow schoolmaster, Eamon de Valera.

Eventually the Irish Catholics; tired of Protestant forces drilling right in their faces, and sick of jobs going to Prods and not Catholics, had reached their boiling point.

According to M. J. MacManus, *"At the call of James Larkin, Dublin workers swarmed out of the slums to engage in unequal combat with the all powerful 'Federation of Employers.'"* There were strikes, lockouts, evictions, riots, and widespread hunger. In August, Larkin called upon the workers to arm. "What is legal for Carson and the Orangeman," he told them, "is legal for us." The response was immediate and enthusiastic. The British army decided to look the other way, and Irish "Citizen Army" was born.

At this time, however, there was no contact between the educated "collar and tie" class, to which Dev belonged, and the soldiers of The Citizen Army, who were comprised entirely of manual laborers.

Before the end of 1913, another army sprang in to existence. At a meeting held in Dublin in November, Eoin MacNeill, Professor of Ancient Irish in the National University and Vice President of the Gaelic League, organized a new body of volunteers. Its purpose was not to take hostile action against the Ulster Volunteers, but to establish themselves, more or less, as a challenge to the organized Orangemen.

Dev was one of the first to join the new body. Here, at last, was something more tangible that the conflicts of political warfare. The young men of the Gaelic classroom were getting together. Men who met on the hurling fields, who had read *Sinn Fein* each week; the same men who gathered in Tom Clarke's little shop on Parnell Street to hear the Separatist doctrine expounded; who had cheered Yeat's *Cathleen ni Houlihan* and Lady Gregory's *Rising of the Moon* at the Abby Theatre. Soon there were 150,000 of them, and at the top, were poets and professors and intellectuals. Behind the whole movement – watching, planning, and secretly directing – were the men of the Irish Republican Brotherhood.

Within a few months, Dev had attained the rank of captain. According to one of his contemporaries at that time, Dev was, "considerably over six feet in height, a very serious looking man in his early thirties, with a long nose and spectacles and a strangely foreign complexion."

The caldron, which had been bubbling since The Citizen Army was formed, began to boil over in 1914. 35,000 German rifles had been successfully smuggled in to the hands of The Citizen Army. The Nationalist Volunteers were still unarmed, but were busy collecting money and making plans to purchase weapons.

In July of 1914, the Volunteers marched from Dublin to Howarth, having just met the yacht *Asgard* in which Erskine Childers, his wife, and Mary Spring-Rice brought a cargo of rifles across the North Sea. This time the British did not look the other way. A column of British troops intercepted the Volunteers, and a scrimmage ensured in which both sides broke rank. One eyewitness described de Valera as "cool and resolute" during the fray.

A few days later, World War I broke out. It wasn't long before a split in the Volunteers occurred. The majority decided to join the British and fight for "right, religion, and freedom," and to defend Ireland from a possible invasion. The remaining Volunteers decided no blood should be shed for any cause other than Ireland. Before the war would end, more than 50,000 Irishmen would die fighting under the British flag.

Dev rose through the ranks of the Volunteers, and eventually was appointed Adjutant of the Dublin Brigade under Commandant Thomas MacDonagh. The two had common interests, and were both Gaelic Leaguers.

One night MacDonagh asked Dev to join the Irish Republican Brotherhood. Dev was hesitant at first, knowing the organization had been banned by the Catholic Church, but later agreed as long as he was asked only to take orders. Dev soon learned that from the moment World War I had broken out; a rising in Dublin had been planned. The only question was when?

James Connolly, hotheaded and impetuous, wanted immediate action, and had to be restrained from marching his Citizen Army to the mansion house during a British Army recruitment meeting. Roger Casement was in Germany looking for arms and attempting to form an Irish Brigade. There was constant communication with John Devoy and other friends of the movement in America. Easter Sunday, April 23, 1916 was finally selected as the date of the rising.

Unfortunately, the British captured Casement when the German submarine carrying him landed on the Kerry coast on Good Friday. Casement had been unable to organize an Irish Brigade comprised of prisoners of war, and was returning with only a single cargo of 20,000 rifles. On the same day, the German arms ship, which had been waiting in vain through out the previous night in Tralee Bay for a signal from the Irish shore, was captured by a British vessel and scuttled by its crew.

A party of volunteers had been dispatched from Dublin by motor car to contact the German ship, but the driver, mistaking the sea for a moonlight road, drove over the pier at Ballykissane. The driver escaped, but the passengers drowned.

Once again, on the eve of an Irish insurrection, everything had gone wrong. Much like Red Hugh's impetuosity at Kinsale; the contrary winds that impeded Wolfe Tone at Bantry Bay; and the plethora of blunders that affected Robert Emmet in 1803. But they had gone too far for the IRB to halt their plans.

Dev had been issued an order by Irish Volunteers Chief of Staff, Eoin MacNeill, to cease any actions of the part of the Volunteers. Dev received this order with a troubled mind.

In theory, Dev agreed with MacNeill that the Rising should be postponed, yet he knew the Rising was inevitable, as the IRB Revolutionary Council had already met and decided to strike at noon the following day. For Dev, that was sufficient.

Padriac Pearse, the leader of the IRB, was his Commander-in-chief and he would obey Pearse's orders, which he thought superseded MacNeill's. Therefore, if there were to be a Rising on Easter Monday, Dev would take part in it, no matter how slim the chances of success.

On Holy Thursday night he slept in his uniform with his revolver lying close to his bedside. Good Friday and Easter Sunday were full of last minute details. On Easter Sunday night, Dev returned home for a few hours, gazed upon his four sleeping children, and gave his wife no inkling of what was to come.

There was no longer a Volunteer Army or a Citizen Army; they had become one called the "Army of the Irish Republic." It was a pitifully small army. As it mobilized in the streets of Dublin that morning it numbered one thousand in all. Of number, fewer than a hundred were assigned to Commander de Valera. Dev and his men of the 3rd Battalion had been given the responsibility to delay the British reinforcements that would inevitably be dispatched from England once news of the Rising reached the authorities.

Dev stationed his men near Mount Street Bridge, placing handfuls of them in various houses, and the remainder stationed in Boland's Flour Mills, which was to be his headquarters. It was there he hoisted the Tricolor.

Once his headquarters were fortified, Dev told his men to get some sleep. Dev went from floor to floor inspecting the sentry posts. Dev didn't sleep much in the few days leading up the rising. He was afraid if he slept his men would desert their post, or fall asleep themselves.

Once he did find the posts deserted, and when he located the sentries they were on their knees in a hut saying the rosary, with their rifles stacked in a corner. Dev reprimanded them, stating there is a time for prayer and a time for duty! One of his men actually went mad waiting for the British to come and shot a comrade, and then was cut down in retaliation.

On Wednesday, the insurrection erupted in other parts of the city as British troops converged on the city from all sides. The British gunboat *Helga* steamed up the river and battered the walls of Liberty Hall. The upper story of the post office was wrecked and many buildings on O'Connell Street were set ablaze by shells fired from the *Helga.*

British troops had finally landed at Kingstown and were marching along the route held by Dev's men. His men had no military experience, but they held good positions, and the British "Sherwood Foresters" walked right in to a nest of Irish Volunteer snipers. The British retreated in confusion. Again and again they would attempt to march toward Haddington Road, but Dev's men beat them back by pouring volley fire in to their ranks.

Using a Gatling gun and hand grenades, the British eventually captured Mount Street Bridge as well as a house that contained most of the Irish Volunteer snipers.

As the fighting raged on the Irish began to lose ground. Communications with the General Post Office had been severed. Pearse had surrendered his sword, the Tricolor had been hauled down from Jacob's Factory, and Cathal Brugha (Charles Burgess) - wounded 17 times - was carried out of the South Dublin Union.

Still Dev's men of the 3rd Battalion continued to fight from the roofs, at barricades, and at street corners. Dev continued to issue orders, but he knew the end was in sight.

It was not until Sunday that the order to lay down arms reached Dev. He marshaled his 117 men, and spoke to them quietly for a few moments. He then marched them to the nearest military post. Leading the way was a Red Cross official carrying a white flag. They crossed Mount Street Bridge, where so many British soldiers had been gunned down by his men, along Northumberland Road

As he marched, Dev noticed Irish women offering tea and sandwiches to the British. He called out to them, "If only you had come out with knives and forks!" Dev approached the British officer in charge and spoke in a tired voice, "You may shoot me, but my men must not be molested when surrendering."

Dev was put on trial eleven days later and sentenced to death. From Kilmainham Jail, Dev wrote several letters. To "Frank," he wrote the following: *"Just a line to say a last good-bye. I am to be shot for my part in the Rebellion. if you can give any advice to Sinead and the little ones I know you'll try. Remember me to your wife, Mother, Aunt Stan, etc... Pray for my soul. DeV."*

Twelve executions had already taken place, and protests were beginning to be raised in the House of Commons and in the British and American press. Dev's mother was working feverishly to produce evidence of his American citizenship in hopes he would be spared from execution. It worked.

After the wounded Connolly was shot as he lay propped up in a chair, and Sean McDermott after he had limped from his cell to the prison yard, the executions ceased. De Valera's sentence was commuted to life in Dartmoor prison.

Six dreary months went by. Later, Dev was moved to Maidstone prison after organizing a short hunger strike. Before the year was out he was lodged in Lewes Jail, where all the convicted insurgents were concentrated. It wasn't long before Dev had the prisoners in revolt, rebelling against their "convict" status. They had demanded the rights afforded prisoners of war. When this was refused, they set out to trash the prison.

It was at this time that America entered World War I. The British Ambassador at Washington reported the effect of the Easter Week executions on opinion in America had been disastrous. "The Irish here have blood in their eyes when they look our way," he said. After some discussion, the British Prime Minister thought the English would look magnanimous to America, and especially the Irish-Americans, if they freed all Irish prisoners.

All night long crowds waited for the train containing the now free Irish prisoners to arrive at Kingstown. As they stepped from the train, a roar of cheering broke out, followed by the Soldier's Song. One tall, lanky figure seemed to attract the most attention. "There he is!" people shouted, "there is de Valera!" His fame at defending Boland Mills had spread abroad. The part he played in the fight for Irish freedom had made him famous; what he would do later would be him a legend.

Michael Collins
The Big Fellow

*"They wouldn't shoot
me in my own county."*

- Michael Collins responding to the threat of assassination

In the days preceding his own death, Michael Collins offered the eulogy for his friend, Arthur Griffith. Only after Collins was ambushed and killed a few days later, did those attending Griffith's funeral comprehend the words uttered by Collins and realize those words would come to apply to Collins as well: *"There seems to be a malignant fate dogging the fortunes of Ireland, for at every critical period in her story the man whom the country trusts is taken from her."*

Michael Collins was born on October 16, 1890 near Sam's Cross in West Cork, a small hamlet situated between Rosscarbery and Clonkilty. As soon as he appeared his Uncle Paddy exclaimed, *"Be careful of this child for he will be a great and mighty man when we are all forgotten."*

Michael's father, Michael John Collins, was 60 years old when he married a local girl, Marianne O'Brien. She was only 23. They were apparently happy and went on to have eight children.

Michael, the youngest, was born when his father was 75. Michael's father was a farmer, and the family lived comfortably on a holding of 90 acres they called "Woodfield" after a hill in the area. Even though there was much conflict between the Irish and English.

Michael's family lived a hard but comfortable life, considering what the average Catholic farmer had to endure at that time.

Michael Sr. had lived through the famine, joined the Fenians, and had a strong belief that the land should be owned by the Catholics. He instilled in his son not only the sad history of the Irish peasantry situation, but also the glory days of the Clan O'Coileain, formerly the lords of Ui Chonaill.

When Michael turned six years old his father died. On his deathbed, his father made his own prophecy about his son: *"One day he'll be a great man. He'll do great work for Ireland."*

According to author Tim Pat Coogan, the death of Michael Sr. left Michael without fatherly control and susceptible to outside influences. Michael attended national school at Lisavaird and fell under the tutelage of schoolmaster, Denis Lyons, who was also active in the Irish Republican Brotherhood, a secret organization dedicated to ousting the British from Ireland. Lyons had a tremendous influence on Collins. Over the years Collins would develop the attitude of the young rebels of the day: mild agnosticism, rejecting orthodoxy, and a love of advanced ideas.

Collins was sent to Clonkilty to study for the post office examinations. He lived with his sister, Margaret, whose husband owned a local newspaper called *West Cork People*. Collins helped out at the paper, learned to type, and wrote articles on sporting events.

In 1906, he passed the Post Office examination and moved to London to work for the Post Office Savings Bank in West Kensington. While in London, Collins aligned himself with the other Irish and joined the Gaelic Athletic Association, playing football and hurling. Collins refused to play soccer. There would be "no soccer for the Gaels," he would say…it was an English game. It became such an issue for the London Irish that the London GAA eventually split.

In 1909, Collins joined the Irish Republican Brotherhood (IRB), and as the years went by he rose in the organization. This was in contrast to his positions of lesser authority in the Post Office. None-the-less, he was adhering to the IRB's policy of infiltrating every possible branch of activity that might be of use to the Brotherhood.

Collins remained at the Savings Bank until 1910 when he moved to a stock brokerage company, Horne and Co., and was placed in charge of the messengers. He would eventually pass the civil service examinations and join the Board of Trade as a clerk in 1914.

Although history tends to portray Collins as a singled-minded, determined individual, he was also a young man in the big city for the first time. He drank, (but not to excess) fought and chased women...and the women seemed to be rather taken with him, although, some found his haughty attitude a bit cheeky. His "holier than thou" disposition would cause him to be known as *"the big fellow."* It wasn't, as most people assumed, for his size, but rather for his demeanor.

In 1916, Collins turned 26 years old. He had developed almost a dual reputation among the London-based Irish community. His enemies saw him as a hot-tempered fellow given to fits of fury. His friends viewed him much differently. When they looked at Collins they saw a generous man who was capable of great kindness.

By now Collins was growing uneasy. London-based Irish were fearful of conscription given the fact that, as residents of England, they were legally eligible to be drafted into the British Army during WW1...and they had no intention of fighting for England.

It wasn't long before the Irish Republican Brotherhood confirmed some long standing rumors...a rising in Dublin had been planned. Collins immediately resigned telling his employers he was going to *"join up."* They assumed he meant he was joining the British army. He had other plans.

On January 15, 1916 he crossed the Irish Sea to Dublin. The IRB assigned him to be Joseph Plunkett's "financial advisor" and "aide-de-camp." Plunkett was one of the main organizers of the pending rebellion. While the necessary amounts of men were being gathered for the uprising, which took some time, Collins went to work for the Plunkett family in their bookstore.

Historians are quick to point out the rising actually began to fall apart even before it began. The rebels knew this, but made the decision to proceed anyway hoping the rebellion would spark national pride that had been lagging for so many years.

On Easter Monday, April 24, 1916, another hopeless Irish rebellion would begin. After Padriac Pearse, Commander of the new Irish Republican Army (made up of the Volunteer Army and the Citizens Army of the Republic), read the proclamation of the Republic to a small crowd outside of the Dublin General Post Office, the rising was underway.

Most of Collins duties were in the operations room where the leaders laid out maps and plans. The battle against the British raged for several days and the rebels actually held out longer than expected.

The beginning of the end came days later when the British gunboat, "Helga," began to shell the General Post Office, which had to be evacuated. Collins was furious there had been no prearranged emergency escape plan out of the GOP. They were trapped.

According to Peter DeRosa, in his book, *Rebels*, Collins made up his mind that if he got out of this alive, he would never again *"be a duck in a British duck-shoot."* With his revolver in one hand, and his clothes singed by burning debris, Collins led his men across Moore Street toward temporary shelter. He soon discovered that the British had sealed off any escape routes. Collins was reported to have sat in a corner waiting for the end.

Eventually Collins and the other rebels laid down their arms when, on April 9, Pearse surrendered unconditionally and ordered a cease-fire.

The captured Volunteers were marched down O'Connell Street between a row of fixed bayonets, and endured the wrath of the Dublin citizens who had suffered because of the wide spread destruction.

The British soldiers mocked and harassed the rebels, forcing some to strip naked. Many of the rebellion's instigators had hoped to escape detection, thus avoiding trial and possible execution. However, Dublin Castle Inspectors usually spotted them.

One particular Inspector named "Burton" spotted Sean McDermott and pulled him out of line. With a sly grim he stated, *"You didn't really think you'd get away from me, did you?"* McDermott was later executed along with other rebel leaders. Collins was standing nearby and overheard the conversation. He swore one day he would take revenge on the Inspector for the execution of his friend and idol.

Collins escaped court-martial and execution because he was unknown to the Dublin Metropolitan Police detectives. He was eventually sent to Frongoch internment camp in Wales. It was at Frongoch that his flair for leadership first became visible, according to Edgar Holt, in his book, *Protest in Arms.* His fellow detainees soon found that he had a considerable talent for organizing resistance to unpopular orders.

In quieter moments, Collins went back to his study of the Gaelic language and Irish history. He was eventually released, along with the other detainees, in the summer of 1916 as there was no concrete evidence against them.

Collins was anxious to return home, but he returned to a different Dublin. The rebels, originally vilified by the public, were now seen as heroes. The many executions had so repulsed the Irish citizens they began to emphasize with their struggle, and to detest the British for executing fellow Irishmen.

Collins quickly revived the IRB and began a plan to achieve Irish independence. In the summer and fall of 1917 the Volunteers began to drill, and were often seen in public in their officially forbidden uniform. It was about this time that President of the Irish Republic, Eamon de Valera, and Collins began to have their philosophical differences. DeValera was Collins' superior, and had fought in the Easter Rebellion, but was saved from execution due to his American birth.

After the rising, deValera had chosen not to rejoin the IRB as he did not agree with their objectives. That was the beginning of the friction between him and Collins. Cathal Brugha (Charles Burgess), deValera's Minister for Defense in the Dail, also began to resent Collins' growing popularity and his influence over the Volunteers.

Collins had worked out a new constitution for the IRB, and was also secretary of the Irish National Aid Association which helped the dependents of the men killed in the Rising as well as imprisoned Sinn Feiners. Sinn Fein, meaning "Ourselves Alone," was a political party which espoused the ideas of the United Irishmen. These activities kept him somewhat apart from the main stream volunteer activities.

The first signs of division were becoming evident between the IRB men, who looked to Collins as their leader, and the Sinn Feiners led by Cathal Brugha and deValera. By 1917, Collins had achieved positions of high power in both Sinn Fein and the IRB.

Collins used his power to organize an intelligence network; begin an arms smuggling operation; secure a national loan to fund a rebellion; and start two underground newspapers.

He also created an assassination squad dubbed "The Twelve Apostles," or simply, "The Squad." These were twelve men who gave up their civilian occupations and devoted their whole time to the dangerous tasks that Collins assigned to them. These tasks included raids on small police barracks and the ambushing and killing of many Royal Ulster Constabulary men in Counties Clare and Tipperary.

Eventually, Britain had enough of these killings, and responded by recruiting a new version of the Royal Irish Constabulary. These were unemployed, battle-hard ex-British servicemen. There were nicknamed the "Black & Tans" because they wore dark-green (almost black) R.I.C. caps and khaki tunics and trousers. Eventually they were given the regular R.I.C. dark-green uniforms, and were no longer distinguishable from the other members of the forces, but the name stuck.

In due time the Black & Tans were accused of some of the most violent acts committed by the Crown forces in Ireland. They also showed they were adept at retaliating with their own brand of terror. They burned and looted public-houses, often drinking their loot. Private houses were also wrecked. The Tans terror grew more intense each month. Gun battles between British troops and Volunteers became commonplace in the Dublin streets.

The terror culminated on November 21, 1920 when Collins' squad assassinated 14 British officers, effectively destroying the British Secret Service. In retaliation, the Black and Tans fired on a crowd watching a football match at Croke Park, killing twelve people including one of the players.

By 1920, Collins was a wanted man. The British had placed a $10,000 reward for his capture. But due to the unavailability of good photographs, Collins was able to travel about Dublin on a bicycle, in view of the British Security Forces, the Royal Irish Constabulary, and the Black and Tans. He operated out of a number of offices in the city, moving only when capture became imminent.

Collins is most famous for masterminding the attack and reprisal method of guerilla warfare, which enabled small "flying columns" of men to strike at British targets and then vanish. Collins knew he could never defeat the British army in a traditional war, but he could chip away at their defenses and deplete their morale through bombings and assassinations.

By 1921 both sides were growing weary of the fighting. On July 12, Eamon deValera went to England to begin treaty talks with British Prime Minister Lloyd George. DeValera had hoped the conversation would lead to an Irish Republic. The talks did not go well, as George had no intention of conceding on the issue of an Irish Republic. Dejected, deValera returned to Ireland.

In September, deValera was elected President of the Irish Republic. He once again offered to negotiate as a representative of a sovereign state. George refused, stating he would only agree to peace talks if it included a process in which Ireland would join the British Empire. DeValera realized that he would not leave such a meeting achieving his goal of a Republic or united Ireland, so he refused to attend.

Instead, he ordered Arthur Griffith and Collins to head the Irish delegation. Both of the men objected, believing they were not capable of conducting such negotiations. Collins quipped that he was a soldier, not a politician.

This move by deValera has been scrutinized by historians for years. DeValera was an experienced negotiator, but he chose to send inexperienced men to parley with a far more experienced British team. This was probably the single worst decision deValera ever made.

Collins, like a true soldier, carried out the order, but dreaded the outcome. He stated, *"To me the task is a loathsome one. I go. I go in the spirit of a soldier who acts against his best judgement at the order of a superior."*

Under tremendous pressure, the Irish negotiating team pressed for a united Ireland. Britain refused anything less than dominion status. Collins eventually signed a treaty that gave Ireland a republic, excluding the North Eastern province of Ulster, which remained under complete British rule.

Collins knew the treaty would not be acceptable to many of his comrades in Ireland. But frustrated though he was, he felt this would bring Ireland closer to eventual total freedom. After signing the treaty, Collins was heard to say, "…I tell you, I have signed my own death warrant."

Upon his return to Ireland, deValera was furious at Collins for giving away Ulster. In protest, deValera resigned his presidency. Arthur Griffith was elected in his stead. A provisional government was formed in January 1922 and Collins was elected Chairman.

Now he and deValera, once friends and colleges, were on opposing political sides as a result of the treaty.

When word of the treaty reached Ireland, the tension between the pro-Treaty and anti-Treaty sides boiled over into complete civil war. Collins made every effort to avoid hostilities. He had no wish to fight with his former comrades-in-arms. But his efforts failed.

Anti-treaty IRA units (called "Irregulars") now led by deValera, immediately took over the Four Courts in Dublin in April. On June 28th, Pro-treaty Free State troops, now led by Commander-in-Chief of the Irish National Army, Michael Collins, began to bombard the building.

It took a week of intense fighting to dislodge the anti-Treaty forces. Before the 10-month war was over, Cathal Brugha would die, as would Collins' closest friend, Harry Boland, who has chosen the anti-treaty side.

Former comrades fought each other and families were split. Unfortunately, it is woven in the tapestry of Irish history that at a time when the Irish should unite against a common foe, they would rather fight amongst themselves.

The pro-treaty Provisional government began to retake cities and towns held by the anti-treaty Republicans. After much fighting, Collins and his better-equipped pro-treaty army had forced the Irregulars out of the main Irish cities and into the country.

In an effort to secure peace between the two factions, Collins decided to make a trip to Co. Cork. No one really knew the exact reason for Collins' trip. Many assumed he was there for peace talks. That might explain why Collins had such a small military escort while heading into strongly held Anti-Treat Republican territory. Collins' men advised him that such a trip was too risky. *"They wouldn't shoot me in my own county,"* he replied.

His escort consisted of a motor-cycle scout, followed by an open Crossley tender containing two former Squad men, Joe

Dolan and Sean O'Connell, and eight riflemen. The Collins party, foolish as it may seem, did nothing to play down their trip through Cork. The motorcycle-scout would often speed ahead and knock on doors saying, *"The Commander-in-Chief is coming."* Obviously, this was very provocative to the local anti-treaty men.

The Collins party stopped at a local public house to ask directions. Unfortunately, the seemingly friendly pub patron who gave them directions was also an Irish Republican Army sentry, who quickly reported to his superiors their prime target had just been spotted on the way towards *Bael na mBlath.*

The Anti-Treaty Irish Republican Army decided that an ambush would be laid at Bael na mBlath in hopes that Collins would return. The ambush party patiently waited. As the darkness set in, many of the ambushers began to give up and leave believing Collins had returned using another route.

Suddenly, Collins' convoy was spotted negotiating the narrow road through the glen. The handful of ambushers who stayed behind then opened fire. Startled, Emmet Dalton, who had been accompanying Collins, shouted at the driver to *"Drive like hell!"* Collins countermanded the order yelling, *"Stop! Jump out and we'll fight them!"*

The car screeched to a halt, and Collins leaped out with his rifle in his hand. The gun battle lasted ½ hour until the ambushers began to flee. Collins called out, *"Come-on boys, there they are, running up the road!"* He then left the shelter of his car and began to pursue the attackers. Now Collins was standing in the middle of the open roadway with no cover.

The shooting began to slacken when Dalton said he heard Collins cry out, *"Emmet!"* Dalton and Sean O'Connell ran from behind the cars to find Collins lying in the roadway, his head resting on his arms, and a gaping wound at the base of his skull behind his right ear.

Realizing the wound was very serious, O'Connell whispered the Act of Contrition into his ear. He thought Collins responded by a slight squeeze of his hand. He then dragged Collins across the road to shelter under the armored car. Dalton continued to fire on the fleeing ambushers, and then returned to Collins and bandaged his wound. But he soon realized it was futile. Collins was dead.

Quickly, the escort searched for a priest to perform the last rites of the Catholic Church. After locating a church, a priest was summoned. The priest looked in the car at the bleeding body, which was leaning against Dalton. Recognizing Collins, the priest turned on his heels and walked back inside the church. One of Collins men, infuriated at the affront, raised his rifle and fired at the priest. Dalton quickly knocked aside the gun barrel and the bullet missed its target.

Collins' men brought his body back to Cork where it was shipped to Dublin. His body lay in state for three days in the rotunda. Tens of thousands filed past his casket to pay their respects, and even more lined the streets of Dublin as the cortege made its way to Glasnevin for the burial.

Michael Collins may have been the "big fellow" in life, but true to Irish martyrdom, he became even larger in death.

Patrick Pearse
Rebel Poet

"...Life springs from death;
and from the graves of patriot
men and women spring living nations."

- Patrick Pearse, delivering the eulogy for O'Donovan Rossa

Like many of the revolutionaries of his day, Patrick Pearse was not a pureblood Irishman. He was born in Dublin to James Pearse, an English stone carver, and Margaret Brady, whose family had fled the famine in Co. Meath.

James did well for himself, thanks to the Gothic revival in architecture, and spent much of his time embellishing Catholic edifices. This allowed the family to live comfortably, and afforded Patrick, and his brother Willie, to be educated at the Christian Brothers School. It was there Patrick received his first classes in the Irish language.

In 1895, while still a teenager, he joined the Gaelic League which had begun to revive the Irish language and literature. Pearse eventually taught Irish at Westland Row, and later graduated from Royal University of Ireland.

After graduation in 1901 he was called to the bar, but never practiced, with the exception of one case in 1905 which involved whether it was "legal" to paint Irish names on the sides of carts.

In 1908, along with friends Thomas MacDonagh, Con Colbert, and his brother, Willie, he founded an Irish language school called St. Edna's at Cullenwood House in Rathmines outside Dublin. The curriculum of the Irish school would not only be the Irish language, but also chivalry, self-sacrifice, *"... charity towards all," "...a love of inanimate nature,"* and, *"a sense of civic social duty. "* He wished that all the youth of Ireland would, *"...spend their lives working hard and zealously for their fatherland and, if it should ever be necessary, to die for it. "*

Over the years, Pearse would devote himself to the revival of the Gaelic language. According to author John L. Murphy, *"all other issues for Pearse at this stage, became secondary to cultural nationalism. "*

Emigration had drained Ireland of its Irish-speaking natives; and the Queen's English was becoming more prevalent. Those who still spoke Gaelic were looked upon as poor and ignorant, not unlike the Native Americans in the USA. Pearse was determined, through prose and poetry, to revive the native Irish language and thought, and to rediscover what he idealized as *"kindly faced, frieze-coated peasants. "* He wanted to master, not the adopted tongue of Dublin revivalists, but rather the Connaught dialect itself.

Through his pen, he was becoming more radical in his view of Irish independence, transforming himself from a supporter of "Home Rule" to an outright Republican.

In 1913, he was one of the founders of the Irish Volunteers, a native Irish militia that would eventually become the Irish Republican Army.

That same year Pearse also joined the Irish Republican Brotherhood. While the IRB and other labor movements attracted Pearse's nationalism, he did not agree with socialist views.

Later, Pearse would organize a secession faction of volunteers which split with John Redmond's Home Rule party after Redmond called for Irish support of the English war effort.

In the summer of 1915, the body of Fenian Jeremiah O'Donovan Rossa was brought home from America for burial. At Dublin's famous Glasnevin cemetery, Pearse delivered one of the most famous graveside orations in the history of the Irish revolutionary movement. *"But I hold it a Christian thing, as O'Donovan Rossa held it, to hate evil, to hate oppression, and hating them, to strive to overthrow them, "* said Pearse. *"...*

Life springs from death; and from the graves of patriot men and women spring living nations. " Pearse ended his oration by reminding all that *"while Ireland holds these graves, Ireland, unfree, shall never be at peace."*

With England preoccupied with World War I, Pearse and the other rebels decided the time was right for an armed insurrection. They hoped their rebellion would spark a national uprising of Irish citizens.

So on Easter Monday, April 24, after reading the proclamation by "the Provisional Government of the Irish Republic" (Poblacht na h-Eireann) on the steps of the Post Office, Pearse took command of the "operations" in the heart of Dublin. As he prepared for war, Pearse must certainly have thought of the poem he previously wrote entitled, *Christmas 1915*:

"O King that was born,
To set bondsmen free,
In the coming battle,
Help thy Gael!"

For the next two days he and his men defended their position from British reinforcements and looting slum-dwellers. However, by the second day it was apparent no national rebellion would occur, and Pearse and the rest of the rebels were all alone.

As the British army closed in on the Republican positions, Pearse spoke of his vision: *"when we are all wiped out, people will blame us for everything, condemn us...but in a few years they will see the meaning of what we tried to do."* By the fifth day, Pearse gave the order to surrender the General Post Office, and on Saturday a general surrender drew an end to the Rising. Patrick's brother, Willie, carried out the white flag.

All of the rebel leaders were court-martialed in kangaroo courts made up of three British officers. The defendants had no lawyers to represent them, and were not allowed to call any witnesses.

To no one's surprise, the court found every defendant guilty, and condemned them to death. During his very brief trial, Pearse told the court, *"You cannot conquer Ireland. You cannot extinguish the Irish passion for freedom. If our deed has not been sufficient to win freedom, then our children will win it by a better deed."*

Later at a dinner party, General Blackadder, who was in charge of the trials, told a friend, *"I have just performed one of the hardest tasks I ever had to do. Condemned to death one of the finest characters I ever ran across. A man named Pearse. Must be something very wrong in the state of things, must there not, that makes a man like that a rebel?"*

From his cell at Kilmainham jail, Pearse continued to write. His letters and poems recorded his devotion to a free and Gaelic Ireland. He also wrote one last letter to his mother stating, *"I will call you in my heart at the last moment."*

Father Aloysius, who was attending the men, gave Pearse at ten-inch brass crucifix to carry with him. As Pearse walked to his execution, he heard two volleys of shots, and he knew that fellow rebels Tom Clark and Tom MacDonagh were dead.

Blindfolded, Pearse was escorted to the prison wall to be shot. At the same time, his brother Willie was being led to the jail to wait his turn. A sympathetic British soldier escorting Willie decided to allow the brothers to say their last farewells. But as he led Willie to where Patrick had been standing, the soldier heard the sound of volley-fire. *"Too late,"* said the guard as he realized that Patrick had just been executed, and he turned Willie around and headed back towards the jail.

Fortunately, no one had told Willie that he was being taken to see his brother one last time, or that the sound of rifle-fire marked the end of his brother's life. Willie would be shot the next day. The brothers were buried in quick lime in Arbour Hill.

St. Edna's remained in operation until 1935 run by Pearse's mother and sister, yet it never achieved the lofty goals set by its founder.

Years later, Michael Collins would criticize Pearse and others for too many words and not enough action. However, Collins would be stirred to action by the failed rebellion. Using fewer proclamations, and less eloquence, Collins would lead his "Flying Columns" to fight a guerrilla war against the English.

While Pearse failed to revive a Gaelic nation, he certainly succeeded in ensuring that *"my fame and my deeds live after me."*

Countess Markievicz
Irish Revolutionary

*"Nature should provide me
with something to live for,
something to die for."*

- **Countess Markievicz**

Sometimes in life, people who are not directly affected by adversity seem destined, for whatever reason, to take up the banner for the downtrodden. That was the case with once of the more colorful rebels in Irish history, Constance Gore-Booth.

She was born February 4, 1868 at Buckingham Gate, London. Constance grew up in Lissadell, on the West Coast of Ireland. Her father, Sir Henry Gore-Booth, was an explorer and philanthropist with a large estate in Lissadell, Co. Sligo.

Despite being born in to a rich Anglo-Irish family, Constance and her sister, Eva, were often taught concern for the plight of the poor dispossessed families along the West Coast. Constance remembered watching the prosperous Protestant farmers with their Scottish names and comparing their lot with the dispossessed Irish-Catholics in their miserable huts. Constance and her sister performed numerous charitable acts for the less fortunate.

Constance and Eva were quite lovely. Sarah Purser immortalized their beauty in a painting, and in poem by William Butler Yeats who was a frequent guest at their estate:

*"The light of evening, Lissadell,
Great windows open to the south,
Two girls in silk kimonos, both
Beautiful, one a gazelle.*

Constance once said of her upbringing in Lissadell, *"We lived on a beautiful, enchanted West Coast, where we grew up intimate with the soft mists and colored mountains, and where each morning you woke to the sound of the wild birds....No one was interested in politics in our house. Irish history was also taboo, for 'what is the use of grieving over past grievances?'"*

In 1887, Constance and Eva were presented at the court of Queen Victoria, in the standard coming of age ritual of the ruling class. Constance was often referred to as "the new Irish beauty."

But Constance was not content to be an ornament, so she traveled to London in 1893 to study art at the Slade School. Then, in 1898, she left for Paris where she attended the Julian School. It was there she met Count Casimir Dunin Markievicz of Poland, an artist from a wealthy family that owned land in the Ukraine. Markievicz was younger, a Catholic, and already married with a son, but his wife was back in the Ukraine and seriously ill. In 1899 she died, and Casimir and Constance were married on September 29, 1901. "Countess Markievicz" then settled in to a life of art and literature.

In 1901 their daughter, Mauve, was born. She would be raised by her grandparents and eventually become estranged from her mother.

In 1903 the Count and Countess moved to Dublin where Constance began making a name for herself as a landscape artist. The couple also became involved in the Dublin social scene. Together they founded the United Arts Club in 1905 to help bring together people of the artistic renaissance. But Constance was still searching for a cause to champion. *"Nature should provide me with something to live for, something to die for, "* she would say.

Then in 1906 something occurred that would change her life. She rented a cottage in the Dublin hills. The previous tenant was Padraic Colum, a poet, and he had left behind old copies of the revolutionary publications "The Peasant" and "Sinn Fein." After reading these, Constance knew she had found her cause. At 36 years of age, and sheltered by her wealthy upbringing, she never realized there were people in Ireland who actually opposed the authority of the British crown.

By 1908 Constance had immersed herself in the theatre, the main path from which the "Inghinidhe na hEireann" (Daughters of Erin) could effectively educate.

She also joined "Bean na hEireann" (an early manifestation of "Cumann na mBan") and lectured to the group that, *"a free Ireland with no sex disabilities in her constitution should be the motto of all nationalist women."*

She prepared women for the battle she knew was coming by telling them they should, *"get away from wrong ideals and false standards of womanhood...we have got to get rid of the last vestige of the harem before woman is free as our dream of the future would have her."*

Constance would also join Sinn Fein, and became a familiar sight at nationalist demonstrations and suffragist rallies.

She went to Manchester, England in 1908 and ran for office with the help of her sister, Eva, who was deeply involved in social reform there. It was no surprise that Constance lost, given her radical politics, the prevailing attitude towards women at the time, and the fact that her opponent was a young Winston Churchill.

In 1909 she founded "Fianna Eireann," named after Finn's legendary warrior band. Her organization, which was similar to the Boy Scouts, began teaching young boys military drill and the use of firearms. Padraic Pearse would say that without Fianna Eireann, *"the Volunteers of 1916 would not have arisen."*

In 1911, Constance became an executive member of both Inghinidhe and Sinn Fein. She would go to jail for the first time for taking part in a demonstration against the visit of George V. Constance.

She also involved herself in the labor unrest of the time, running a soup kitchen during the lockout of union workers in 1913 and supporting labor leaders James Larkin and James Connolly.

All this political activity took a toll on her family. Her daughter was being raised by her own mother, and Casimir eventually left for the Balkans where he served as a war correspondent, and later joined the Imperial Russian cavalry during World War I. Casimir's departure allowed Constance to immerse herself fully in the nationalist movement. Soon she was taking rifle practice, determined to be as good as any of the men.

As World War I began, Dublin became a pressure cooker of social and political upheaval. Home rule had been promised by the English then put on indefinite hold. Irish boys who volunteered to fight for Great Britain were dying by the thousands on the Western Front, and in England there was talk of conscripting Irishmen.

The pot boiled over on April 24, 1916 when Irish rebels seized the General Post Office, as well as other areas of Dublin. Assembling at Liberty Hall before noon, Padraig Pearse, Commandant and Chief of the Army of the Republic and President of the Provisional government, cycled to the meeting.

He wore the green uniform of an Irish Volunteer, a South African-style slouch hat, and a sword. Connolly and Clarke were there, as was Joseph Plunkett, dying of tuberculosis, and wearing bandages on his throat the result of an ineffective surgery.

Sean MacDiarmada was there, leaning on his cane, partially crippled from childhood polio. And the Countess was there. While most women during the uprising participated as nurses or by running messages through the streets, Constance was second in command to Michael Mallin of Connolly's Citizen Army. She was dressed in a green blouse, knee britches, an ammunition belt, and the same style of slouch hat as Pearse, only her hat had feathers.

She supervised the setting up of barricades as the rising began and was in the thick of the fighting all around St. Stephen's Green. At one point, when a young girl was wounded by several British bullets and undergoing surgery, Markiewicz left the room, returning in a minute to tell her, *"Don't worry, Margaret, my dear, I got the wretched blighter for you."*

The story of the failed rebellion has been told and retold. Plunkett planned on 5,000 rebels, but only 1,000 showed up.

The rebellion was only a few hours old when the countess spotted several British soldiers outside the rebel emplacement. She leveled her rifle and fired. Two men fell to the ground. After holding the St. Stephens Green for six days, the rebels were forced to retreat to the Royal College of Surgeons.

The retreat did nothing to dampen the Countess's enthusiasm. *"We've done more than Wolfe Tone already!"* she told her troops.

Eventually, the undermanned, under-equipped rebel force was beaten, and they were forced to evacuate the burning General Post Office on Friday, April 28. Pearse ordered total surrender on Saturday, April 29.

A young woman from Cumann na mBan was sent to the College of Surgeons to alert the rebels of the surrender. The Countess was stunned. *"We could hold out for days here. Let's die at our posts!"*

Despite her boast, she finally acquiesced. The English officer who accepted their surrender was Capt. Wheeler, a distant relative of Markievicz. He offered to drive her to jail. *"No offence, old feller, but I much prefer to tag along with my own,"* she replied.

The rebels had held out for 6 days, the longest stretch of fighting since 1798. Sixty-four rebels, 130 British soldiers and police officers, and more than 300 civilians died. Hundreds more were wounded. The heart of Dublin was a smoking ruin. Three-thousand people, including 79 women, were arrested. Many had nothing to do with the rebellion. There either looked suspicious or were just in the wrong place at the wrong time

As the Countess was marched to jail at the head of her small command, she heard shouts of "mad dogs" and "shoot the traitors." The citizens of Dublin were furious at the rebels for shutting down their city for a week. Many who had relatives fighting overseas saw the rebellion as a traitorous act.

They rebels were taken to Dublin Castle and from there the Countess was transported to Kilmainham Jail. She was the only one of 70 women prisoners who was placed in solitary confinement. She fully expected to be executed. On May 3rd she sat in her cell and listened to the volley fire of the first round of executions, each followed by a single shot as the commander of the firing squad put a single bullet in their heads.

At her trial she told the court, *"I did what was right and I stand by it."* She was sentenced to death, but General Maxwell commuted this to life in prison on "account of the prisoner's sex." She told the British officer who brought her the news, *"I do wish your lot had the decency to shoot me."*

Countess Markievicz was released from prison during the General Amnesty of 1917. Soon afterwards she kept a promise she made to herself during the uprising and converted to Catholicism.

Her revolutionary fire still burning, she was jailed in 1918 by the British during an imaginary "German Plot," aimed at defeating the anti-conscription forces in Ireland. She was sent to Holloway prison along with Maud Gonne, and Mrs. Tom Clarke.

While in prison, her name was placed as a Sinn Fein candidate for the St. Patrick's Division in Dublin. She became the first woman elected to the British Parliament, running as a Sinn Fein candidate. Like Sinn Fein candidates before her, she did not take her seat, refusing to take an oath of allegiance to the King.

Sinn Fein decided to boycott the British Parliament and form its own Dail Eireann. Constance claimed her seat, this time as Minister for labor in Eamon DeValera's first cabinet.

When the treaty was signed, Ireland became divided. She would go to jail twice more during the course of the Anglo-Irish War of Independence, and was released from jail to attend the Anglo-Irish Treaty debates.

She strongly opposed the treaty and had an angry exchange with Michael Collins the day the anti-treaty forces walked out of the hall. She called the pro-treaty advocates *"traitors."* Collins replied by using an even worse label...he called her *"English."*

When the civil war broke out, Constance again took up arms under Oscar Traynor, and later Cathal Brugha (Charles Burgess) and helped defend Moran's Hotel. Later she toured the U.S. raising funds for the Republican cause.

After the Civil War, she regained her seat in the Dail, but her Republican politics ran afoul of the Free State government, and in 1923 she was jailed for a fifth time. This time she was taken to a seldom-used Dublin workhouse where, along with 92 other women prisoners, she went on hunger strike, calling it off only after orders from her superiors.

By 1926, her sister, Eva, had died, worn out by her many pacifist causes. Constance herself was growing weary, but she continued to fight on, drilling her Fianna boys and working for Eamon DeValera's Fianna Fail party.

When the winter brought a coal strike, she trudged up and down tenement stairs to bring food, fuel, and necessities to the impoverished Dubliners. By now, she had little more than they did. It was said she knew how to delegate authority, but she could never delegate kindness. For this reason, the poor of Dublin called her "Madame."

Constance died on July 15, 1927 in the public ward of Sir Patrick Dunn's Hospital with her family in attendance. She thought she had appendicitis; others believed it was cancer. Many thought it was due to overwork and exhaustion.

The City of Dublin gave her a huge funeral and 300,000 people lined the streets of Dublin to say farewell. Eamon deValera gave the graveside eulogy, while her beloved Fianna boys stood guard.

The Banshee:

Foreteller of Doom

In some parts of Leinster,
it has been said her wail can
be so piercing it shatters glass.

- Leinster Folklore

Most Baby-Boomers can recall the first time they saw a Banshee…even if they weren't exactly sure what it was. It was in the 1959 Disney film, "Darby O'Gill & the Little People." A fun but stereotypic Irish flick starring a very young actor named Sean Connery.

In one of the more intense scenes, the Banshee arrives, shrouded in a black cape, combing her long, silver hair, and emitting loud, devilish wailings as she floats through the air terrorizing the people below. She manifested in order to warn a family of the impending death of a young woman. Whether she was there to warn the family or take the woman's soul is debatable.

The floating Disney apparition terrified children only slightly less than the Wizard of Oz's "Wicked Witch of the West."

The shadowy imagine that scared the bejeezes out of children was a *Bean Sidhe* (Banshee). The term is an anglicization of the Irish *bean sí*, or the Scots Gaelic *bean shìth*, - both meaning "woman of the fairy mounds."

She was a supernatural being from ancient Celtic folklore whose mournful crying, or "keening," at night was believed to foretell the death of a member of the family. If you heard the wailing, someone in your family would die very soon, or perhaps suffer a most terrible fate. Either way…it wasn't good.

In some parts of Leinster, it has been said her wail can be so piercing it shatters glass. In Kerry, the keen is a "low, pleasant singing," whereas on Rathlin Island in Co. Antrim, it sounds like, "a thin, screeching sound somewhere between the wail of a woman and the moan of an owl."

According to Irish lore, each family of ancient Milesian stock had their own private Banshee who warned them each time a member of the family was about to die. Sort of like having your own private ghost.

It is said this solitary fairy-woman forewarned only those of the five major Irish families: the O'Neills, the O'Briens, the O'Connors, the O'Gradys and the Kavanaghs;

In any event, she heralds the demise of only those who are of noble lineage, and it is with great dread when her piercing keening is heard.

Intermarriage has since extended this select list to many, many families of Irish descent, and she has followed the old race across the ocean to distant lands. It is said her mournful wails can be heard in the United States, England, Canada, Australia, or wherever the Irish have emigrated.

In many respects, this mysterious creature resembles traditional Irish mourners of old (i.e. the "Keeners"). Those who have seen her describe the spirit as drawing a comb slowly through her hair, similar to tearing the hair out in anguish, which the ancient mourners used to do.

The comb is related to the centuries-old Irish tale that if you ever see one lying on the ground you must never pick it up. If you do, the banshees - having placed it there to lure unsuspecting humans - will spirit you away.

Apparently the manifestation of the Banshee usually happens thusly: when a member of the family is dying, the night before the death, the Banshee will wail piteously in frustration and rage. The family she has come to visit will always hear her, as would others in the area. It's a rather blood-curdling experience for those who have the misfortune to be in the vicinity.

The creature will pace the dark hills above the soon-to-be-departed's house. Her appearance sharply contrasts against the black night – and her white figure emerges with silver-grey hair streaming to the ground. A grey-white cloak of a cobweb texture clinging to her tall thin body. Her face is pale, her eyes red with centuries of crying for all the Irish dead.

The creature can appear in one of three guises: a young woman, a stately matron, or a raddled old hag. These represent the triple aspects of the Celtic goddess of war and death, namely *Badhbh, Macha* and *Mor-Rioghain*. She usually wears either a grey, hooded cloak or the winding sheet or grave robe of the dead.

One of the largest reports of this wailing was in 1938, when the Giants' Grave in County Limerick, Ireland, was excavated and the bones were moved to a nearby castle. Those who heard the crying throughout central Ireland said that it sounded as if every Banshee in Ireland was keening.

The wailings of many Banshees in unison is unusual, but not unique. There have been other reports of several Banshees manifesting together which usually forecasts the dramatic illness - and perhaps death - of a major religious or political figure.

In Irish mythological history, the Banshee tradition may link to the fierce Morrighan as the "Washer at the Ford," a legend of Cuchulain. In this story, the Morrighan appeared as a young woman who prepared for an upcoming battle by washing the clothing--or perhaps the shrouds--of those who would fight and die.

"Then Cuchulain went on his way, and Cathbad that had followed with him. And presently they came to a ford, and there they saw a young girl thin and white-skinned and having yellow hair, washing and ever washing, and wringing out clothing that was stained crimson red, and she crying and keening all the time. 'Little Hound,' said Cathbad, 'Do you see what it is that young girl is doing? It is your red clothes she is washing, and

*crying as she washes, because she knows you are going to your
death against Maeve's great army.'"*

--"Cuchulain of Muirthemne."

In 1437, King James I of Scotland was approached by a
banshee who foretold his murder orchestrated by the Earl of
Atholl. This is an example of the banshee in human form. There
are records of several human banshees, or prophetesses, visiting
the great houses of Ireland, and the courts of local Irish kings As
per usual, it is followed shortly by some form misfortune in that
particular family.

Most people don't believe in ghosts, vampires, or the bad
luck caused by broken mirrors. But then again, they aren't
foolish enough to tempt fate either.

If one is unfortunate enough to hear the wail of Banshee late
at night, it is a good idea to run like mad in the other direction...
and then pray she hasn't come for you.

Maureen O'Hara
Wild Irish Rose

"O'Hara? She's the greatest guy I ever knew."

- John Wayne, when asked about his relationship with Maureen

Forget Betty Grable. In 1959 the National Association of Hosiery Manufacturers awarded Maureen O'Hara the title of *"the most beautiful legs in America."* Just another of the many accolades that O'Hara would gather in her long and illustrious career that would transport her from a Dublin suburb to the glamour of Hollywood.

Maureen FitzSimons (not Fitzsimmons!) was born on August 17, 1920, in the village of Ranelagh, near Dublin. She was the second of six children born to Charles FitzSimons and Marguerite Lilburn. Her mother operated a chic couturier salon adjacent to the Shelbourne Hotel, and was an accomplished contralto.

Maureen's father was a clothier in Dublin who had part ownership in an Irish soccer team called the "Shamrock Rovers." Her older sister, Peggy, who Maureen called *"the pretty one,"* would become a Sister of Charity nun, after refusing a singing scholarship to La Scala in Milan. The rest of the children (Florrie, Margaret, James, Charles), including Maureen, were encouraged to participate in the performing arts and were given lessons in singing, dancing, elocution, and deportment.

Her first love was soccer, so playing the role of the prim and proper little girl was not to her liking. Her mother would often dress Peggy and Maureen in matching outfits. However, since Peggy was tall and willowy, it only emphasized the fact that Maureen was *"roly-poly,"* according to O'Hara.

One day two teachers looked at her little tummy and asked her is she was hiding a football. Maureen became so enraged at the comment that she blurted out, *"You two old biddies, one of these days you're going to boast that I was in your class and that you were my teachers!"* It was during such encounters that she learned to be self-assured, determined, and confident. She often said that playing outdoors with her brothers also gave her the ability to hold her own.

Still in her early teens, she studied at the London School of Music, and the London College of Music and Drama (and earned an ALCM degree) Later she auditioned and was accepted into Dublin's prestigious Abbey Theatre School when she was only 14. However, her father didn't believe that acting was a very practical career. So at his insistence, she enrolled in secretarial and bookkeeping courses at "Miss Galway's Business School." Maureen once boasted a shorthand and typing speed of 90 words per minute.

While at the Abby Theatre she was offered a screen test in London. According to Maureen, the experience was a fiasco. Charles Laughton viewed the screen test and concurred; however when she turned a certain way he noticed her profile, and then her eyes. Immediately he asked his partner, Eric Pommer, to view the test. He agreed with Laughton, the screen test was horrible. Regardless, Laughton saw something in her and signed her to a seven-year contract with the newly formed "Mayflower Pictures." Since she was only 17 at the time, the contract was signed by her parents and witnessed by a local parish priest. This contract marked the official start of her movie career.

Laughton then starred her in his London film, *Jamaica Inn,* (directed by Alfred Hitchcock). Laughton was so impressed with his young protégé that he brought Maureen to America to star with him in *The Hunchback of Notre Dame.*

Before the filming of *Hunchback,* Laughton had insisted Maureen change her name from Maureen FitzSimons to Maureen O'Hara. FitzSimons was much too large for the marquee.

Maureen didn't like the idea one bit and *"fought like mad."* But eventually she capitulated. She was under contract to Laughton and had little say in the matter. After viewing *Hunchback*, New York Times film critic Bosley Crowther wrote: *"She is like the emerald shower which succeeds the initial explosion of a skyrocket."*

Due to her stellar performance in *Hunchback*, RKO purchased her contract. With Hollywood as her new direction, she was cast as "Angharad" in John Ford's *How Green Was My Valley*. Those who failed to notice her in *Hunchback* couldn't help but be mesmerized by her performance in *How Green Was My Valley*.

It wasn't long before O'Hara would become one of Hollywood's favorite leading actresses, and one of its highest paid stars. In 1942, just before she made *The Black Swan* with Tyrone Power, she signed a $200,000 per year, seven-year contract. It was one of the biggest contracts in Hollywood at that time.

Despite the high salary, Maureen wasn't thrilled with being bound by such a contract. *"We had to do what we were told,"* said O'Hara. *"If you didn't...you were suspended...(and) put off salary for the entire time it took to replace you and make the film. Who would pay your grocery bills? So many films we made crying in our heart as we went to work every day."*

Throughout the 1940s and 50s she appeared in several action films, but was best known for her color swashbuckler films such as *At Sword's Point, The Black Swan, Against All Flags*, and *Sinbad the Sailor*. Her athletic ability, and her character's willingness to stand up to any man, made her wildly convincing as a female swashbuckler. She also filmed *Miracle on 34th Street*, which remains a Christmas classic.

The 1940s also saw the innovation of color movies which showed off Maureen's red hair and brilliant hazel eyes. So much so that she was dubbed, *"The Queen of Technicolor."* In fact, the inventor of the Technicolor process, Herbert Kalmus, was so taken with how well O'Hara's beauty and coloring enhanced his product, that he would send her a bouquet of multi-colored roses after she completed filming each new Technicolor movie.

It's hard to believe that the studio once recommended she color her hair (and even undergo rhinoplasty). During the 40's she married Will Price, and had her only child, Bronwyn Brigid, who was born in 1944. Unfortunately, her marriage to Price ended in 1952 due to his alcoholism and physical abuse.

In the 1950s she continued in her swashbuckler roles and began doing rollicking westerns as well. During the filming of *Rio Grande* on location in Moab, Utah, Harry Carey Jr. once remarked, *"She was so gorgeous. It took your breath away to see her every morning."*

Because of her own athletic prowess, Maureen developed a healthy respect for stuntmen. Chuck Roberson, John Wayne's stuntman for more than 30 years, referred to her as *"My little Irish stunt girl"* and once stated, *"Wet or dry, Maureen O'Hara was one of the best looking women I ever had the pleasure of knowing, and more than that, she was a damn fine stuntman in her own right."*

During the 60s Maureen moved in to more maternal roles in *The Parent Trap*, *McLintock!*, and *The Rare Breed*, the last two directed by Andy McLaglen, son of veteran character actor Victor McLaglen. At the time, she did not realize that her last movie with John Wayne would be *Big Jake*.

In 1968 she had met and married Charles Blair, a famous pilot and family friend. Blair had also become good friends with John Wayne. Once when Wayne was visiting, he and Charlie were playing chess…and hatching a plot. It was at that time that the two most important men in her life approached Maureen and said, *"Don't you think it's about time you stayed home?"* Both were expecting an argument from her, but she replied, *"Fine…I quit."* She then happily settled in to life as Ms. Blair, full-time wife.

The Blairs retired to the Virgin Islands in 1973 where Charles owned and operated the airline *Antilles Air Boats*, and published a magazine entitled, "The Virgin Islander." Together they ran the company until Charlie was tragically killed in an air crash in 1979, off the coast of St. Thomas.

This was particularly devastating for Maureen who was recovering from cancer surgery at the time. With little time to grieve, Maureen quickly assumed control of his airline, becoming the first female president of a scheduled airline in aviation history. Eventually she sold the airline, as she and Charles had planned, to focus on her other interests.

When Maureen arrived in Hollywood, John "Pappy" Ford claimed her as his prime "Rosebud." A name he bestowed upon the elite group of actresses who appeared in his films. She soon joined the unofficial "John Ford Stock Company," a group of actors who Ford molded to their full potential.

The most famous of the group was John Wayne, who Ford discovered while Wayne was attending college at USC and working as a 3rd assistant prop man at the studio. They were a tremendously talented group of professionals who were tough enough to deal with Ford's eccentricities, and smart enough to recognize his genius. Those lucky enough to join his "stock" company, besides Wayne and O'Hara, were: Ward Bond, Victor McLaglen, Mildred Natwick, Ben Johnson, Harry Carey, Jr., Chill Wills, John Agar, Paul Fix, Grant Withers, Anna Lee, and Jack Pennick. A plethora of stuntmen were also added to the company including the famous Yakima Canutt.

Ford was a character, and often delighted in toying with reporters. His biggest yarn surrounded his actual name. He would tell reporters his real name was either Sean O'Fienne or Sean Aloysius O'Fearna. At other times he would state he was born John Martin Feeney. (Maureen claims his full name was "Sean Aloysius Kilmartin O'Fearna.") His older brother, Francis Ford, had entered the movie business, and as John followed he took his brother's adopted name of "Ford." Therefore Sean O'Fienne (O'Fearna), or John Feeney, became John Ford. Is any of it true? Perhaps, but with Ford you never knew.

The Quiet Man began as a short story written by Maurice
Walsh, which originally appeared in the Saturday Evening Post
in 1933. The lead character was a quiet inconspicuous fellow
named Shawn Kelvin, who didn't like to draw attention to
himself. The lovely lass, with whom he eventually fell in love,
was a rather timid woman named Ellen O'Grady.

In the script-writing process, screenwriter Frank Nugent
transformed these rather retiring main characters into the
stoic and brave Sean Thorton, and the fierce and fiery Mary
Kate Danaher. Only the bullying brother remained relatively
unchanged, although "Big Liam O'Grady" had become "Red
Will Danaher."

Shawn/Sean would remain a "Quiet Man," but in the hands
of John Ford the character would represent silent strength, with
hidden fears and desires. He was quiet, but full of secrets. Nugent
had taken a rather touching story about a man who returns to his
Irish birthplace in an attempt to reclaim his Irish identity, and
created an Irish version of *The Taming of the Shrew.*"

This idea of filming a movie about a "Yank" who returns to
Ireland appealed to Ford's Irish ancestry. Three years later, after
the initial publishing of *The Quiet Man*, Ford bought the option
to the story for $10.00. But he would have "a tough row to hoe."
It would take Ford from 1940 to 1951 to raise the money to
make *The Quiet Man.*

One would have thought that a director who had already won
three Best Director Oscars (for non-western films) would have
no problem gathering the funds. Not so. Every major studio had
turned it down. Nobody wanted a "silly little Irish story," they
wanted westerns. And even though John Wayne and Maureen
O'Hara had agreed to star, the studios still weren't interested.
Maureen eventually told Ford, *"Look, if we don't hurry up
and make it, Duke will be playing McLaglen's role, and I'll be
playing the widow woman!"*

Finally, John Wayne approached Herb Yates, President
of Republic Pictures, and asked if he would let Ford direct

The Quiet Man. Yates read the script and was not impressed. However, Yates would consider financing Ford's Irish film if the proposed cast for *The Quiet Man* would first do a western. Yates figured that he could recoup the money he was certain he would lose on *The Quiet Man.* Ford agreed. The result was the classic, and financially successful, *Rio Grande*, which was based on another Saturday Evening Post story. It was also the first pairing of Wayne and O'Hara.

After much haggling with the studio, Ford agreed to a modest budget of under $2 million. In order to help his long time friend, Wayne agreed to a reduced fee of $100,000 to star. Maureen also agreed to reduce her fee to $75,000, much less than her normal salary.

Finally, Ford and his cast and crew were off to Ireland for six weeks of filming. A trek such as this was rather unusual 50 years ago, as so many films were made on Hollywood back-lots. For example, when Ford filmed *How Green Was My Valley*, an entire Welsh village was actually built in Malibu, California. Never the less, in this case, Ford demanded authenticity. So, mostly all of the outdoor shots were filmed on location in Ireland.

When the cast and crew arrived in the tiny village of Cong (Co. Galway) for filming, it caused quite a stir. Generators had to be brought in to run the lighting and sound, as the village had no electricity. Ford even used local villagers as background for authenticity. He also employed Maureen's brother, Charles, to render legal advice and find filming locations. Charles was a lawyer, and a member of the Abbey Players. He also landed the role as "Forbes," the IRA man in the movie.

Even though Maureen was one of Ford's favorite actresses, and as close to him as one of his own children, she was still treated with the same *"calculated roughness"* as any other actor. *"We used to say 'who's in the barrel today?' because the person who was getting hell might not be the one he was after. He might be watching someone else and their reaction – their anger at what he was doing."* But that was Ford's directing style, and it elicited mixed emotions from his actors. Maureen once said, *"we loved him, and we could kill him. We all sang for him. With Ford all you could do was forgive him and love him. That's all you could do with the man...and sing a song for him."*

There have been many stories written about the filming of *The Quiet Man*, too many to list here. Once, Maureen dared to confront Ford on the set of *The Quiet Man* during a scene in which wind machines were being used. *"Ford had this bloody wind machine behind me. Anybody else would have put it in front. And he went in for a close-up, take after take. And my hair was hitting my eyes like whiplash! I complained, and Ford said something, and I finally blurted out 'What would a bald-headed sonofa_____ like you know about hair blowing in the eyes.' And I thought, 'Oh my God, what have I done, I'm going to get fired?' I saw him look at everybody on the set. They were dying to laugh, but they couldn't move. And Ford had this decision to make: laugh with the crew or kill me. He decided to laugh, and I thought, 'Thank God, I'm saved.'"*

Maureen even fractured her wrist in one scene when she hauled off and smacked John Wayne across the face during their first encounter in his new cottage, "White O'Mourn." Anticipating a powerful wallop, Wayne deflected the blow, but the result was an injury to Maureen's wrist.

Still a mystery today is the famous "whisper" scene at the end of the film. Apparently whatever Maureen said to Wayne was at the direct instruction of Ford who hoped to elicit an honest element of surprise from Wayne.

Wayne, Ford, and O'Hara made a solemn vow never to reveal the words. Many people have speculated, but no one knows for sure. Ford, jokester that he was, would occasionally create lines for prying reporters, journalists, and co-workers. But he never revealed the truth. Even Maureen's own family doesn't know.

The Quiet Man would go on to receive seven Academy Award nominations (Best Picture, Best Supporting Actor - Victor McLaglen, Best Screenplay, Best Art Direction, Best

Sound, Best Cinematography, Best Director). It would win the Best Cinematography and Best Director Oscar, the fourth for John Ford. It was also the first "Best Picture" nomination the Republic Studios had ever received in their 17 years in existence.

John Ford passed away in Palm Desert, California on August 31, 1973. He remains the only director to have won four Best Director Oscars. His key to success, according to film critic Leonard Maltin, was that he made movies to please himself, not movie executives.

The John Wayne/Maureen O'Hara pairing would continue for several more movies, while their off-screen relationship remained platonic. *"We were just good buddies, for 35 memorable years,"* explained Maureen.

Once, when the two were filming a scene together, Wayne thought she wasn't giving it her all. Maureen explained that she was trying to share the scene with him *50-50. "To hell with that,"* Wayne shouted, *"you try to steal it!"* Then Wayne walked away, but turned around and said, *"That is...if you can!"*

Before Wayne died in 1979, when asked about his relationship with Maureen, he would say, *"O'Hara? She's the greatest guy I ever knew!"*

Maureen died in 2015, at the age of 95, and was buried at Arlington National Cemetery next to her husband.

(Note: this article was reviewed, edited, and approved by Ms. O'Hara prior to her death).

James Cagney
Song and Dance Man

"Everything I know,
I learned in Vaudeville."

- James Cagney

James Cagney's father was an alcoholic, and prone to what the family called, *"Dad's fits."* According to the author, John McCabe, in his book, *Cagney*, in his drunken stupor, James Francis Cagney, Sr. would begin a low keening, an Irish form of ceremonial lamentation, which would begin in the bowels and rise into a near shriek. This would be accompanied by a slow rocking from side to side.

Whenever the family heard this sad, guttural cry his wife, Carolyn, would come running and massage his neck and forehead until the wailing stopped.

At times, when Jim was very young, and his mother was out, he would be the one to administer the soothing massage. Cagney later said, *"...what a sound! It was a cry of agony, and I can still hear it. I used in once in a while in my pictures when I had to portray someone who had fallen into mental disrepair. That was Pa. Sixty shots of rye whiskey a day for years had really done their work. He was the most loveable guy who ever lived, but when one of his fits was on him, we learned to stay away and let Mom take over."*

James Cagney, Sr. was born in 1875 in New York City's Lower East Side in a high crime district known as "Five Points." He told James, Jr., or *"Jamesie-O"* as his father called him, little about his ancestry except to say that the original family name used to be O'Caigne and that they came from Co. Leitrim, Ireland. James Jr. surmised that his father wanted to hide his ancestry, but he never really knew why. James Jr. never had the time or the inclination to dig up his roots. He once said, *"...as I didn't have children of my own blood, I figured what the hell. I tend to live in the present anyway."*

James Jr's mother, Carolyn Elizabeth Nelson, was a large, redheaded woman who was very proud of her Norwegian heritage. Carolyn's father, the bad-tempered Henry Nelson, was the captain and only occupant of a tiny river barge. He insisted on being called "Captain" until the day he died, even though he commanded absolutely nobody.

Carolyn's mother was a *"bright, but self-effacing"* Irish-American woman, according to the author, John McCabe. Carolyn adored her parents. Carolyn married James Cagney, Sr. when she was eighteen and he was twenty-one. James Sr. worked as a telegraphist and bookkeeper. His downfall came when he took a job as a bartender at the local pub. *"A lot of people tend to get drunk,"* he told a friend. *"I tend to celebrate, and I like to celebrate all day and into the night...if I can make it that far."*

When he was still new on the job, he once tried to quiet an angry intoxicated patron who had been bothering the customers. For his effort, the usually gentile Cagney received a fist in the teeth, knocking out twenty-one, which he counted as he spit them out on the sidewalk.

Besides drinking rye whiskey, and spending time with his family, his other hobby was baseball. He often combined the two, and was still able to pitch such decisive fastballs that he was nicknamed, *"Jimmy Steam."* As the years rolled by, James Sr. saw more of the saloons and less of the baseball diamond.

On July 17, 1899, James Francis Cagney, Jr. was born in the top floor of a small brownstone apartment on East Eight Street. He was the second of five children. His brother, Harry, had been born in the same apartment just a year earlier. James Sr.'s bartending job forced the family to relocate to uptown Yorkville in 1901 where brothers Edward and William were born in 1902 and 1904 respectively. His sister, Gracie, was born in 1905, but died 10 months later of pneumonia.

Years later, Cagney would recall his days on East sixty-Ninth Street. *"That always sticks in my memory as a street of stark tragedy, there was always crepe hanging on a door or two somewhere on the block. There was always the clanging of an ambulance bell. Patrol wagons often came..."*

The Cagney neighbors included Germans, Italians, Hungarians, Irish and Jews. By his teens, James could speak fluent Yiddish, a talent he used in several of his films. Although Cagney himself never got into serious trouble, several of his friends ended up in prison. His closest friend was Peter Hessling, known to all as *Bootah*. His family was even more poverty-stricken than the Cagneys, so Bootah resorted to criminal activity to survive.

Both Cagney and Bootah had played on various scrub baseball teams. Eventually the two would go their separate ways when Bootah dropped out of school and disappeared.

A few years later, Jim's semi-professional baseball team was invited to play inside the walls of Sing-Sing prison. There he would run into to his old friend, Bootah, doing time for shooting a policeman in the arm. Before the game was over Jim would encounter three more pals from the old neighborhood; "Dirty Neck" Jack Lafferty, Patsy Donovan and "Guts" Finster.

On July 21, 1927, Bootah was given the electric chair. He had decided to pull one more job before going straight. In the process of holding up a well-heeled Italian man, a policeman coincidentally rounded the corner and stumbled on the crime in progress. He was shot dead by Bootah. The cop had left work early to go home and take care of his sick wife and their four children. Cagney wept when he heard the news.

Before the drink really took hold of James Sr., he was an energetic, amusing, and playful character. Each day when he left for work, the entire family would see him to the front door. He would kiss his wife; blow kisses to his four sons; doff his green tweed cap in a comical fashion; make the sign of the cross; check his fly to see that it was buttoned, and walk out the door, often singing a ballad. He loved his wife, and adored his children. And they worshipped him, warts and all.

Even though James Sr. had his fits, James Jr. would always remember his family, poor as they were, full of *"...laughter. Songs and laughter."* James Jr. said that it was rare when his father was a fall-down drunk; most of the time he was a quiet drinker. *"You never knew he had it in him except by the angle of his hat. He would always tip his hat a little over one eye."*

The Cagney boys learned the art of boxing from of all people, their mother. Carolyn, known as "Carrie," went to many amateur prizefights when she was young. She quickly realized that sluggers usually got the bad end of the deal, whereas boxers, who could dance, would avoid being hit.

She gathered the boys together two afternoons a week and taught them to fight. She knew they would have to know how to defend themselves in the streets. Carrie was fiercely protective of her sons, and shared her own father's bad temper. She once used a six-foot bullwhip on a night watchman who had mistakenly beaten up Harry for some minor infraction. After thoroughly thrashing the man, she was forever known on her street as *"Kill 'em Carrie."*

She especially focused on James, who was the runt of the family, and he turned out to be her prize pupil. Eddie, five years younger than James, and Harry, the oldest, were kind souls. They soon grew to depend on James for protection from the neighborhood gangs.

Jim never looked for conflict, but didn't avoid it either. The neighborhood kids teased Jim, calling him "red," because of the color of his hair, or "runt" due to his size. He hated being called the latter.

By the time Jim was 9 years old, his father had turned to gambling. He'd stumble home haggard and hung over early in the morning, after disappearing for 3-4 days on a drinking and gambling binge. Then he'd give Jimmy a quarter, and send him down to the local pub for a quart of red-eye.

The family poverty, tough street life, and their father's alcoholism and gambling began to make the Cagney boys very resentful. One day the Cagney brothers devised their own motto, *"We love everybody, but don't give a damn about anybody."* They lived by those words.

Soon it was time for Jim to help support the family, and at 17 he got a job as a bellhop at the Friar's Club, while attending Stuyvesant High School.

Upon graduation he was hired as a junior architect at a local firm. His mother encouraged him to continue his education, so he enrolled in Columbia University for a course in fine arts.

He and brothers, Harry and William, were sent to Lenox Hill Settlement House to take courses in public speaking. Occasionally, the settlement would stage plays and allow the neighborhood kids to take part. After playing bit parts as a Chinese Pantomime, and a Japanese Emperor, he landed his first starring role in a one-act play called, *"The Lost Silk Hat."*

In the fall of 1918, a Spanish influenza epidemic swept the Eastern Seaboard, and James' father, his constitution already weakened by alcohol abuse, died at the age of 42. Carrie was devastated. For all of her husband's faults, she loved him dearly.

Jim Jr. walked over to St. Francis Rectory to ask an assistant pastor to officiate the memorial service at the local funeral home. The pastor agreed, but on the day of the service he did not show. Jim took the priest's absence very hard. With the exception of a few family christenings and funerals, Jim never appeared in a Catholic Church again.

Shortly after the death of James Sr., baby daughter Jeanne, was born. In his sixth month at Columbia, he withdrew from school to work full-time and help out with the family expenses. He secured a job at Wannamakers Department store and became friends with a salesman who was a former vaudevillian. He told

James that a local vaudeville theatre needed a replacement for a boy who had left the cast. Cagney auditioned and got the role in the show, *"Every Sailor."*

What he didn't realize was that he had to dress as a woman... actually a comic female impersonator. Regardless, at $35 a week, it was too good to pass up. For this role he also had to learn to dance...

After the show ran for eight weeks, he returned to work at a brokerage house. But in the summer of 1920 he auditioned for a Broadway musical called *"Pitter Patter"* and was hired as a chorus boy. For a few bucks more he became the dresser for the main star.

It was in this show where he met his future wife, Frances Willard "Billie" Vernon, a chorus girl from Iowa. Billie was intrigued with Cagney. Instead of playing cards between numbers like the rest of the chorus, Cagney read books. Impressed that Jim was both cute and smart, the two were married in 1921, after the close of the show. Several vaudeville shows followed such as, *"Ritz Girls of 1922,"* and *"Snapshots of 1923."* During their early years together, James and Billie often toured the Vaudeville circuit, sometimes together, sometimes not.

Jim's big break in the motion picture business came in 1930 when Al Jolson recommended him to Warner Brothers for a part in *"Sinner's Holiday."* Recognizing a rising star, Warner Brothers signed him to a contract, and in 1931 gave him his first big role as Tom Powers in *"The Public Enemy."*

Cagney burst onto the screen with the now famous scene in which he squashed half a grapefruit into Mae Clark's face. Audiences were at first stunned, then intrigued by his brash performance. Fan mail poured in. Warner Brothers had found a new star.

Jim went on to film a series of gangster pictures, as well as many musicals. His most famous role was as George M. Cohan in "Yankee Doodle Dandy." He proved his versatility by tackling military roles, as well as *"The Man of 1000 Faces,"* the Lon Chaney story. Will Rogers had the best quote about Cagney, *"Every time I see him work, it looks to me like a bunch of firecrackers going off all at once."*

Cagney's first trip to Ireland was in 1959 to film the movie, *"Shake Hands with The Devil,"* about an unrepentant Irish revolutionary. The title derives from an Old Irish saying, "Shake hands with the devil and you'll never get it back." Filmed at Ardmore Studios in Bray Ireland, Cagney portrayed a character named, Sean Lenihan, a great surgeon and medical professor who was also a commandant in the Irish Republican Army. His character was obsessed with the notion that *"Ireland must be free, sea to sea."*

Cagney brilliantly portrayed a man who would kill anyone who stood in the way of his plans to free Ireland from British rule, yet, as a physician, he was dedicated to saving lives.

According the author John McCabe in his book, *Cagney*, the details of the plot were numerous and convoluted, and the supporting players from the Abbey Theatre added much depth to the film. A review in the Irish Times stated Cagney was quietly savage as the IRA leader, and that the drama was heightened, *"...by making the Commandant a good deal larger than life. Cagney, however, brought such superb artistry to it that even in the final scene you could cast him as your emotions dictated - for his was the face, according to your choice, of a fanatic or the implacable Irish dead."*

When the filming ended, Cagney was reluctant to leave Ireland. He had hoped to conduct some research on his family history, as well as tour the entire country. Unfortunately, another project was waiting for him back in the states.

Cagney was a self-taught actor and a keen observer who varied his roles with mannerisms and eccentricities of men he had known. Most notably were the quirks and gestures he learned from his father. He abhorred method acting. *"You don't psych yourself up for these things, you do them. I'm acting for the audience, not for myself, and I do it as directly as I can."*

In the 1930s, 40s, and 50s, Hollywood took notice of the large number of Irish-American actors working in the industry. Originally called "The Club" or "The Boys Club," the group consisted of original members James Cagney, Spencer Tracy, Frank McHugh, and Pat O'Brien. Later, the group included Ralph Bellamy, Frank Morgan (real name Francis Wuppermann), Lynn Overman, Bert Lahr, Lou Calhern, Jimmy Gleason, Allen Jenkins and Bob Armstrong. Even George M. Cohan and Will Rogers were in the gang from time to time.

Even though "The Club" had a very non-descript name, since most of the founding members were Irish-Americans, columnist Sidney Skolsky, in jest, called them *The Irish Mafia*, and the name stuck.

Cagney never understood the joke. *"That there was some Irish blood can't be doubted, but Bellamy has not one drop of Irish blood, Frank Morgan was German, and Lynn Overman is also a Teutonic name. I am one-quarter Norwegian."*

Regardless, theirs was strictly a social club. Many of the members worked for Warner Brothers, and would show up in each other's pictures from time to time, but that was the extent of their influence. As the members began to move away, or pass away, the "club" became mostly an opportunity for friends to swap old stories.

Politically, Cagney was a longtime New Deal Democrat who, in later years, became a conservative because of what he perceived as a moral confusion threatening American's values.

In 1940 a Los Angeles politician, before the House committee on Un-American Activities, accused him of Communist sympathies. He defended himself and was exonerated. The issue arose from his fund-raising activities for many causes, including providing food for striking California farm workers and facilitating the purchase of an ambulance for the Loyalist side in the Spanish Civil War.

The actor remained fairly private on public issues, except one; ecology. In 1958 he made radio appeals for preserving the nation's resources. *"Outside of my family,"* he said, *"the prime concern of my life has been nature and its order, and how we have been savagely altering that order."*

In World War II, Cagney was chairman of the actor's group of the National Victory Committee, appearing in many benefits to sell War Bonds and in long tours to entertain the Armed forces in this country and overseas. At the same time, he was also president of the Screen Actors Guild.

In 1961, at the top of his game, Cagney retired to his Duchess County farm in Upstate New York after making the Billy Wilder movie, *One, Two, Three.*

Undoubtedly weary from his hectic schedule, he finally had the time to sail and raise horses, as well as devote time to painting and poetry.

In the true Irish sense, Cagney always stayed close to the land. A dream he had since his childhood days when he visited a relative's farm in the pastoral flatbush section of Brooklyn. Despite two decades of offers from major directors, Cagney steadfastly refused them.

When he traveled east to see his brothers, he began to spend more time at The Playhouse, a local New York theatre club. Being in New York seemed to stimulate his writing of verse, and he had vague thoughts of returning to Ireland and researching the O'Caignes. Ireland's troubles disturbed him more and more. After his experience with the movie, *Shake Hands with The Devil,* he wrote:

"The men of Tyrone and all the six counties
(Intransigent seems to describe them)
Supply all the bounties from all of those counties
So England continues to bribe them

Elizabeth I, the queen called virgin
Set up the haves and have-nots
By usurping the lands of the old Irish clans
And gave them to Anglos and Scots.

Essex and Raleigh and Cromwell,
All Englishmen of distinction,
Had an overall plan for the old Irish clans
And the overall plan was extinction.

So you want us to take them to our hearts
And treat them as brother to brother.
A poor foolish dream and futile, my friend,

For they're not Irish, they're 'other.'"
His hoodlum on-screen persona clashed with his true nature.
He was a modest, private man, with little or no ego.

In a Hollywood atmosphere that can epitomize boorish
behavior as well as a lack of self-discipline, Cagney remained
married to Billie for 65 years, drank only occasionally (never
to access), and shunned the Hollywood lifestyle, preferring the
company of close friends and family.

He and Billie couldn't have children of their own, so they
adopted James, Jr. and Cassie. Their life on Martha's Vineyard
was wonderful, according to the children. But as the children
grew to adulthood they became estranged from their parents.
Soon they were demanding a share of the Cagney estate even
before their parents had passed on.

Cassie was offered property at Twentynine Palms, California,
but she felt it was inadequate. Jim then gave her a condominium,
which *"was gone after awhile"* so she demanded another one.

James Jr., married and had several children, divorced, and
remarried, all this after his stint in the Marines. Eventually he
told his father he wanted the Cagney home, Roaring Brook, the
218-acre farm on Martha's Vineyard. Jim deeded it to his son in
1976, and in 1983 Jim Jr. sold the Cagney home.

Although he understood, Cagney was very sad as his last
connection to Martha's Vineyard was gone. Jim Jr. stopped
visiting his parents after he sold Roaring Brook. He became
drug and alcohol addicted and died of a heart attack in January
1984, at the age of 42.

But James Cagney persevered, and under physician's orders to be more active, he came out of retirement in 1981 for a role in the movie *"Ragtime,"* in which he was teamed with his old friend, Pat O'Brien.

He made one last made-for-TV movie in 1984 called *"Terrible Joe Moran."* Wheelchair bound, and suffering the effects of several strokes, Cagney died of a heart attack on March 30, 1986.

Throughout his career, Cagney was often asked how he wished to be remembered. Most writers assumed he would want to be known as *"Cagney the tough-guy,"* or perhaps *"Cagney the movie star."* But to their surprise, he would always respond, *"I'm just a song and dance man."*

John L. Sullivan vs. James J. Corbett

Two Great Irish-American Heavyweights

*"My name is John L. Sullivan
and I can lick any man in the house!"*

**- The "Boston Strongboy" shouting to the fight crowd
at the Dudley Street Opera House**

James John Corbett (1866-1933) transformed the sport of boxing from a brutal test of raw strength to an art form.

Born September 1, 1866 in San Francisco, California, the son of Patrick and Catherine Corbett of Co. Mayo and Dublin respectively, he defied his parents by ignoring their wishes to become a priest.

As a youth, Corbett earned a reputation as a street fighter, baseball player, and gymnast. Jim's father owned a livery business, where several sets of boxing gloves were kept in the yard. Jim and his brothers Frank and Harry, often sparred with the hack-drivers.

Jim played baseball for the "Alcazars" until an injury to his right hand ended his career. Whatever that injury was, it certainly didn't stop a boxing career. His brother, Joe, became a famous pitcher for the Washington Senators, Baltimore Orioles, and St. Louis Browns.

His baseball ambition thwarted, Jim devoted his energies to boxing. He attended Sacred Heart College and secured a job as a clerk in a San Francisco bank. But he eventually left his "respectable" bank job for the lure of the boxing ring. His devastated parents were convinced that boxing would bring only shame and humiliation. Jim began hanging around the San Francisco Olympic Club.

With little actual boxing experience, he unknowingly challenged a fellow he called "Blackbeard" to a boxing match. Little did Corbett know that he picked a fight with the club Heavyweight Champion. When Jim awoke a few minutes later, he was sitting in his corner with someone waving smelling salts back and forth under his nose. Embarrassed that he had been knocked out, Jim attempted to run around the ring to show the members he was OK. Still groggy from his beating, he fell flat on his face.

After his humbling defeat at the Olympic Club, Corbett began to train seriously. He knocked out Frank Smith when he was 18, and then fought a three-fight series against Joe Choynski.

He and Choynski met three times in a three-month span in 1889. The first bout was a "no contest" after four rounds as it was broken up by the police. The second bout was a 27-round epic battle set on a barge in San Francisco Bay to avoid the authorities. The seams from Choynski's gloves cut Corbett in round three. Later in the fight Corbett broke his left hand, but still managed to summon enough power to knockout Choynski with a left hook. The third fight Corbett won with a four-round decision.

After beating Jake Kilrain, a very respectable heavyweight, Corbett fought a 4-hour, 61-round heavyweight contest in 1891 against Peter Jackson. The fight was ruled a "no contest."

Before his career would end, James J Corbett would become the first world heavyweight boxing champion under the "Marquis of Queensbury" rules (when gloves replaced bare knuckles).

His classy appearance, sleek physique, and boyish good looks would bring a whole new audience to the sport...women. He earned such nicknames as "Handsome Jim," "Pompadour Jim," and finally, "Gentleman Jim." In short, Corbett brought respectability to what had always been a barbaric spectacle.

However, Jim was not the congenial, polite upstart as portrayed by Errol Flynn in the 1942 movie, "Gentleman Jim." He made enemies as easy as he made friends. He was described by acquaintances as: aloof, moody, arrogant, quick-tempered, inconsiderate, an adulterer, a bully, and a racist. An inveterate womanizer, screen legend Mae West was apparently one of his love interests.

His first marriage to Olivia "Ollie" Lake in 1886 lasted two years until she became fed up with his infidelity and left.

He then married Vera Stanwood only two weeks after his divorce from Ollie. His infidelity continued. He also abused Vera, threatening to kill her, and once tortured her with a lighted cigar. Despite the abuse and infidelity, Vera stayed married to him for 38 years.

Corbett was faithful to his immediate family, and set up his brother, Harry, in a restaurant called "Corbett's" in San Francisco. He cleared his father's mortgage on his livery business, and sent his parents back to Ireland on a holiday. He was also known to pay for friend's weddings and funerals. He and Vera had no children, and he enjoyed "exchanging banter" and playing ball with the local kids.

Once Corbett had reached the pinnacle of his boxing career, he was struck by tragedy. In 1898 his father murdered his mother, and then turned the gun on himself. A motive was never discovered, other than "insanity" as was reported by the papers of the day. Friends and neighbors said the father, a heavy drinker, had been acting strangely in the few weeks leading up to the murder-suicide.

John Lawrence Sullivan (1858-1918) was a second generation Irish-American born October 15, 1858 in the Roxbury section of Boston, Massachusetts. His father, Michael, was born in Laccabeg, Abbeydorney, Co. Tipperary and was part of the great famine exodus to America. His mother was from Co. Westmeath.

Like Corbett, Sullivan's parents had hopes he would become a priest. He briefly attended Boston College, but dropped out to work as an assistant plumber. His plumbing career ended when he got into a disagreement with his employer and broke his jaw.

Needing to earn a living, Sullivan entered weightlifting exhibitions where he was known to lift and throw kegs of beer. He was amazingly strong.

Sullivan made his name one night at the Dudley Street Opera House. Heavyweight boxer, Tom Scannel, offered to fight anyone in the audience. At the encouragement of the crowd, Sullivan accepted, and climbed on stage. Scannel offered to shake hands, but then sucker-punched Sullivan in the jaw. Infuriated, John L. struck him one-half dozen blows sending him into the orchestra pit. He then turned to the crowd and roared, *"My name is John L. Sullivan, and I can lick any man in the house!"*

Contemporary reports describe his strength and stature in mythical proportions. His massive size must have come from his mother, Mary, who weighted 13 stone, whereas his father only weighed 9 stone (but was known as a *scrapper*).

John excelled at semi-pro baseball, which led the Boston Red Sox to offer him a $1,500 per year deal. He declined as his prospects in the ring looked more promising…even though boxing at that time was largely illegal.

Sullivan began winning fight after fight and in 1880 he hired Billy Madden as his manager. Madden decided that in order to push for a title fight, Sullivan needed to pay a visit to New York, *"and show the fight people there what I could do,"* said Sullivan. *"Madden was a great ballyhoo artist and offered any man $250 who could stand against me for four rounds. Steve Taylor accepted and I easily beat him."*

John was quickly accepted by the New York "fancies" and began dressing rather elegant. He would appear at various functions and proclaim at every opportunity *"I can lick any man alive."*

Much like Corbett, Sullivan would earn a rather shady reputation. He hung around with bad characters, and survived a disastrous marriage. Before fights he was known to bring prostitutes in to his hotel and register them as his wife. It was even alleged that before the fight with Jim Corbett he sneaked "Miss Mardi Gras" into his hotel room at 1:45 a.m.

Sullivan developed a routine after pummeling his adversaries; he would help them to their corner, fuss over them until they came to, and slip them a couple of bucks. Then, raising his arms for silence, he made a few remarks suitable to the occasion, ending in the quaintly formal sign-off which was to be his trademark: *"Always on the level, yours very truly, John L. Sullivan."*

Finally, in 1882, Sullivan got his shot at the heavyweight title when he was matched against the reigning champion Paddy "The Trojan Giant" Ryan in Mississippi City, Mississippi. Both boxers had similar backgrounds. Ryan was born in Tipperary. He immigrated to America where he worked as a bartender.

At ringside for the Ryan-Sullivan fight were Oscar Wilde, Frank and Jesse James, as well as Red O'Leary, New York's most notorious bank robber. Betting was very heavy with Sullivan at 2 to 1 odds.

This particular fight is remembered for the fighter's elaborate colors flying in each of their corners, as well as worn by their supporters.

Ryan's colors were designed by New York's leading artist, and were comprised of white silk with a red, green and blue border, representing the colors of America, Ireland, and New York State. In the center was an eagle standing on a globe with a blue background and white stars. On the center of the globe was a white band inscribed with the name "Paddy Ryan, Champion of America." In the left-hand corner was the Irish harp, and in the right was a sunburst, representing the Fenian movement of which Ryan was a member. In the lower left-hand corner was an American shield and in the right the word "Excelsior" over a golden sunset representing the seal of New York State.

Sullivan's colors were also elaborate. His was comprised of white silk with a plain green border. In the upper left-hand corner there was an American flag, and in the right an Irish flag. The two lower corners also contained American and Irish flags. In the center was an American eagle. Between the two fighter's flags, Ireland was well represented that day.

At that time in boxing history the referee was selected at ringside, as no boxer trusted any referee chosen ahead of time. There were too many temptations from gamblers to bride the officials.

When the corners could not agree on a referee, Sullivan shouted, *"let them pick their own referee. All referees look alike to me!"* Two referees were then selected. It was the only time in boxing history where two referees officiated at the same fight.

None-the-less, Sullivan pounded his opponent in eleven minutes and was declared the winner after Ryan was unable to rise. After the fight Ryan confessed, *"I thought a telegraph pole had been shoved against me endways."*

The Fight!

While Sullivan had earned his stripes fighting bare-fisted in dingy, back room saloons, and on the decks of barges in the Hudson River, James J. Corbett fought mostly in private clubs.

The two had met before, in a four-round exhibition the year before. Sullivan demanded they fight in full evening dress, hoping to embarrass Corbett. When the two dropped their coats and hats, they looked like two well-healed guests at a formal dinner who decided to take their disagreement outside. The crowd jeered and booed the two dandies who danced around, pulling their punches, so as not to actually injure each other. After the exhibition, Jim turned to his trainer, *"I know I can whip this fellow."*

Sullivan hadn't fought for three years since the Kilrain bout. He was growing older, and the excesses of life were catching up to him. He was constantly hounded by challengers, and by the press, wanting to know when he would fight again. So he came up with a plan.

He announced *"I hereby challenge any and all of the bluffers who have been trying to make capital at my expense."* Sullivan insisted any challenger be willing to lay down a $10,000 bet.

He was banking on the fact that no one could come up with that amount of money. It was a great plan. He could silence his critics - having made a legitimate challenge - and return to his sedentary life as the reining heavyweight champ. Two of the top three challengers backed down. Not so, Gentleman Jim, who with his manager, scurried around town and came up with the $10,000 from various sporting people. The challenge was met, and the fight was scheduled.

In the weeks leading up to the fight, Corbett was expected to be nothing more than Sullivan's punching bag. After all, who could possibly stand up to the strongest man in Boston? Even his financial backers had their doubts. Corbett goaded Sullivan by stating, *"he can't hit me in a week, and he'll be the worst licked man you ever looked at."* Sullivan grew to dislike Corbett even more because of his taunting, often referring to him as a *"damned dude."*

On a humid night on September 7, 1892, in New Orleans, Louisiana, just after a downpour, the referee brought the two together in the center of the soggy ring.

Thirty-Four year-old Sullivan, now past his prime, was clad in green tights and high shoes and weighed in at 212 lbs.

Twenty-Four year-old Corbett, who stood a few inches taller (but looked considerable smaller), weighed 178 lbs. and wore drab-colored trunks, with a belt made of the colors of the American flag. Both were wearing gloves for the first time.

While listening to the fight instructions, Corbett said to the referee, *"what if he does this in the clinches?"* and then shoves his elbow in to Sullivan's Adam's apple and pushed his head back. The referee said that would be a foul. Sullivan glowered at the upstart. A gong, used for the first time in boxing history, sounded the start of the fight.

It didn't take long for Corbett to frustrate Sullivan with his speed and agility. During the first few rounds, Sullivan rocked Corbett with two shots to the head, but Corbett answered with his lightening left jabs and broke Sullivan's nose.

By the 7th round Corbett went for Sullivan's gut, doubling him over in agony. Gentleman Jim began to pound on Sullivan round after round, and by the 18th, the champ was a mess. Reporters of the day referred to John L. as "wearing a blood mask."

Sullivan was outclassed, and beyond his prime, and it showed. Corbett hit him with two shots to the heart, and only the bell saved Sullivan in that round. Several times, hoping for the knockout, Sullivan swung so hard that when he missed his target he spun himself all the way around, leaving him vulnerable to punches from Corbett.

Corbett had used extraordinary concentration and patience as he systematically dismantled Sullivan. By the 21st round Corbett moved in for the kill, and Sullivan was trying to merely survive and protect himself from the onslaught.

A perfectly timed right from Corbett caused the Boston Strong-Boy to pitch forward and fall on his face. Sullivan tried to get up, but could only roll over on his right side. The fight was over.

Supporters bearing John L's colorful banners threw them in to the ring, covering Sullivan like a shroud. It took four strong men, helped by Corbett, to carry Sullivan to his corner. Sullivan leaned over to his second, World Lightweight Champion, Jack McAuliffe, and asked, *"what the hell happened, Jack?"* To which McAuliffe replied, *"You're not the heavyweight champion anymore."*

Corbett would go on to fight many more bouts, using his left jab with deadly accuracy. He successfully defended his title with a third-round knockout over Charley Mitchell.

On St. Patrick's Day, March 17, 1897, Corbett was knocked out by British boxer, Bob Fitzsimmons, in the 14th round at Carson City, Nevada after Fitzsimmons stopped him with the now famous "solar-plexus punch."

Jim took the loss hard, and for a while was nearly suicidal. After failing in two comeback attempts in 1900 and 1903 against former sparring partner, James J. Jeffries, Corbett left boxing for a career in vaudeville.

In 1932, while riding a New York subway, Corbett was struck with intense abdominal pain. He was able to leave the train and hail a taxi home. His physician later diagnosed him with liver cancer.

James "Gentleman Jim" Corbett died at home, in Vera's arms, in 1933 at the age of 66. Gene Tunney once said of Corbett, *"he had the keenest and most analytical brain that ever graced a prize ring."*

What Corbett lacked in aggression and punching power he made up for with his mastery of the scientific side of the sport. No less than seven fighters would assume the name "Corbett" in tribute to their hero.

Gentle Jim left us with this thought, *"When your nose is bleeding and your eyes are black and you are so tired you wish your opponent would crack you one on the jaw and put you to sleep, fight one more round. Remember that the man who always fights one more round is never whipped."*

As far as John "The Boston Strongboy" Sullivan, he did what no man had done before. He challenged America to a fight, offering thousands of dollars to any man, anywhere, who could stay on their feet for four rounds.

Wherever he went, the Irish came out in droves to cheer. Never a proponent of ring science, he just simply slugged his opponents into submission, and he became a very rich man. One of his few opponents who lasted three rounds with Sullivan once exclaimed, *"it was like being hit by a runaway horse."*

His career would have its ups and downs, as would his reputation. Even when he was old and gray, John took to the road, shaking hands along the way. *"Come shake the hand that shook the world!"* he would bellow. He knew the Irish needed a hero they could touch.

Legend has it that if you shook his hand, you could then boast to your mates, *"...come shake the hand that shook the hand that shook the world!"* Boxing had taken on a broad appeal, and, according to author, Michael Hayes, Sullivan was seen as the man who brought it from the shadows.

After the Corbett fight he swore off liquor and became a temperance lecturer. He retired to his Massachusetts farm, having squandering most of his $1 million, and died in 1918 at the age of 60. Before he was buried, the frozen ground had to be blasted with dynamite to carve out his grave. Jake Kilrain, who served as a pallbearer quipped, "Old John would have approved."

Mike "King" Kelly
America's First Sports Superstar

*"Show me a boy that doesn't
participate in baseball and
I will show you a weak, sickly,
hot-house plant, who will feel
sorry, as he grows older,
that he was ever born."*

- Mike "King" Kelly, 1881

Mike Kelly was a dandy. He was flamboyant, boisterous, and a snapper dresser. He would become the first sports hero in modern history…and the people adored him.

Kelly would never be seen in public unless he was sporting the latest fashions, complete with patent leather shoes and a twirling cane topped with a giant jewel.

Occasionally his pet monkey would accompany him by riding on his shoulders. His face adorned billboards, proclaiming him *"the nation's best dressed man."* Kelly flaunted his wealth, always bought drinks for the house, and twiddled his large black mustache for the Chicago ladies. His Irish wit and charm captivated women who found him irresistible.

His fans loved him so much they bought him a house and a carriage drawn by two white horses to take him to and from the park. Kelly played baseball by day, partied by night, and seldom slept in his own bed. One of his former managers said, *"there's not a man alive who can drink Mike Kelly under the table."* It was not a compliment. Regardless, Kelly always showed up to play.

Little is know about the early years of Michael Joseph Kelly. He was born in New York City on New Year's Eve, 1857, to

Michael Kelly and Catherine Kylie. His parents had been among the 1 million refugees from Ireland who escaped the Great Famine in the 1840s. They settled in New York City where Mike, and his brother, James, were born.

Mike's parents took education seriously. This was due to the maltreatment they received at the hands of the British in Ireland. *"They may not have had the advantages of an education themselves, British misrule, prevents that, but they knew the value of education,"* Kelly relayed years later in his autobiography.

The occupation of Mike's father is unknown, most likely manual labor like many Irish immigrants. But later, at the outbreak of the Civil War, he joined the 125th Regiment of the New York State Volunteers. Catherine Kelly waited for news of her husband, but heard little in the three years he was gone. Meanwhile, she sent Mike off to school at the age of five. She finally received news that her husband had survived the war and was coming home.

The 125th had 910 enlisted men when they marched off to engage the Confederate army on August 13, 1862. At then end of the three-year enlistment 39 men would be dead, and 90 would desert. Kelly's father had stayed, fought, survived, and returned to his family. He then re-enlisted and moved the family from Troy, New York to Washington, D.C.

Many years later Mike would recall watching a parade down Pennsylvania Avenue, featuring Union generals George McClellan and Judson Kilpatrick. *"So much gold and gold lace I never saw before,"* he told his ghostwriter. *"For years I remembered them, and it was the ambition of my life to go and do likewise."*

Mike was introduced to baseball at the age of 10. He was already the fastest runner in his school, and he quickly acclimated to this new sport. Baseball, or "Town Ball" had been played by soldiers on both sides during the civil war. When the soldiers returned home at war's end, they brought the game back with them.

In 1868, baseball was strictly an amateur sport, played by differing rules from region to region. There were some men who received money "under the table" to play, but, by-and-large, the game was informal recreation for gentlemen.

Mike loved the game and played whenever he had the chance. Eventually, he was given the opportunity to make some money at it, and at the ripe old age of 15 he made his professional baseball debut with the independent Troy "Haymakers."

According to author Marty Appeal, in his book, *Slide, Kelly, Slide*, the baseball that Mike was introduced to was actually known as "burn ball." One of the main differences between today's game was that a runner, if hit by a thrown ball, was out. *"Many a time have I been hit in the small of the back, and for a moment imagined that my back was broken,"* Mike recalled. Kelly eventually joined a Washington team that was organized enough to actually have a name, the "Keystones." Since Mike was just learning the game, he experimented with all of the positions.

Around 1876, Mike's father became ill, and the family was forced to relocate to Paterson, NJ. Searching for a team so he could continue playing, Mike joined the Paterson, "Olympics" for one year.

The Kelly family hadn't lived in Paterson very long before Mike Sr. died, followed shortly by his wife. Mike, and his brother, James, became orphans, and it was at that time Mike's schooling came to an end.

Needing to support himself, Mike got a job at the Murray Silk Mill earning three dollars a week hauling baskets of coal from the basement to the top floor. His developing strength and large physique allowed him to carry more coal than his co-workers. This allowed him to finish work early so he could play ball in the later afternoon. Oftentimes he even sneaked out of work by jumping from the second story window just so he could meet his mates for a baseball game.

When Mike turned 19, he still was torn between becoming a baseball player or an actor. His burgeoning interest in acting began when he befriended a fellow Keystone teammate named Dave Walling, who Kelly called *"an able batsman and an adept fielder."* Walling could have gone on to have a pretty good baseball career, but instead he created a successful act on the variety stage. Mike admired the theatre and became obsessed with it through out his life. Eventually Kelly would try his hand at acting which supplemented his income during the off-season.

Kelly similarities in the two professions; both were not considered very respectable back in the day. In fact, no self-respecting individual would be caught dead staying in a hotel that catered to actors or ballplayers. They were considered low class. But with actors, Mike found kindred spirits, and many of his closest friends would come from the theatre.

He also knew he had to earn a living, and struggled with the decision to stay on at the mill or pursue his dreams as a ballplayer and or actor. He chose the dream.

Kelly moved to Ohio and hooked up with the Columbus "Buckeyes." Playing catcher, he was quickly noticed by a baseball scout and was signed the very next year by the Cincinnati "Red Stockings" of the National League.

At 19 years old, standing 5' 10", 157 lbs, and just one year from playing on the sandlots of Paterson, NJ, Mike Kelly made the big leagues.

Playing for the Red Stockings was a challenge for Kelly. He was now playing with the best of the best and it was intimidating. He started off slow, but never wavered in his enthusiasm. His teammates liked him and called him "the kicker," which meant the guy who cheered on his mates and riled his opponents.

Kelly also proved to be a bit of a klutz in Cincinnati. He basically fell down a lot, often tripping himself while fielding a ground ball or running to catch a fly. His teammates said he couldn't run a 100 yard-dash without hitting the dirt at least once. But just when Kelly's awkwardness was about to be his downfall, he had the game of his life. Against the Boston

Beaneaters he hit two doubles, a triple, and his first major league home run. He had finally found his stride.

From then on it wasn't uncommon for Kelly to drive in every run his team scored. *"He would jump into the air 10' from the sack,"* a teammate recalled, *"dive directly for it, dig one of his spiked shoes into the bag and then swerve clear over on his side. Few 2ⁿᵈ basemen had the nerve to block his hurricane dives."*

Kelly played primarily in the outfield and hit .283 his first year. The following season he batted .348, and the Kelly legend was born.

One of the earliest base-running tales of Kelly occurred in 1879 when Cincinnati was playing Chicago. Kelly swatted a double to left field. The ball was scooped up by the Chicago left fielder and thrown to the second baseman. Kelly, having rounded second on his way to third, appeared to the fans to have been tagged out by the second baseman. An argument ensued with all of the Chicago infielders gathering at second base to protest. Knowing that no one had called "time-out," Kelly proceeded to dash off to third and then to home plate for the score.

In 1880, Chicago player/manager Adrian Constantine "Cap" Anson persuaded Kelly to join the Chicago White Stockings. The city of Chicago had just been rebuilt following the devastating fire of 1871 that swept through the city.

As the 1880s beckoned, Chicago was the fastest growing major urban center in America. New York had a population of 1.2 million in 1880, with Philadelphia second at 847,000. Neither city had a major league franchise at the time, which left Chicago (population 503,000) as the largest big league town in the land.

It was no coincidence the losing White Stockings suddenly began to win games. "Cap" Anson had an eye for talent. As Kelly's ability grew, so did his confidence...and his swagger. His reputation for base running was becoming legendary. He stole at least 50 bases for four consecutive years, once stole six bases in one game, and in 1887 he stole a total of 87 bases.

Kelly loved to play to the crowd and that's where his amateur acting experience surfaced. He tipped his hat after stealing a base, and often talked with fans while playing in right field. He was especially popular with the Chicago Irish who resided in the 5th, 7th and 8th wards on the southwest side of town, near the stockyards and the lumberyards. They came in droves to cheer for their man, "Kel."

With success came money, and Kelly became a fashion plate. He was known to dress in pointed, patent leather, high button shoes and to wear a high silk hat, cocked off to one side. He also liked to drink...a lot. Kelly also liked tobacco, playing cards, and betting on the horses. According to author Marty Appeal, Kelly liked to *"flaunt his nocturnal habits."* He considered it *"manly."*

Mike Kelly was now on his way to becoming a household name. Within a few years Kelly's name would come to equal, or even surpass, the great bare-knuckle fighter, John L. Sullivan.

The New York Evening Journal once said, *"Mike Kelly was the trickiest player who ever handled a baseball. There was nothing he would not attempt...Baseball rules were never made for Kel."* The reference to skirting the rules is best evidenced by the following tale: Kelly would often take advantage of the game's only umpire by skipping 2nd base on his way to 3rd when the umpire wasn't looking. And occasionally, when he shifted from outfield to catcher, he would use his mask to cover the plate so the runner couldn't see it. Anything was fair game for Kelly. Anything it took to win.

In the off-season, Kelly would return to Paterson, NJ and buy drinks for his friends at local taverns, telling thrilling tales of big league baseball. He eventually met and married Angus Hedifen, a local girl from Paterson, NJ whose parents were natives of Scotland. They remained married for 13 years.

In the seven years Kelly was with Chicago they won five pennants. In 1881 and 1882 he led the league in doubles. In 1884 through 1886 he led the league in runs scored, and in 1884 and 1886 he had the league's highest batting average.

Kelly not only won games with speed and skill, but as noted previously, he also won with intelligent, creative, and sometimes outrageous play.

Although primarily an outfielder, Kelly saw a significant amount of time behind the plate as a catcher. On one occasion, Kelly was behind the plate with two outs and a runner on third. The batter grounded to the shortstop, who threw to first base. The runner coming from third saw Kelly drop his mitt, apparently indicating the batter was out and the inning was over. Somewhat confused, the runner slowed down. But the batter was actually safe. The first baseman whipped the ball the Kelly who caught it bare handed and tagged the runner for the third out. Mike was a good actor.

Once, while playing the outfield in a twilight game, at the top of the ninth with two outs and Chicago ahead by one, he raced back to the fence for a fly ball. He leaped into the air, clasping both hands together as if to make a spectacular catch. He then nonchalantly jogged towards the bench as the umpire called the batter out. The game apparently over, both teams headed into their respective locker rooms. Once in the locker room, Manager Cap Anson asked Kelly for the game ball, reminding him that the owner, Mr. Spalding, didn't like to waste them. *"The ball?"* Answered Kelly. *"How the hell would I know? It went a mile over my head."* Acting.

Kelly was Cap Anson's greatest and most challenging star. Asked if he drank during games, Mike answered, *"it depends on the length of the game."* One game was actually delayed as Kelly and several wealthy gentlemen sat in the box seats and toasted one another. The only thing Kelly consumed faster than alcohol was Anson's patience.

His on-field antics could be overlooked if it meant winning games, but his drinking and carousing was another matter. Cap

Anson once said, *"He was a whole-souled, genial fellow with a host of friends, and but one enemy, that one being himself. Time and time again I have heard him say that he would never be broke, but money slipped through Mike's fingers as water slips through the meshes of a fisherman's net, and he was fond of whiskey as any representative of the Emerald Isle."*

With his antics on the rise, and his value diminishing, in 1897 White Stockings President A.G. Spalding sold his star player to the Boston Beaneaters of the National League for a record sum of $10,000. This was the first 5-figure sale in baseball history. Player contracts had often been peddled, but no one of Kelly's stature had ever been actually *sold*. Kelly was not happy. *"Horses are sold,"* he said, *"not ballplayers."*

The City of Chicago was stunned and boycotted their team. Cap Anson, who had endured Kelly's behavior for years, was finally rid of him. He no longer had to babysit his spoiled protégé. With the new $10,000 Boston contract and a $5,000 bonus, Kelly was dubbed the *"$15,000 Beauty."*

Despite Kelly's displeasure at being sold, the pairing of Mike Kelly and the City of Boston was a match made in heaven. Boston had always embraced its heroes warmly.

The coming of Kelly to Boston led fans and newspapers to begin calling him the "King of Baseball." From this came the natural progression to "King" Kelly. Kelly was always a big draw in Boston when he played against the Beaneaters. The Boston Irish faithful often made a point of waiting for the Chicago games, just for a chance to see their man. Now he was one of them.

Kelly was named captain of the Beaneaters which immediately caused problems. The role of captain was a far more visible one, and Kelly was not about to curtail his drinking habits. He was hardly a perfect selection to set an example. Despite the pressure that his heightened celebrity brought, Kelly responded in his usual style, entertaining the crowds while helping to win ballgames.

Schoolchildren began gathering near the ballpark for a chance to get his signature. This was the beginning of an American tradition - the autograph. Another tradition began with Kelly, only this came from the art world. An artist named Frank O. Small painted Kelly sliding into second base head-first before a cheering crowd. This painting was reproduced and sent to every Irish pub in Boston, replacing the famous "Custer's Last Stand."

Kelly continued his chicanery. As an outfielder he often kept an extra ball in his trousers and would use it when a ball was hit over the fence, pretending that he had actually caught it.

Perhaps the most repeated story was the now famous "Kelly now catching" story. This occurred during a game when Kelly was actually sitting on the bench and someone else was playing catcher. It was the last of the ninth with two out when the batter hit a foul tip near the Boston bench. Kelly, seeing that the Boston catcher couldn't reach the ball, yelled out *"Kelly now catching"* and caught the pop fly barehanded. Captains, apparently, could make substitutions, and the rulebook didn't say when a substitution might occur. Once again, Kelly had outsmarted everyone.

Despite his trickery, it was his dashing and daring on the bases that won the hearts of the Boston fans, and was truly worth the price of admission. He knew just when to run, and he perfected a hook slide that allowed him to elude tags. He wouldn't hesitate to kick the ball out of an infielder's glove either.

It wasn't long into his first season with Boston that a fan in the South End Grounds, yelled, "slide, Kelly, slide!" as Mike danced off first. Another fan picked up the chant, and then another. Soon, the "Slide, Kelly, Slide" chant would fill the south end grounds each time "Kel" reached first with second base empty. This rallying cry would take its place among the great expressions of baseball, and even seep into the slang of non-baseball fans.

In 1889, a silly song called "Slide, Kelly, Slide" was written for Miss Maggie Cline, a popular vaudeville and dance-hall singer. It actually had little to do with Kelly, but became very popular as a little baseball ditty. It would be sung by the fans whenever he reached base. Eventually the song would be recorded on cylinder, and later on 78 RPM. The song made Maggie Cline a star, and added to the legend of Mike "King" Kelly.

Unfortunately, without Cap Anson around to monitor him, Kelly's drinking worsened. He put on weight and had trouble catching the high flies. The press, who had been among his biggest supporters, turned on him and criticized his manner of play. Kelly reacted with anger to their condemnation and began to quarrel with reporters.

In 1889, players on all of the teams became upset over what they perceived as a lack of attention to their very real concerns, mostly surrounding salary caps. Most of the players, including Kelly, defected and formed their own "Players League."

Kelly became one of the "bosses" of the new Boston "Reds" franchise team. Unfortunately, the new league was doomed from the start. The National League waited for the Players League to announce their schedule, and then scheduled competing home games on almost every date.

This was financially devastating for both leagues. Eventually the Players League surrendered, and both leagues went back to the business of playing ball.

Things were now very uncomfortable for Kelly in Boston. He had burned too many bridges during the war between the leagues, and he found himself suddenly unemployed.

He headed back to Cincinnati, where his major league career began 13 years earlier, and joined the lousiest franchise in all the major leagues. They made him manager and captain...and he proceeded to do everything wrong.

Kelly got tossed out the game opener for arguing with the umpire, and later got into a fistfight with one of his own players. He chose to play on Sundays, which was strictly prohibited, and enforced, by the local authorities. Kelly didn't care one wit. He had no game plan, and no set roster, and often played anyone wherever they wanted to play. Attendance at the games was abysmal.

His personal antics, overlooked in Boston, were not tolerated in Ohio. Kelly was not the "draw" he had once been, and he managed to struggle through 82 games before the team went broke and folded.

The Boston Reds thought he had some stuff left and quickly signed Kelly and welcomed him back "home." But after playing four games with the Reds, he snubbed them by jumping to the Boston Beaneaters for a more lucrative offer.

Kelly played a mediocre year. It was becoming obvious that nearly 20 years of alcohol abuse was taking its toll. At 34 years old he was no longer swift and had become somewhat flabby. His arm became noticeably weaker each year.

His final days with Boston would not be proud ones. He pulled a few cheap stunts while playing catcher and the umpires would have none of it. Kelly's once cute stunts were now seen as desperate acts from an aging athlete.

In the winter of 1892-93, King Kelly walked away from Boston baseball forever. He was quickly picked up by the New York Giants in 1893 as a bit of a novelty, but he didn't fair very well there either.

By now Kelly was merely trading on his name, not his skills. His drinking increased and the Giants' manager ordered Kelly to the Turkish baths each morning to dry out before each game. He was now the number four catcher and his play was described as "listless."

At the end of the 1893 season, Kelly was quietly released. He drifted into the minor leagues the next few years, managing Allentown in the Pennsylvania State League and Yonkers in the Eastern League. But even Mike knew his baseball days were over, and he finally hung up his cleats.

Living *high on the hog* has its disadvantages. Before long all of Kelly's earnings had been spent. He had lost it all at the

Faro table or racetrack, buying the finest clothes, and buying countless rounds of drinks for his cronies. Mike was flat broke.

He realized that with his athletic career over, his future earnings could be based on potential success as an actor. People still wanted to see the great King Kelly. So he did what other sports celebrities of the time had done before him, he headed for the stage.

His first show was booked for Monday afternoon, November 5, 1894, and he left New York City the night before on the Fall River Line to travel by boat up Long Island Sound to Boston. An unexpected fall snowstorm slowed the journey. One account said Mike loaned his topcoat to a stowaway. None-the-less, Mike became ill.

Upon arriving in Boston, Mike complained to a sportswriter that he didn't feel well. He was taken to a friend's house and put to bed. Old friend and former Beaneater, Dr. George Galvin, was summoned from the local hospital.

Assuming the worst, Mike's friend's tried to contact his wife, Agnus, but a second snowstorm knocked out telegraph service. By the time Dr. Galvin arrived, Mike was having difficulty breathing. Diagnosed with pneumonia, Mike was moved to Emergency Hospital. As the stretcher was being lifted through the hospital door, Kelly apparently slipped off the stretcher and on to the floor. *"This is my last slide,"* he said.

Mike appeared to be recovering in the hospital, but still suffered bouts of fever and delirium. A few days later, Mike's condition suddenly worsened and Father Hickey of St. James Catholic parish was summoned to administer the last rites. On November 8, 1894, Mike "King" Kelly died. He was only 36 year old.

Sports Editor Jim Price, who knew and watched Kelly's career, would exclaim years later: *"Kelly was a genius in sizing up a situation and finding a weak spot in the enemy's armor. Some called him a dirty player, but Mike constantly was thinking up wiles to befuddle and entrap his slow-witted opponents. While he was the brainiest catcher of his day, his hold on the fans was far more as an offensive player. Like (Babe) Ruth, he burned the candle at both ends, and he could make headlines outside of the ball field. A handsome Irishman, with wavy black hair and a cavalry trooper's mustache, Kelly was all for wine, women, and song."*

During his 16 years in the majors he played an astounding 758 games in the outfield, 583 as catcher, 96 at third base, 90 at shortstop, 53 at second base, and 25 at first base. He even made 12 pitching appearances, compiling a record of 2-2.

The legend of Mike Kelly remained for a time, but eventually those that remembered him passed on. His famous painting, which hung in Boston Saloons, would eventually come down. And the quirky song, *Slide Kelly Slide* which survived well into the 1920s, would fade into history.

The saga of "King" Kelly became eclipsed by the likes of young upstarts like Ty Cobb and Babe Ruth. Only hard-core baseball historians know the quintessential rags to riches (to rags) story of one of the greatest baseball players in history.

Mike "King" Kelly was inducted into the Baseball Hall of Fame on April 25, 1945.

Halloween
An Irish Tradition

"This night they dance with ghosts,
and the pooka is abroad,
and witches make their spells…"

- W.B. Yeats, Fairies and Folktales of the Irish Peasantry, 1888

Between 1000 BC and 100 BC the Celtic people of Northern France, the United Kingdom and Ireland celebrated the New Year with a druid festival.

It was at this time that *Ball*, the Celtic god of spring and summer, ended his reign. It was also the time when the Lord of the Dead, Samhain (pronounced "Sah-wen"), began his reign. (Some scholars believe that there was no such God, and that Samhain merely means "summer's end.")

The Celts were a pastoral people, as opposed to an agricultural people. The end of the summer was significant to them because it meant the time of year when the structure of their lives changed radically. The cattle were brought down from the summer pastures in the hills and the people were gathered into the houses for the long winter nights.

As is common in history, when territory wars occurred, the vanquished often assumed the customs of the conquerors. When the Romans conquered the Celts in 43 AD, Roman autumn celebrations such as the one honoring Pomona, goddess of fruit and trees, and "Feralia" which was celebrated in late October honoring their dead, were integrated with Samhain. Thus, the apple, which was the symbol of Pomona, became associated with Halloween (i.e. the practice of "apple-bobbing" at parties). The apple is referred to in Celtic Emhain Abhlach, "Paradise of Apples," where the dead, having eaten of the sacred fruit, enjoyed a blissful immortality.

The festival began on *Oidhche Shamhna*, the eve of November 1 when the souls of the departed supposedly revisited their old homes to comfort themselves with food and drink provided by their kinfolk. *All Hallow's Eve*, at the beginning of winter and the dying time of the old year, was a night when the dead stalked the countryside causing trouble and damaging crops.

The Celts believed that when people died, they went to a land of eternal youth and happiness called *Tir nan Og* (sometimes referred to as "Summerland.") They did not have the concept of heaven and hell the Christian church later brought to them. The dead were believed to be dwelling with Fairy Folk, who lived in the numerous mounds or *sidhe* (pronounced *shee*) that dotted the Irish and Scottish countryside.

In the Celtic belief system, turning points such as the time between one day and the next, the meeting of the sea and shore, or the turning of one year into the next were seen as magical times.

The turning of the year was the most potent. Celts believed that on the night before the new year, the boundary between the worlds of the living and the dead became blurred. The Irish also believed in the intertwining of forces: darkness and light, night and day, cold and heat, death and life.

Celtic knotwork represents this intertwining of forces. It was during these events that the fairies would swarm from their mounds. Any crops left on the vines at this time were considered "blasted by the fairies" and unfit for human consumption.

Some believed the fairies were actually the spirits of the dead, while others were convinced they were the legendary *Tuatha de Dannan*. The Tuatha were a tribe of people who came through the mists and invaded Ireland during the "fifth wave" of invasions. They were students of the occult and came from "four cities somewhere in the north."

In order to establish dominance in Ireland, the Tuatha first defeated the Fir Bolgs, the tribe of people who had ruled Ireland. Later, the Milesians would invade Ireland and defeat the Tuatha, who fled underground, where many in ancient times believed they still dwelled. Hence, they became the fairies.

Interestingly enough, in some Celtic legends, the Irish actually invite the fairies, or dead, by opening up the fairy mounds to welcome them back to the land of the living for one day. They even go as far as to set a place at the table in case their now deceased loved-one decided to join them for supper.

Much like the concept of *evil*, the Celts did not have demons and devils in their belief system. The fairies, however, were often considered hostile and dangerous to humans because they were seen as being resentful of men taking over their lands. They became as close to evil as the Celtic belief system could conceive.

On this night, the fairies would sometimes trick humans into becoming lost in the fairy mounds, where they would be trapped forever. Even William Butler Yeats had the fairy faith and incorporated much lore into his poetry. In his book "Fairy and Folk Tales of the Irish Peasantry (1888), he wrote, *"On November Eve they are at their gloomiest, for, according to the old Gaelic reckoning, this is the first night of winter. This night they dance with ghosts, and the pooka is abroad, and witches make their spells, and girls sit at a table with food in the name of the devil, that the fetch of their future lover may come through the window and eat the food."*

Celts thought the presence of the otherworldly spirits made it easier for the Druid, or Celtic Priests, to make predictions about the future. For a people entirely dependent on the volatile natural world, these prophecies were an important source of comfort and direction during the long, dark winter.

To commemorate the event, the Celts dressed up in frightening costumes made from animal heads and skins. The Celts hoped that wandering ghosts would think they were fellow spirits and would not harm them. This allowed the Celts to wander freely without fear.

The Celts would also place bowls of food outside their homes to appease the ghosts and prevent them from entering. Then they would parade to the outskirts of town leading the ghosts away. The Celts would douse all of their hearth fires, and then build huge bonfires from sacred oak branches to scare away the evil spirits. Crops, animals, and even humans were sacrificed into the flames to quell these wandering souls. The remaining bones were then collected and read to predict the fortune of the upcoming year, which began November 1. (It is not surprising to discover that the original name for "bonfire" was "Bone fire").

When the celebration was over, they re-lit their hearth fires from the sacred bonfire to help protect them during the coming winter. Some sources state the main Druidic fire was kept burning at Usinach, in the middle of Ireland. Others say it was at *Tlachtga,* 12 miles from the Royal Hill of Tara. Traditional Halloween fires were still being lighted in Scotland as late as the 19th century.

In the 800s, the influence of Christianity had spread into Celtic lands. In the seventh century, Pope Boniface IV designated November 1 All Saints' Day, a time to honor saints and martyrs.

It is widely believed today that the pope was attempting to replace the Celtic festival of the dead with a related, but church-sanctioned holiday. The celebration was also called "All-Hallows" or "All-Hallowmas" (from Middle English "Alholowmesse" meaning All Saints' Day) and the night before Samhain was called "All Hallows Eve" and eventually, "Halloween."

Even later in 1000 AD, the church would make November 2nd "All Souls' Day," a day to honor the dead. It was celebrated similarly to Samhain, with huge bonfires, parades, and dressing up in costumes as saints, angels, and devils. Together, the three celebrations; the eve of All Saints Day, All Saints' Day, and All Souls' Day, became known as *Hallowmas.*

As European immigrants came to America, they brought their varied Halloween customs with them. Because of the rigid Protestant belief systems that characterized early New England, celebration of Halloween in colonial times was extremely limited. It was much more common in Maryland and the southern colonies.

As the beliefs and customs of different European ethnic groups, as well as Native Americans, meshed, a distinctly American version of Halloween began to emerge. The first celebrations included "play parties," public events held to celebrate the harvest, where neighbors would share stories of the dead, tell each other's fortunes, dance, and sing. Colonial Halloween festivities also featured the telling of ghost stories and mischief-making of all kinds. By the middle of the nineteenth century, annual autumn festivals were common, but Halloween was not yet celebrated everywhere in the country.

In the second half of the 19th century, America was flooded with new immigrants. These new immigrants, especially the millions of Irish fleeing Ireland's famine of 1846, helped to popularize the celebration of Halloween nationally.

Ireland has always remained close to its Celtic roots, and the Irish have been careful to keep their traditions alive wherever they went. Taking from the Irish and English traditions, Americans began to dress up in costumes and go house to house asking for food or money, a practice that eventually became today's "trick-or-treat" tradition.

The Celts believed that the presence of the otherworldly spirits made it easier for the Druid, or Celtic Priests, to make predictions about the future. These predictions or the telling of fortunes, over the centuries evolved into divination fortune-telling practices dealing with marriage, weather, and the coming fortunes for the New Year.

Young women believed that, on Halloween, they could divine the name or appearance of their future husband by doing tricks with yarn, apple parings, or mirrors. These were performed via such methods as "ducking for apples" and "apple peeling." Ducking for apples was a marriage divination. The first person to bite an apple would be the first to marry in the coming year. Apple peeling was a divination to see how long your life would be. The longer the unbroken apple peel, the longer their life was destined to be.

Another tradition was to cook such objects as a thimble, a ring, or a coin in a cake and serve it to guests. The person who got the coin would find wealth, the ring would lead to marriage, and the thimble meant no marriage. Divination fortune telling therefore evolved directly from the early Celtic practice of bonfires and bone collecting to tell the future.

The Irish can also lay claim to helping to invent "Trick or Treating." One version is that the Irish would imitate the fairies and go from house to house begging for treats. Failure to supply the treats would usually result in practical jokes being visited upon the owner of the house. Another version of Irish trick-or-treating was that a group of villagers would go from house to house begging for food for a community feast. Those who gave generously were promised a prosperous year, those who gave little or none were threatened and cursed.

Still another theory traces it to the early Celts who left food and milk on their doorsteps to appease the wandering dead and to obtain their blessing for the coming year.

Another tale deals with "Muck Olla," a shadowy Druidic figure who would seek vengeance on those who failed to contribute in his name. Some say "Muck Olla" was merely a "non-druid boogey man from Yorkshire, England.

In Co. Waterford, Halloween is called "Oidhche na h-aimleise," "The night of Mischief or con." It was a custom for boys to assemble in gangs and descend on farmers to levy a sort of blackmail, good-humoredly asking for, and as cheerfully given, according to Kevin Danaher in his book "The Year in Ireland: Irish Calendar Customs." It can also be traced to All Souls' Day in England where poor citizens would beg for food. People would give them pastries called "soul cakes" in return for their promise to pray for the family's dead relatives. The distribution of soul cakes was encouraged by the church as a way to replace the ancient practice of leaving food and wine for roaming spirits.

The practice, which was referred to as "going-a-souling" was eventually taken up by children who would visit the houses in their neighborhood and be given ale, food, and money. The more soul cakes the beggars would receive, the more prayers they would promise to say on behalf of the dead relatives of the donors. This was a sure way to expedite a soul to heaven who might be floating in limbo at the time. Today, children dress up and go from house to house for candy. Harmless pranks are pulled on neighbors or friends.

With the Protestant reformation in England, church holidays diminished in importance...especially Halloween, as it was closely associated with the Catholic Church calendar.

'Guy Fawkes Day" would become an important addition to the English holiday calendar, and many of the Halloween traditions shifted to the annual commemoration of his death.

On November 5, 1605, Fawkes was apprehended, hung, drawn and quartered for a failed attempt to blow up the King and parliament by planting gunpowder under Buckingham Palace. Since Fawke was a Catholic, his botched assassination attempt was seen as treason and part of a "popish" plot against the Protestant government.

On the first anniversary of Fawke's execution, English Parliament declared a day of public thanksgiving. Even today, weeks in advance of November 5th, English children prepare effigies known as "Guys." They set their "Guy" out on street corners and beg "a penny for the Guy" from passing strangers.

The eve of November 5th is known as "Mischief Night," when children are free to commit pranks on adults. Then on the night of November 5th, the Guys" are burned in bonfires, just as the ancient Celts burned their huge fires on November 1st.

To this day, services are offered on November 5th by the Church of England in thanksgiving for the safety of the seat of government and the apprehension of Fawkes. It is celebrated with fireworks (possibly representing the explosion that never occurred) and bonfires.

In Lewes, England, effigies of the pope are burned. Usually someone will dress up as the Pope and parade through the streets where he is pelted with fruits and vegetables – so much so that he must wear a face guard. It's not difficult to see that the English adapted Halloween to suit their political needs, and to separate it from the Catholic Church. The Fawkes celebrations appear to be ritual dramas that underscore English independence from the Pope.

The most recognizable aspect of Halloween is the carving of the pumpkin or Jack O'Lantern. Another link to old Ireland, the Jack O'Lantern legend goes back hundreds of years in Irish history.

Jack was a miserable miserly old thief and drunk who liked to play tricks on everyone. One day he tricked the Devil into climbing an apple tree. As soon as he did, Jack placed crosses around the trunk of the tree. Unable to get down, Jack made the devil promise him not to take his soul when he died. When Jack finally did die, he went to the pearly gates of heaven, but was refused entry because he had been mean and cruel and led a miserable, worthless life. He then went down to Hell. The Devil kept his promise, and refused him entry as well.

Jack was now very scared as he realized he had no place to go. His only option was to wander forever in the darkness between heaven and hell until Judgement Day. When he asked the Devil how he would be able to see in such darkness, the Devil tossed him an ember from the flames of Hell to help him light his way. Jack then placed the ember in a hollowed out turnip (one of his favorite foods that he often stole). Jack then roamed the earth for eternity.

In the bogs and marshes and fields in Ireland, one can sometimes see a lonely light drifting through the mists. To follow it leads to darkness and dangerous places…and some never return. The Irish would carve out a turnip themselves, and then put a light inside in hopes that if Jack came wandering by he would be scared away.

When the Irish came to America, they brought the legend of the Jack O'Lantern with them. The immigrants quickly discovered that a pumpkin was larger and easier to carve.

Halloween is a true combination of Pagan, Christian, and Celtic harvest festivals, as well as various stories, myths, legends, and some political agendas thrown in for good measure.

Many legends are based on truth, some are not. There are as many versions of ancient Halloween tales as there are leaves on trees. Part of this is due to the fact that the ancient druids were storytellers, not writers, so there is virtually no written record.

So much like the children's game where one child tells a story and passes it on to the next, who passes it on to the next, etc… until the final version bears little resemblance to the original, so goes the history of Halloween.

Christmas in Ireland

The wren, the wren, the king of all birds,
St. Stephen's Day was caught in the furze,
Although he is little, his family is great,
I pray you, good landlady, give us a treat.

- Sung by "The Wren Boys" on Christmas Day

Christmas is one of the most revered holidays in Ireland; a chance to slow down the pace of life, and spend time with family, much as it was hundreds of years ago. Christmas is a time to celebrate history and tradition in many lands, and Ireland is no exception.

According to the World Book, Christmas in Ireland, on Christmas Eve, the Irish place lighted candles in their windows to light the way for Mary and Joseph, who wander forever on Christmas Eve.

But in the days when the English tried to suppress Catholicism, the candles were a signal to passing priests of a house where Mass could be said in safety.

It is the custom for a daughter named "Mary" (or for the youngest child of the house) to light the candles. When British authorities questioned this practice, they were told that Joseph and Mary wander the world every Christmas Eve looking for a place to stay, just as they did in Bethlehem so many years ago. The candle served as a sign that the travelers were welcome to take refuge.

The British authorities allowed the practice to continue, attributing it to "Irish superstition." Tradition aside, many of the faithful Irish did actually believe that the Holy family might visit their home on Christmas Eve. So more elaborate preparations were made which included sweeping the floor, stoking the fire, and setting the table for three. Many of their front doors were left unlatched or wide open. A dish of water was then placed on the windowsill for the Holy Family to bless; the water was then kept throughout the year and used for curing illnesses.

There is another custom that unfolds on Christmas night – the telling of stories. The oldest member of the family gathers everyone around the hearth, or the table, and recounts the story of Mary and Joseph.

There are also stories about the family, the famine, and the great heroes and villains of Irish history. Story telling is part of Irish culture.

While the Swedes have 25 versions of the Cinderella story, the Irish have 311 and are still counting, according to "Christmas in Ireland" by World book Encyclopedia. There is, of course, a story behind all of the story telling.

For centuries, Irish children were deprived of an education by a combination of poverty and English law. The English kept the Irish uneducated in order to keep them subjugated. Knowledge is power, and the English were not about to let the Irish have either. To combat this, the Irish conducted classes in secret in the countryside. Hidden behind bushes and hedges, priests taught a few children from every generation to read and write.

One of the principle reasons for the rapid spread of Christianity throughout Europe was the willingness of Christian leaders to incorporate the rituals, beliefs and customs of other religions. Few of the ancient displaced religions were more assimilated than the Druids, Wiccans and Pagans.

Alban Arthuan is one of the ancient Druidic fire festivals which occurred on December 21st through 22nd. Alban Arthuan coincides with the Winter Solstice and means "The Light of Arthur" in reference to the Arthurian legend that states King Arthur was born on the Winter Solstice.

Alban Arthuan is also known as Yule, derived from the Anglo-Saxon "Yula," or "Wheel of the Year" and marked the celebration of both the shortest day of the year and the rebirth of the sun. The custom of burning the Yule Log, the tradition that is most familiar to people today, was performed to honor the great mother Goddess. The log would be lit on the eve of the solstice, using the remains of the log from the previous year, and would be burned for twelve hours for good luck.

Decorating the Yule tree was also originally a Pagan custom; brightly colored decorations would be hung on the tree, usually a pine, to symbolize the various stellar objects which were of significance to the pagan – the sun, moon, and stars – and also to represent the souls of those who had died in the previous year.

The modern practice of gift giving evolved from the pagan tradition of hanging gifts on the Yule tree as offerings to the various Pagan Gods and Goddesses. Some scholars believe that many of the current traditions surrounding "Father Christmas" (or Santa Claus) can also be traced back to Celtic roots. His "elves" are the modernization of the "nature folk" of the Pagan religions, and his reindeer are associated with the "Horned God" (one of the Pagan deities).

In Ireland, the Christmas season can be divided into two distinct halves. The first half, the weeks of Advent and Christmas Eve and Day, are primarily spiritual, a celebration of church and family. The second half of the season, the twelve days of Christmas (December 26 to January 6) are basically just for fun. And the fun begins early on the "first day of Christmas," which is called St. Stephen's Day and honors the first Christian martyr who was accused of speaking against the laws of Moses and stoned shortly after the Crucifixion of Christ.

In Ireland, St. Stephen's Day is a national holiday, celebrated with great relish. However, the celebration has little or nothing to do with the first saint. For hundreds of years, December 26 has been the day of the "Wren Boys." "Hunting for wren" or "going on the wren" is a peculiar custom, similar to Halloween, which survives on the Isle of Man, in part of Spain, and throughout Ireland.

Originally, hunting the wren began a day or two before Christmas or even on Christmas night; small bands of boys eagerly peered into bushes and under eaves of houses for the tiny wren bird. Once a wren is spotted, the boys chase the hapless bird until it was either caught or dropped from exhaustion. The dead bird was tied to the top of a holly bush (or to the end of a wooden pole) which was decorated with ribbons and bits of colored paper. Early in the morning of St. Stephen's Day, the boys gathered to "go on the wren."

The dead bird attached to the pole was carried around by the band of boys who were disguised in some form of costume. Straw masks were worn, or faces blackened with burnt cork. It was common for the boys to dress up in old clothes, usually women's dresses, which were saved through the year for this purpose.

The boys carried the bird from house to house in the neighborhood, knocking on doors, and begging (or demanding) admittance where they would dance and play instruments. They boys would also entertain the house with the Wren boys' song:

The wren, the wren, the king of all birds,
St. Stephen's Day was caught in the furze,
Although he is little, his family is great,
I pray you, good landlady, give us a treat.

On Christmas Day I turned a spit;
I burned my finger. I feel it yet,
Up with the kettle, and down with the pan;
Give us penny to bury the wren.

Although some families gave the Wren Boys food, the requested treat was usually money. In some cases the Wren Boys assume particular characters and present skits. One boy would play the part of an Irish chieftain, who might be named after the most prominent family in the neighborhood. Another boy would play the role of "Sir Sop," an English chieftain.

The part of servants and officers in attendance to the two chieftains were played by the other boys. The Irish chieftain was always well dressed, while Sir Sop was clothed in straw with a matching straw hat. The Wren Boys acted out the skit at each house, interspersing the dialogue with songs and dances.

Irish historians offer several explanations for the origin of the custom of hunting the wren on St. Stephen's Day. The hunting of the wren has been connected to the pagan custom of sacrificing a sacred symbol at year's end. Pagan symbols of the winter solstice are interwoven with Christian symbols of Christmas throughout Europe.

In Great Britain, for example, dead robins are still occasionally pictured on Christmas cards and decorations. In Ireland, the wren has been revered and accorded a place of honor as the "king of birds." An ancient Irish folk tale describes a contest staged among all birds to see who could fly the highest. Each bird, in turn, did his best, but the eagle soared higher than the rest. But victory was snatched from the proud eagle when the little wren - who had been hiding on the eagle's back - suddenly appeared and flew higher still. Thus it won, and became the "king of all birds."

However, the wren soon lost it crown. According to one legend, St. Stephens was hiding from enemies in the bush. A wren betrayed his whereabouts with its noisy chattering. Thus, the wren was hunted on St. Stephen's Day and stoned, like St. Stephen, with pebbles and sticks.

Another legend, dating from the late 700s when the Vikings were invading Ireland, holds that Irish soldiers were betrayed by a wren as they were sneaking up on sleeping Viking raiders. The wren began to eat breadcrumbs left on the head of a Viking drum. The rat-a-tat-tat of the bird's pecking on the skin of the drum woke the drummer boy, who sounded the alarm. The Irish soldiers were defeated by the Vikings, and hapless wren has been persecuted for its treachery ever since. Today, much of money collected by the Wren boys (and girls) is given to charities.

Mummers were originally itinerant actors who performed folk plays door-to-door on St. Stephen's Day and during the Christmas season. In Ireland, mummers are often called Christmas Rhymers, and the dialogue of the play is always recited in verse:

Room, room, brave gallant boys
Give us some room to rhyme
To show a bit of our activity
At the Christmas time...

Although mumming is an import from Great Britain, Irish mummers' plays have a distinctly nationalistic flavor and are an important part of the nation's folk culture.

Modern mummers usually belong to amateur groups, which stage the traditional plays before an audience. The plays are usually simple tales revolving around a duel between two great heroes. One of the heroes takes a "fall," but is miraculously cured by "the Doctor."

The characters in Irish mummers' plays emerge, for the most part, from Irish and English history. The heroes are usually saints – St. Patrick or even England's St. George. The villains include the likes of Oliver Cromwell or King William. Other characters – Father Christmas, Beelzebub, the Devil, the Doctor, or even the Wren – are mixed in to keep the plot moving, to sing the narrative, or perhaps, just for fun. Like the Wren Boys, they usually donate the proceeds from their performances to public charities.

The twelve days of Christmas – the interval between Christmas Day and Twelfth-night or Epiphany – is an important part of the holiday season in Ireland. The entire nation relaxes and enjoys less serious holiday events.

After Christmas Day, "going for the wren," mummers and country dances, the second major event is Holy Innocents' Day. Many people attend Mass on December 28 to commemorate the slaughter of the male children of Bethlehem. King Heron, believing a Messiah destined to become the new "King of the

Jews" had been born, decreed that all male children under the age of two be out to the sword. Joseph, warned by an angel, saved the Infant Jesus by fleeing to Egypt. In Ireland, Holy Innocents' Day was thought to be filled with bad omens. It was referred to as "the cross day of the year" (La Crostna na Bliana) where evil things could occur in memory of the senseless slaughter of children. In some counties, people refused to transact any business on that day. Holy Innocents' Day is no longer fraught with danger, but the slaughter of innocent children is still remembered with prayers and church services.

The next important day after Christmas is New Year's Eve (and New Year's Day). The Irish have a somewhat ambivalent attitude towards New Year's. The younger generation has begun to celebrate the event, but it is still of no great importance to the older generation.

In Ireland, the customary way to note the passing of the old year was to eat a large meal on New Year's Eve. The meal was to guard against hunger in the coming year. New Year's Eve, which in Gaelic is called *Oiche Coille,* thus became known as "the night of the big portion," or *Oiche na Coda Moire.*

A variety of New Year's customs evolved around the theme of keeping hunger at bay. In some sections of Ireland, the man of the house, armed with a cake or loaf of bread, struck the inside of the door three times saying:

Out with misfortune, in with happiness,
From tonight to this night twelve months,
In the name of the father, and of the Son,
and of the Holy Ghost.

Spinsters and girls of marriageable age traditionally placed ivy and holly leaves under their pillows on New Year's Eve. The leaves were thought to induce dreams of the man a girl was fated to marry. Before falling asleep, the girl whispered into her pillow: "Oh, ivy green and holly red, tell, tell whom I shall wed."

It is not difficult to understand the motives behind most Irish New Year's customs if one considers the extraordinary hardships that the Irish have endured, especially during the times of the famine. But over the years, many of the old customs have disappeared.

The Irish take down their Christmas decorations on January 7. The tree, holly, and other greenery are discarded.

In the past, the greenery were burned, as it was considered bad luck to simple put them in a trash bin. Although the season has ended, much of the spirit of Christmas in Ireland remains throughout the year in their history, customs, and traditions.

Joyce Kilmer
Catholic Poet & Soldier

"The sixty-ninth is on its way,
France heard it long ago,
And the Germans know we're coming
To give them blow for blow.
We've taken on the contract,
And when the job is through
We'll let them hear a Yankee cheer
And an Irish ballad too."

- "When The Sixty-Ninth Comes Back",
by Sergeant Joyce Kilmer, 165th Infantry (69th NY),
Company H

Alfred Joyce Kilmer wasn't Irish. But according his two grand daughters, he liked to believe he was.

Kilmer was actually of German descent, his ancestors immigrating to America in 1710. But he preferred to refer to himself as *"half-German, half-human."* His mother was named Annie Kilburn, and although she was of English descent, Kilmer assumed there had to have been some Irish on her side… somewhere.

Even Kilmer's own son said his father tended to exaggerate the amount of Irish blood in his veins. So, according to his grand daughters, *"…all we have is Joyce's word that he had Irish ancestors…"*

Regardless of whether Kilmer had any Irish blood, he certainly embraced the ideals of the Irish warrior/poet. Joyce was born at New Brunswick, New Jersey on December 6, 1886. He graduated from Rutgers College in 1904 and received an A.B. from Columbia in 1906. Before Kilmer gained fame as a writer, he worked briefly as a salesman for Charles Scribner's

Sons, and as an editorial assistant for Standard Dictionary. He
was preoccupied with the idea of belonging to the *"intellectual
aristocracy,"* and was known in his youth as a *"young radical"*
and something of a socialist.

His first volume of poetry, *A Summer of Love*, which showed
the influence of William Butler Yeats and other Irish poets,
gained him fame and earned his a spot in "Who's Who" at age
25. Kilmer also wrote book reviews for *The New York Times*
and *The Nation*, and became a special writer for *The New York
Times Sunday Magazine*. He worked on the staff of The New
York Times for five years.

Kilmer was deeply religious and converted to Catholicism in
1913. His point of view on all matters of religion, art, economics,
and politics, and even faith and morals, was strongly Catholic.
His religious faith, as well as his love of nature, is evident in his
writings. He also showed a sense of humility and dignity, and a
worship of the simple things. His love for nature, and devotion
to family, was also apparent. His most famous poem, "Trees," is
evidence of the combination of his respect for God and nature:

Trees
*I think that I shall never see
A poem lovely as a tree.
A tree whose hungry mouth is prest
Against the earth's sweet flowing breast;*

*A tree that looks at God all day,
And lifts her leafy arms to pray;*

*A tree that may in Summer wear
A nest of robins in her hair;*

*Upon whose bosom snow has lain;
Who intimately live with rain.*

*Poems are made by fools like me,
But only God can make a tree.*

In 1917, Kilmer enlisted as a private in the Seventh Regiment, National Guard, New York. He did this even though he was married, the father of two children, and not required to serve. He had hoped to write a book about his experiences.

According to his granddaughter, Anne Kilmer, Joyce took the war very seriously, and thought it was, *"romantic for a poet to be a fighter."* Anne said it was actually his mother's idea, and that she pushed him into the war. At the time of his enlistment, he was considered the premiere living American-Catholic poet.

At his request, and with assistance from the famous Father Francis P. Duffy, he transferred to the 165th Infantry, also known as the "old" 69th New York Irish Brigade, a unit of the Rainbow Division.

Even though the 69th was called "The Irish Brigade," no one was turned away from joining due to their ancestry or religious preference. But when you had Irishman recruiting Irishman, it makes sense that the regiment would end up 90% Irish.

The 69th New York, comprised of 3,500 soldiers, boasted more men than were in the entire Union Irish brigade during the Civil War. Still predominately Irish-Catholic, the duty roster also included non-Irish names such as Rodriguez, Menicocci, Ivanowski, Dambrosio, and Kaiser. There were at least 60 Jewish soldiers, some of whom were born in Ireland.

Once overseas, vacancies due to casualties or transfers would be filled regardless of ethnicity. Never-the-less, the regiment kept its identity, and was always known as "The Fighting Irish."

As mentioned previously, the 69th (later renamed the 165th Infantry) became part of the "Rainbow Division." This unit was formed exclusively from National Guard units activated for service in the war. Twenty-six states and the District of Columbia contributed to the units. The division received its name from Division Chief of Staff Major (later General) Douglas MacArthur, who stated that the division stretched like a rainbow, covering the country from one end of the sky to another. MacArthur eventually rose to command the Rainbow Division.

Among the infantry regiments which joined the 69th at Camp Mills (to form the 42nd Division) was the 69th's old Civil War adversary, the 4th Alabama of the Confederate States Army (now the 167th Infantry). On several occasions, the members of both outfits took a crack at re-fighting the Civil War, but eventually old animosities were set aside. They realized they had a bigger fight ahead of them in France.

While the regiment was at Camp Mills, Kilmer was transferred to Company H., Headquarters Company, and assumed the position of Senior Regimental Statistician. When he arrived in France, he quickly attained the rank of Sergeant, and was attached to the newly organized Regimental Intelligence staff as an observer. He spent many nights on patrol in the dangerous "no-man's land" gathering information that would be of tactical importance to the Regiment and the Division.

On Christmas, 1917, the regiment found itself in the old Roman town of Grand, where Father Duffy would celebrate midnight mass. On the morning of the 26th, the 165th started down a road built by Caesar's Legions on their way to the assigned area, Longeau. Underfed and poorly clothed for the blizzard-like conditions, the men marched over mountain passes for four days and four freezing nights. It was a matter of pride to the men of the 69th that no one fell out. Only those who were rendered unconscious from exhaustion were picked up by the ambulances.

After this grueling march, Kilmer sat down and wrote what some consider to be his best work, *Holy Ireland*, based on some of his experiences. *Holy Ireland* was an excellent example of Kilmer's idealistic Irish theme, which he treated with humor and affection, according to historian Christopher Morley. This theme repeats itself many times in his verses, especially in *Holy Ireland*.

The story begins with twelve Irish-American soldiers who had just completed a long march, taking refuge in the home of a French widow and her three children:

"Where is Sergeant Reilly?" it said. We lazily searched. There was no Sergeant Reilly to be found. "I'll bet the old bum has gone out after a pint," said the voice. And with the curiosity of the American and the enthusiasm of the Irish we lumbered downstairs in quest of Sergeant Reilly. He was sitting on a low bench by the fire. His shoes were off and his bruised feet were in a pail of cold water. He was too good a soldier to expose them to the heat at once. The little girl was on his lap and the little boys stood by and envied him. And in a voice that twenty years of soldiering and oceans of whisky had failed to rob of its Celtic sweetness, he was softly singing: "Ireland Isn't Ireland Any More." We listened respectfully.

"They cheer the King and then salute him," said Sergeant Reilly. "A regular Irishman would shoot him," and we all joined in the chorus, "Ireland Isn't Ireland Any More."

The lads were then treated to a lovely meal, but not before the soldiers discussed their mutual Catholic faith with the widow and the need for "Madame's little daughter" to make her First Communion.

After dinner, in which Madame really could not afford to feed the soldiers but did so anyway, the soldiers sat in awe of this plain, hard-working woman as she tended to her youngest child. *"There are mists, faint and beautiful and unchanging, that hang over the green slopes of some mountains I know. I have seen them on the Irish hills and I have seen them on the hills of France. I think that they are made of the tears of good brave women."*

As the soldiers lay down for the night, they discussed how lucky they had been to find Madame, and her little family, who treated them so well. They marveled over how they were accepted as part of her family, and relived the moment when Madame and her young daughter sang Catholic hymns for them in French. *"I tell you, Joe, it makes me think of old times to hear a woman sing them church hymns to me that way. It's forty years since I heard a hymn sung in a kitchen, and it was my mother,*

God rest her, that sang them. I sort of realize what we're fighting for now, and I never did before. It's for women like that and their kids.

"It gave me a turn to see her a-sitting there singing them hymns. I remembered when I was a boy in Shangolden. I wonder if there's many women like that in France now—telling their beads and singing the old hymns and treating poor traveling men the way she's just after treating us. There used to be lots of women like that in the Old Country. And I think that's why it was called 'Holy Ireland.'"

On July 30, 1918, during the Battle of Ourcq, Kilmer had attached himself as adjutant to Major William Donovan, commanding the First Battalion. Donovan's adjutant, Lt. Oliver Ames, had been killed in combat the day before.

Hoping to take the high ground of Muercy Farm, Major Donovan ordered Kilmer and a few other soldiers to advance into a wooden area to locate enemy machine guns. While doing so, Kilmer suddenly collapsed and lay still. A bullet fired by a German sniper had struck him in the head. In the blink of an eye the warrior/poet was gone.

Lt. Ames and Sgt. Kilmer were buried side-by-side, in a little creek bed on that farm, near a little copse known as the "Wood of the Burned Bridge."

Lt. Harold E. Allen, Intelligence and Operations Officer, 165th Inf. told the New York Times on 4/29/1919 that, *"Sergeant Kilmer was a skilled observer, a splendid soldier and an accurate reporter of what he saw...probably the best non-commissioned intelligence officer in the 42nd division."* Kilmer was posthumously awarded the French "Croix de Guerre" for bravery.

Much of Kilmer's work expressed his deep religious beliefs. Such expressions of faith fell out of favor in the latter 20th century, which explains why much of his work is little read today. It is even difficult to find a collection of his poems in today's mega-bookstores. But in the 1920s, Americans revered Kilmer as a symbol of *"soldierly courage and poetic idealism."* One can only imagine how Kilmer's poetry would have evolved had he not been cut down on that fateful day in France.

Farewell!
Comrade true, born anew, peace to you!
Your soul shall be where the heroes are,
And your memory shine like the morning star.
Brave and dear,
Shield us here.

"Farewell," by Sgt. Joyce Kilmer
(written to the cadence of "Taps.")

"Being Irish, he had an abiding sense of tragedy, which sustained him through temporary periods of joy."

— **W.B. Yeats**

Bibliography

- Appeal, Marty; *Slide, Kelly, Slide*, Scarecrow Press Inc., 1999
- Ashbury, Herbert; *The Gangs of New York*, Avalon Publishing Group, 2001
- Barron, Elwyn; *Deeds of Heroism and Bravery*, New York, Harper & Brothers Publishers, 1920
- Bartlett, Thomas; *The 1798 Rebellion, An Illustrated History*, 1998
- Bartlett, Thomas; *A Military History of Ireland*, Cambridge University Press, 1997
- Bennett, Richard; *The Black and Tans*, New York, Barnes and Noble Books, 1959
- Cagney, James; *Cagney by Cagney*, Doubleday & Co., 1976
- Connell, Evan , *Son of the Morning Star*, Promotory Press, 1984
- Connolly, S. J.; *The Oxford Companion to Irish History*, Oxford University Press, 1998
- Convis, Charles; *The Honor of Arms*, Western Lore Press, Tucson, 1999
- Coogan, Tim Pat; *The Man Who Made Ireland: The Life and Death of Michael Collins*, Roberts Rinehart, 1990
- Cusack, C. F.; *The Illustrated History of Ireland*, Gramercy Books, New York, 2002
- DeRosa, Peter; *Rebels: The Irish Rising of 1916*; New York, Doubleday, 1990
- Farson, Dennis; *The Man Who Wrote Dracula*, St. Martin's Press, New York, 1975
- Heath, Ian; *The Vikings*, Osprey Publishing, 1985
- Holt, Edgar; *Protest in Arms* 1916-1923, Coward-McCann, 1969
- Keneally, Thomas; *The Great Shame*, Doubleday, 1998

- MacDonagh, Oliver; *The Hereditary Bondsman*, Palgrave-MacMillan, 1988
- MacManus, M.J.; *Eamon DeValera*, New York, 1946
- MacManus, Seamus; *The Story of the Irish Race*, Devon-Adair Company, 1974
- Madden R. R.; *The Life and Times of Robert Emmet*, Excelsior Catholic Publishing House, New York, 1879
- McCabe, John; *Cagney*, Knopf, 1997
- Messenger, Charles; *Northern Ireland: The Troubles*, New York, Gallery Books
- Miller, Robert Ryal; *Shamrock & Sword*, University of Oklahoma Press, 1989
- Myler, Patrick; *Gentleman Jim Corbett*, Robson Books Ltd, 1998
- Nicole, David; *The Normans*, Osprey Publishing,1998
- O'Brien, Maire and Connor Cruise; *A Concise History of Ireland*, New York, Beekman House
- O'Connor, Frank; *The Big Fellow*, New York, Picador USA, 1979
- O'Connor, Sir James; *History of Ireland 1798-1924*, London, 1926
- O'Grady, Kelly; *Clear The Confederate Way!*, Savas Publishing Company, 2000
- Stoker, Bram, *Dracula*, 1897

Periodicals

1. Cahill, Ann; *Tuberculosis – A Consuming Death*, The Newsletter of Stoker's Dracula Organization, Spring 2001
2. Callaghan, James; *Meagher on the Green*, Civil War Times, December 1998, Cox, James; *The Great Fight: 'Mr. Jake' vs John L. Sullivan*,
3. Smithsonian magazine, December 1984
4. English, Thomas; *America's Colleen – Maureen O'Hara*, Irish America Magazine, February 1987
5. Gannon, James; *Irish Rebels, Confederate Tigers*, Irish America magazine, February/March 1999
6. Greaney, Michael, *The Last of the Norman Invasions*, Military History magazine, December 1998
7. Hind, Philip; *Encyclopedia Titanic*, 1996
8. Johns, Wesley; *The Fenian Fiasco*, The History of Buffalo: A Chronology
9. McIntryre, Dennis; *Dracula Back in Dublin*, The Newsletter of Stoker's Dracula Organisation, Autumn 2000
10. O'Beirne, Kevin; *Into the Wheatfield*, Military Heritage, October 1999
11. Smith, P.G.; *Fenian Invasion of Canada*, Military History Magazine, 2000
12. Wheeler, Richard; *Witness to Gettysburg*
13. Williams, Donald; *The "Clear The Way" Regiment*, America's Civil War Magazine, March 2000

CPSIA information can be obtained
at www.ICGtesting.com
Printed in the USA
FFOW03n1545200218
45108539-45534FF